SURVIVING BREAKDOWN

A positive approach to coping,
healing and rebuilding your life
after a nervous breakdown

Elizabeth Wilde McCormick

VERMILION
LONDON

First Published in Great Britain in 1988 by Unwin Hyman.
Revised edition published by Optima in 1993.

1 3 5 7 9 10 8 6 4 2

This revised edition published in the United Kingdom in 1997 by Vermilion, an imprint of Ebury Press

Random House UK Ltd
Random House
20 Vauxhall Bridge Road
London SW1V 2SA

Random House Australia (Pty) Ltd
20 Alfred Street, Milsons Point, Sydney
New South Wales 2016, Australia

Random House New Zealand Limited
18 Poland Rd, Glenfield,
Aukland 10, New Zealand

Random House, South Africa (Pty) Limited
Endulini, 5A Jubilee Road, Parktown 2193, South Africa

Random House UK Limited Reg. No. 954009

A CIP catalogue record for this book is available from the British Library.

ISBN 0 09 181512 6

Printed and bound in Great Britain by Mackays of Chatham, plc

Papers used by Vermilion are natural, recyclable products made from wood grown in sustainable forests.

The phrase 'nervous breakdown' is used widely to describe a condition where someone can no longer cope with life as he or she has previously known it. Breakdown can be a vivid dramatic experience, but, much more commonly, it is a long drawn out process - something many more people experience than is generally realised. 'Burnout' and exhaustion, severe depression, phobic anxiety and the depleting weariness of worry, unhappiness and indecision can all be part of the language of breakdown.

Surviving Breakdown: Coping, Healing and Rebuilding Your Life after Nervous Breakdown is a comprehensive, sensitive and *positive* discussion of a still very much taboo subject, written for those who feel they might be heading towards or are in the middle of a breakdown, as well as their friends and family who want to understand and help.

The author explores the many different forms of breakdown and their various stages, and first-hand accounts of 25 men and women interviewed over a long period of time describe exactly how it feels. The book tells you how you can know if you're 'on the edge', what you can do to help yourself if you are having a breakdown, and who you can seek out for help. A series of exercises helps you assess your vulnerability, understand your fears, avoid stress, recognise fatigue and exhaustion; and poems written by people during breakdown offer an amazing insight into what can be a profound and imaginative experience.

The message of this book is that breakdown can be breakthrough.

By understanding our breakdown and why it happened, we can become more aware of ourselves and our needs and so move forwards in a positive and constructive direction in our lives.

Elizabeth Wilde McCormick is a psychotherapist in practice in London and Suffolk. She is a training tutor in Cognitive Analytic Therapy at Guy's Hospital, and tutor in Transpersonal Psychology at the Centre for Transpersonl Psychology. She is the author of *The Heart Attack Recovery Book, Change For the Better* and *Healing the Heart,* all self help books based on her experiences as both therapist and human being. She is married and has a large extended family of children and stepchildren.

Acknowledgements

Many people have contributed to the formation of this book, both indirectly and directly. There are two main psychological themes. One is of the individual coming into life as a seed with an inherent programme of growth, and that the thrust of the person's life will be towards living out the potential of the original seed. This concept comes from the work at the Centre for Transpersonal Psychology, whose founders, Barbara Somers and Ian Gordon Brown have inspired and encouraged me in my own expression of what is transpersonal. To them, and to all my colleagues, I am grateful for all the sharing and evocation of individual language. The other theme comes from my work with Dr. Anthony Ryle at Guy's Hospital in brief psychotherapy, and embraces the concept of giving people an island of self knowledge by the reformulation of the difficulties or blocks that have come in the way of individual growth. Within this island people may begin to experience the self and gain enough strength and control to choose change in ways of behaviour that have become redundant. My thanks go to Tony Ryle, and to Annalee Curran, Norma Maple and Dilys Davies who all helped with reading this manuscript and offering suggestions, support and a forum to express frustrations.

To Dr. Vanya Orlans at the Stress Centre, Birkbeck College I am grateful for her question: 'Who is it who has the breakdown?' which sent me on a thoughtful journey; and to Dr. Roland Littlewood at the Middlesex Hospital who showed me how to think anthropologically, beyond the personal and individual.

Dr. Anthony Fry, Dr. Lillian Beattie, Dr. Norman Paros, Dr.

Acknowledgements

Anthony Ryle, Claire Rayner, Sally Berry of Arbours Association, Helen Plaut all have their voices within these pages and all helped me to distil ideas and facts for the work in writing. So also did Dr. Glin Bennet, Mardi Robinson, Karin Syrett, Ean Begg, Dr. Pat Shipley, Ann Shearer, Renate Ogilvy, Christopher Perry, Sheila Willson, Ian Fenton, Harriet Griffey and Sheila MacLeod.

My thanks also go to John Eldred and Paddy Bazeley at the Samaritans who talked to me for the purposes of this book, and who, over the years have opened up and amplified the different meanings behind the suicidal impulse.

Dr. Peter Nixon showed me how to understand the use of effort and its effect upon homeostasis, how to pay attention to the effects of prolonged fatigue and exhaustion, and to embrace the real meaning of being under stress, both in myself and in others.

Gill Mansbridge read much of the first draft of the manuscript over one weekend and helped with suggestions and encouragement, and also educated me more fully into feminist thought.

Many, many thanks go to Esther Caplin, my editor, who tirelessly and with great sensitivity went with me through the editing process. Her generous sense of boundaries allowed for both the necessary editing structure and changes, as well as including the more rambling and chaotic expressions of breakdown, which is what breakdown is like for most people. I am grateful for the inclusion of people's stories with their individual detail.

A large debt of gratitude goes to the men and women who volunteered to talk to me about their breakdowns, and have the meetings recorded. Their generosity lives on within these pages. Each person expressed the wish that others might be helped by the reading and sharing of their experiences. For this revised and updated edition, several of the people originally interviewed responded with current news of their lives since having a breakdown. My heartfelt thanks go also to the people who have worked with me in therapy who also gave permission for their stories to be included in this book. Without such footsteps and the wish to share and communicate, this book would not be possible.

Josephine Hugo transcribed many of the tapes with sensitive concern and in absolute trust. She also typed most of the first two drafts, taking her typewriter to Southwold for electricity when most of Suffolk was cut off after the hurricane in October 1987, just a few weeks before my delivery date. My thanks to her and her husband Glyn for the sanctuary of their garden while delivering and collecting material. My thanks also to Dorothy Najafzadeh and her colleagues who worked on the final presentation. Since its first publication in 1988, *Breakdown* has been well received by professionals and reviewers, and letters and feedback from readers speak of its help and comfort during lonely and painful times. The second edition of *Breakdown* was published by Optima in 1993 and now we have this third edition retitled *Surviving Breakdown* and published by Vermilion.

Without my family and friends the peace and solitude in which to write would not have been possible. I am deeply grateful to my husband John, to my children Simon, Kate and Nicky Wilde, To Irene Oxenham, to close friends and family who gave me the space in which to write and complained little about the neglect which the solitude required for writing brings about.

I also acknowledge my own experience of breakdown and what it has shown me, and honour the truth and integrity of the self, without which we would know nothing.

Elizabeth McCormick

The author and publishers would like to thank the following for permission to quote: Spring Publications for the extract by James Hillman from *Suicide and the Soul*. Faber & Faber Ltd for the lines from 'East Coker' Part III from *Collected Poems 1909–1962* by T. S. Eliot; the extracts by Alice Miller from *The Drama of the Gifted Child* and C. S. Lewis from *A Grief Observed*. Collins Publishers and Pantheon Books, a Division of Random House, Inc., for the extract by C. G. Jung from *Memories, Dreams, Reflections* (recorded and edited by Aniela Jaffe, translated by Richard & Clara Winston).

Foreword

It is difficult to change oneself. Most of us, most of the time, prefer to cling to our familiar view of the world and of ourselves even if it does not serve us too well, rather than to risk the confusions and anxieties of revision. Our internal government only falls when it can no longer govern and even then the ensuing anarchy may lead to the reimposition of an even more restrictive and authoritarian regime rather than to constructive change.

It is for this reason that change often only occurs in response to painful and frightening experiences, when we have no choice. Such occasions offer the chance of breakthrough and this book will be of great value to those people faced with this opportunity.

Liz McCormick has written an excellent book, a book which manages to be both very sensible and very moving. It is sensible because she presents a balanced view of the experience of being unbalanced, avoiding facile optimism and not underestimating the difficulties or claiming unique virtue for any one way of dealing with the situation. It is a moving book because of the extensive use made of patients' own words, words which convey the authentic experience both of the pain and fear and of the courage and capacity to grow. It is an optimistic book because it is based on the author's personal and professional experience of the real possibilities revealed by breaking down, and because it will offer to many readers a chance to make the best use of the various kinds of breakdown described in the book.

Dr. A. Ryle DM FRCPsych

Senior Research Fellow,
United Medical and Dental Schools
of Guy's and St Thomas' Hospitals,
London

Consultant Psychotherapist,
Guy's and St. Thomas' Hospitals,
London
1983–1992

Contents

Contents

To Pam
and
To Christopher

I said to my soul, be still, and let the dark come upon you
Which shall be the darkness of God. As, in a theatre,
The lights are extinguished, for the scene to be changed
With a hollow rumble of wings, with a movement of darkness
on darkness,
And we know that the hills and the trees, the distant panorama
And the bold imposing facade are all being rolled away –
Or as, when an underground train, in the tube, stops too
long between stations
And the conversation rises and slowly fades into silence
And you see behind every face the mental emptiness deepen
Leaving only the growing terror of nothing to think about;
Or when, under ether, the mind is conscious but conscious
of nothing –
I said to my soul, be still, and wait without hope
For hope would be hope for the wrong thing; wait without
love
For love would be love of the wrong thing; there is yet faith
But the faith and the love and the hope are all in the waiting.
Wait without thought, for you are not ready for thought;
So the darkness shall be the light, and the stillness the
dancing.
Whisper of running streams, and winter lightening.
The wild thyme unseen and the wild strawberry,
The laughter in the garden, echoed ecstacy
Not lost, but requiring, pointing to the agony
Of death and rebirth.

from 'East Coker' Part III   *Collected Poems 1909–1962*
by T. S. Eliot

Introduction

The thread running throughout this book is the concept of the individual as a seed, planted in the garden of life and trying to grow and form the potential for which it was intended. None of us know what that is until we begin our life and experience ourselves in different ways. If we have had to develop a 'survival' self to cope with what is expected or demanded of us, and at the expense of the seed, we tend to live on automatic, aware that something vital is missing. At some point our real 'seed' self will try to break through, to lead us towards living as we were intended. Learning what is our 'seed' self and what is our 'survival' self is a major part of this book.

When we enter a personal 'no go' area where nothing we've learnt before helps us cope, we can experience breakdown - 'burnout' and exhaustion, severe depression, phobic anxiety, and the depleting weariness of worry, unhappiness and indecision. Some breakdowns are long and prolonged. Others are acute, requiring hospitalisation. Breakdowns are always frightening, painful, difficult experiences, but the outcome does not have to be negative. This book is about making the best use we can of our breakdown, how it can come to be evaluated, experienced, contained and understood; it's about how we can help ourselves to thaw out from the worst times and to rebuild a more real sense of who we are.

Crisis, in the form of breakdown, offers us an opportunity to reappraise our learned survival pattern. We may then let go of old defences that have become redundant, old patterns that are not needed any more or parts of ourselves that are over-extended and inflated because of too much use at the expense of other, unknown parts of ourselves. We can then allow unknown parts of ourselves to be revealed, to become more known and trusted, more developed and understood, so that they are part of everyday life. For this we need a great deal of time. And we need to claim this time. If we just patch ourselves up after a breakdown and go back to the same old ways, we are still vulnerable to breakdown in the future, when we may not be so robust or optimistic. Processing what has happened to us after a breakdown and getting help with rebuilding is essential for our development. All breakdowns happen for a reason. And it's not all gloom! We may also find parts of ourselves that surprise us and which give us the capacity for great joy. Crisis and illness have the potential to make us whole. Breakdown can become breakthrough.

There are many ways of viewing a breakdown and what causes it. The way breakdown is approached has a profound effect on the person suffering and on the outcome of the experience. For example, a medical view will look for a cause and seek a cure; a sociological or anthropological view will look to forces in society which produce reactions amongst individuals, particularly minority groups such as adolescents, women and the elderly; political and feminist views will be directed towards the power structures between groups and at the position of powerless minority groups for whom the unconscious language of symptoms or behaviour is the only expression available; and the different psychological schools will take their particular bias into their view - existential, analytic, behavioural, humanistic or transpersonal. Each view is helpful for certain problems but not for others. There is no one way of viewing breakdown, and it is important that whatever the view held, it does not become rigid or reductive, for this limits the meaning of the personal experience and can lead to a state of limbo, of being stuck.

It is also important that people are not put down for their experience of breakdown. This can be a deterrent to getting work, or to being trusted, accepted and socially welcomed. If the intensely personal experience of breakdown is judged only as an individual's inability to cope we make that individual load much heavier. When an individual breaks down it is all of us who break down. For individual breakdowns have implications for the whole community - for our politics, religion, family structures, social mores and community care.

Because I work with individuals as a therapist my view in this book is directed to the individual's life and what the struggle is about for each person: how much of their suffering is to do with their own path in life, how much they are carrying from the past in terms of family ancestral myth and how much is to do with current cultural pressures. But the wider issues are not forgotten. I am interested in helping individuals and those closest to them to understand the roots of their suffering and make the necessary journey of processing, healing, gathering and restoring; to look at what it means to have broken down, what is being asked of them, what needs to be let go of and what is trying to break through, and how their experience can be used in as creative way as possible.

This book attempts to amplify the many expressions of breakdown and to remove the stigma, shame and deeply wounding guilt that burdens sufferers and often their families. It is written for people who feel they might be heading towards or who are in the middle of a breakdown. It is also for people who know they've had a breakdown and who want to help themselves and to know whom to go to for help. Lastly, it is written for the families, friends and some professionals involved with someone having a breakdown who want to understand, help and support.

This book grew out of a meeting between my professional self as psychotherapist and my own personal inner journey. Towards the end of 1985, at a mid-life point when things seemed to be going well generally, I began to suffer from a breakdown in health. A recurrent infection that was to last for over a year brought me into contact with countless professionals, some of whom performed operations and invasive tests to find out what was happening within my body. Two colleagues recognised exhaustion and breakdown and offered asylum.

My 'no go' area was being seen as week and vulnerable by others, and by myself, which for me meant being left behind and humiliated. All my life I had avoided this place and built my life, very successfully - for many people were taken in - by being strong, competent, always available, reliable; I would never let anyone down. So I always fought any kind of stopping and in the end my body took over. When I had to take three months off I faced what felt like the end of the world for me. No work, no income, no security, no future; and what I believed to be the end of respect, affection, prestige, identity. It was made worse by the fact that I felt I ought to know better, because I had worked with exhausted heart patients and knew all the signs and theories, and because I had had the benefits of a great deal of personal therapy and was in the middle of analysis. I can see now that I had used these particular ways to become 'safe' from vulnerability, a concept I know is shared by many professionals who choose this particular kind of work for these reasons.

It was very hard for me to acknowledge that I had no idea what was happening to me or where I was going. At the time it felt like a cruel joke, aimed at removing everything I had developed and I plunged into an abyss of meaninglessness and despair. There were terrifying demons and tortuous ideas. At times there was no light, no meaning; at times I did not want to live. Then, slowly, and without fanfare of any kind, another awareness began to stir itself and made itself known. I began to feel 'real', and awake. The strengths I began to appreciate were the strengths that had come from inside when all outside had been given up. I could feel myself beginning to shed the old skins of the past, which were ready to be shed, and what was underneath was a bit raw at first, fragile, but it was ready to be given the light of consciousness and is now part of everyday living.

I kept a journal during this time and I began to talk to different people who had experienced breakdown in different ways.

This book is made possible by the combination of all these experiences, from my personal and professional life; by the patience and generosity of my colleagues to whom I talked for the purpose of this book, and by the men and women who share with me their individual journeys of breakdown. Twenty-five men and women talked to me confidentially in a series of taped interviews. I am deeply grateful to them all, and to my clients and patients who gave permission for their stories to be included in this book. All names and circumstances have been changed in order to protect identities, but all the words and conversations are reproduced verbatim where the tape recorder allowed. Several of the profoundly deep experiences shared with me did not record on the tape. The poems throughout the book were written by Charlotte, Peggy and Pam whose stories you will read. They reflect an often forgotten side of breakdown, that of individual language, and the world of the imagination. When

4

consciousness is struggling the world of the imagination is prime. Its language of metaphor and symbol, image and colour speaks universally. It touches us all in a deep place, and can connect us to something greater than ourselves. And in 1992, whilst preparing for a second edition of this book, I wrote to all the people who had taken part and asked them for an update on their stories. You will find these updated stories in each section, their individual journeys, six years on. And now, in 1996, the book is about to have its third incarnation, with Vermilion books, for which I, and those who have found the book useful, and a comfort, are grateful.

I have been deeply moved by the stories in this book and I still feel this way every time I read them. They tell us about the human capacity for courage, endurance, hope, and they tell us that human beings are not the sum total their problems, neuroses, psychoses, depressions and 'madnesses', but people engaged in journeying, mythmaking, soulmaking.

I believe that each individual life has meaning, the meaning that we give it. I believe in saying 'what does this mean, why is this happening, what is its purpose, what do I need to do, seek, develop, in order to fulfil the purpose? And if I can find none, how do I live without in the dark? How do I touch the darkness, dare to be without the light? And if I do not dare these things what is there for me ... where are the places I may go, who can I speak to, who will be with me?' I do not seek to glamorise breakdown into something it is not, nor put upon the individual the burden of finding meaning and purpose when he or she has already a heavier load than most. But I do want to offer hope: that it is possible to go beyond the crisis of a breakdown, and find out what it really is we want to say or change in our life, what we want to connect or re-connect with, and how we can find help to do these things, If we can make some sense of what happens to us then maybe it can become more bearable. I would like to hope that something said or shared on these pages will start the reader on a journey of their own. When we are able to recognise the universality of our suffering we are never so alone or isolated.

1
Breakdown – breakthrough?

WHAT IS A NERVOUS BREAKDOWN?

We are led by medicine itself, through its notion of health, to live beyond ourselves, driven and exhausted, in threat of breakdown, owing to the denial of human frailty. When the physician cautions to slow down, his own 'go, go, go' and *furor agendi*' prevents his warning from having effect. 'Getting better' means 'getting stronger'; health has become equivalent to strength, strength to life. We are built up to break down and then be rebuilt as we were before, like a machine caught in accelerated feedback. The soul seems to make itself heard only by speaking the physicians language – symptoms.

James Hillman, *Suicide and the Soul*

The phrase 'nervous breakdown' is used widely by everyone, lay and professional. It is an extremely loosely defined term, suggesting a condition where an individual can no longer cope with life as she or he has previously known it. The spectrum of personal struggle could range from someone coping with the effects of bereavement or change to someone who is seeing visions and having delusions. In nervous breakdown some people experience a physical 'stopping' of what we might call healthy normal functioning; they may curl up in a ball, become mute, be unable to stop crying, or make a suicide attempt. Others may experience a gradual decline, becoming increasingly depressed, anxious, withdrawn and upset by daily living, or they may become numb, acting automatically and not feeling at all. Nervous breakdown can be a vivid dramatic experience but much more commonly it is long and drawn out, something many more of us experience than is perhaps realised. It is not a mental illness although it carries the same taboo, but part of our development as sensitive human beings on the journey of life.

What do we mean by 'nervous'?

Let us look at the term 'nervous breakdown' more closely. The word 'breakdown' is clear, we all understand this, but the use of the word 'nervous' is misleading. The nerves cannot break down. What can be put under huge pressure is the nervous system: the system responsible for transmitting messages from outside stimuli or our own thoughts, through the brain to the tissues and muscles of the body. It is commonly understood that negative thoughts produce negative feelings, and that negative thoughts are learned from our experience of what happens to us from the moment of birth. Just as we learn, so we can unlearn negative or harmful patterns and replace them by positive or new patterns. We are ultimately in charge of our own nervous system, when we become conscious of how to use it effectively; what to put into it and what not to put into it. If, as the term 'nervous breakdown' implies, we have overstretched our nervous system to the point at which we feel it will snap, this is an indication that our use of the nervous system is limited and needs a wider range of choices. It does not mean, as is often implied, that we are inadequate, weak, or mentally ill.

The word 'nervous' is often used pejoratively. 'It's just your nerves', 'a hopeless case of the nerves', 'another nervous woman making a fuss' or 'his nerves couldn't take it.' In our society 'nervous' implies jumpy, vulnerable, weak, sensitive, unreliable, soft, twitchy, out of control and sometimes neurotic, daft, mad. Nervousness is sanctioned for those working in the arts, but not for those 'in charge', for instance politicians, teachers, doctors, lawyers, businessmen. This division between those who are seen as weak and those who feel they must appear strong in order to stay in charge, polarizes each of these qualities and diminishes the range of emotional expression for each group.

If power structures are based on the example of the 'strong' group, the 'weaker' minority group becomes diminished and negatively judged. Whatever the 'strong' group cannot acknowledge in themselves has to be projected onto a 'weaker' group. The 'weak' group, who have no power, can only express themselves through symptoms of one kind or another. Symptoms are their voice. The minority groups, such as adolescents, women and old people, tend to be seen as 'nervous' and prone to disorders loosely labelled of a nervous kind, far more frequently than any other groups. Taking a broad overview we could say that the 'strong' group take their personal crises in forms that are somehow more acceptable to society: the 'stress' illnesses such as heart attacks, ulcers and burnout, or in the drama of accidents and divorce. Because our society in the 1990's admires the more masculine, focused, rational and logical approach, people who have made their identities with this kind of consciousness find it very difficult to acknowledge their more feminine, diffuse, creative, feeling, vulnerable and sensitive sides. Because it is the power groups who make the labels we carry, 'nervous breakdown' tends to refer to any kind of behaviour or episode that is not rational or in control.

A more positive view is that a nervous system that is as delicate as finely tuned radar antennae gives us great potential for useful and creative sensitivity. That these qualities are not yet as admired as others in our society should not deflect anyone exploring from their own nature. Once valued and experienced, the rewards of being in touch with one's inner life and nature, and finding meaning and purpose from this, are beyond price.

A 'thin' skin

Some of us are born with a 'thin' skin. We notice everything; everything affects us, often deeply, we bruise and are hurt easily, more so than our thicker skinned brothers and sisters. Whilst a thicker skinned person has to learn a greater sensitivity in order to be able to make relationships, a thin skinned person needs to learn how to use this gift, and not go into hiding from life. Learning self protection, when it is needed, learning to find and know one's own voice and use it assertively, and learning how to be open in the most valuable and creative way, is a necessary part of learning to live with this valuable asset.

Imagination

Another contributor to what is judged as 'nervousness' is a vivid imagination. People who relate to life visually and who make quick connections with images and stories are more likely to take emotional situations and human contact to a deeper level, sometimes being flooded with images and reminders. Imagination and sensitivity need appropriate containers, channels for their energy. Without proper channels of expression these two powerful qualities can turn inwards into the person and contribute to illness or what are called neuroses. Because, as we have said, our society tends to overvalue the rational and logical approaches, communications which are not of the verbal or written kind can often be dismissed as meaningless ramblings or neurotic outpourings, rather than an individual attempt to come forward with whatever language is available. Throughout this book we will be looking at the individual language of breakdown: the way in which people in very different situations tried to tell of their plight in the only way available.

Labelling the qualities of sensitivity and imagination as nervousness puts out a candle flame. When we do this we are all poorer. Where would we be without the contributions of those amongst us who offer another dimension beyond the rational: the poets, artists, writers, healers, communicators, mystics, story tellers, dreamers and visionaries who cannot function without their imagination, sensitivity or thin skin? It is for this reason that the word 'nervous' serves no purpose in looking at breakdown.

How can we view breakdown?

We live in a time of increasingly stressful demands on us, both as individuals and as a society, but few places to go for asylum when we need it. It is estimated that 45 per cent of visits to a GP are for sufferings which are 'psychosomatic'. Another estimation is that at any one time one out of four people will be experiencing some sort of mental distress. For most this means persistent feelings of anxiety, irritability, tension or depression, feelings often expressed through smoking or drinking too much, or by being aggressive or withdrawn. Common physical problems like headaches, stomach pains and

9

rashes may be linked to emotional disturbance. Others suffer from one phobia or another.

When we have no means of coping in a conscious way with the build-up of our individual stresses, our reactions are taken over by the unconscious which expresses itself in symptoms of different kinds. We then tend to go to the doctor, in fact we actually need symptoms in order to consult a doctor, and he or she, because of medical training, will be obliged to look at physiology first. This can be a paradox. Often, although this may not be expressed, both parties know that what they are up against is the effect of long term distress. This may be due to difficult relationships, perhaps, or to the wear and tear of poverty, grief, loss, poor housing, too much or too little work, harassment; or the struggle to deal with change without the input of appropriate education or understanding. For this we do not need technological tests, pills or operations, although sadly these are sometimes the only experiences of care or being looked after that some people ever have. Doctors are increasingly asked to be the new wise people and healers, not only in relation to the body, but to how we cope with life. At present their training does not properly allow for this, and many people break down because the help they need is not available.

Breakdown to breakthrough

Part of the stress that people suffer is due to the speed with which our society has developed technologically and because of all the new influences such as space and air travel, nuclear weapons and their implications, terrifyingly sophisticated crime, complex consumer choices, one marriage in three ending in divorce. What we need are people able to help us with our growth and development within the life we find ourselves. We are not machines but there is a temptation amongst leaders and professionals to suggest that we run ourselves along machine-like lines, with little room for wonder, imagination, spirituality, pondering, contemplation, or questing of an inner kind. The natural thrust of the psyche is towards wholeness, and what may emerge as a crisis and breakdown may be the necessary precursor to breaking through to some new or previously eclipsed part of ourselves which is now needing to be reclaimed or seen consciously for the first time.

We need midwives of a different order, who help with the crises emerging from the meeting between the individual self and outside life. These are crises primarily of an inner kind. The crisis of breakdown is rarely helped by anything that comes from outside the individual unless in the form of loving guidance from understanding others. The journey of breakdown is one an individual undertakes alone and within the privacy of his or her personality. The art of the midwife, wise and old, is to be alongside during the months of gestation with her total belief in the life inside the mother, hidden but in evidence; gentle midwifery helps and encourages through the long waiting and gestation, transition and finally the birth itself. The task of midwifery in breakdown is to bring the hidden new life inside the person safely into consciousness. Breakdown becomes breakthrough.

A wise midwife knows when to call in the services of all the modern advances of medical technology and pharmacology. Sometimes the suffering during breakdown is great and involves severe and debilitating depression or psychosis, terrifying hallucinations or violent acting out, and it is during these times that the services of doctors should be sought.

But many people experiencing breakdown do not see a doctor and their experience does not necessarily get called 'nervous breakdown'. Conversely some people find themselves being treated unnecessarily, having medical tests or even operations for symptoms which come primarily from their struggle with life. At present the art of midwifery for breakdown seems to be practised by counsellors, psychotherapists, analysts, some doctors and psychiatrists, a few priests, or not at all. The question of who will become the new midwives is important for all of us, for their presence is sorely needed. Some breakdowns could be avoided with more understanding of the natural process of giving birth to change or throwing off the outdated order in one's life.

Our society is at risk of becoming too rational and too technical, lacking the dimensions of imagination, spirit and meaning, and becoming soulless. The concept of soul is not limited to religion but refers to the deepening of events into experiences; soul makes meaning possible; soul is communicated through love and a sharing of spirit. When we are allowed to experience the suffering of what is sometimes called 'psychopathology' we meet the psychic forces that live inside us and force us on our individual journey in life. That journey has no other meaning than we give it, out of ourselves. Caring to know what

11

our journey is about, finding out how to journey meaningfully makes the difference to whether we see breakdown as a disaster or an opportunity to look at ourselves in a deeper, more meaningful way. After facing the thoughts and demons which have scared and dominated us we never have to be so controlled by them again. Through this kind of journeying we are able to look at our passage to breakdown and beyond, to breakthrough, as painful but necessary, if we are to develop towards being a whole person living out our potential.

Breakdowns are triggered by different factors

1 They may be a reaction to a major life event, such as loss, divorce, bereavement, moving, examinations or a change in status. We never know how we will cope with something new. Sometimes we find reserves that we didn't know we had and sometimes we don't. As families move away from each other more frequently we often lack the support to help us through the change.

2 They may be a reaction to a catastrophic life event for which no one could be prepared, such as a hijack, rape, murder or mugging, earthquake or flood disaster. There are now specialist groups, formed out of the experiences learned due to the Falkland War, Zeebrugge and Lockerbie disasters, to help with this particular trauma.

3 They may occur because we have been living 'lopsidedly', have become too rigid and need to restore a greater sense of harmony. Nature's laws are such that she acts in a balancing, restorative way, she dislikes the tension caused by polarity. The more we live at one end of a polarity, the more its opposite will pull. The psyche acts through the unconscious to restore balance.

4 The breakdown may occur as part of our development. We need crisis to help us to change, release a part of ourselves that we haven't used properly. Typical times for this are during adolescence and mid life.

5 We may be a 'scapegoat': the person who collects all the 'shadow' side of a family or group. This often happens when one member is particularly sensitive and vulnerable and perhaps different from the others in a family or close group. They may have projected upon them all that the others don't want and become the 'black sheep'

or 'problem child'. Any young person suffering in this way is expressing the unconscious statement of family problems. Similarly in a group or community of people if one person begins acting out or becoming ill it is the group as a whole that should be viewed. Families and groups can become too rigid and lopsided and when this happens one person may carry all the unwanted, unconscious aspects.

6 Breakdowns may occur because people are poorly equipped to deal with life or life itself seems to offer so little. Living in poor housing or run-down areas that no one has the energy or inclination to bother about, being caught in the poverty trap, having little or no family support or few friendships or having very few inner resources can all make people vulnerable to breakdown.

When adversity is shared with others or is endured because of a common goal or ideal people can harness all their very best energies. But when too much seems stacked against them people can become dispirited and feel helpless and hopeless. Breakdowns suffered in this group seem to be more to do with social imbalances than part of an individual journey. When the flavour of society through political or economic strategies is 'get on your bike' or 'make your own way', there will be a polarity between people who achieve through personal endeavour and people who cannot keep up and fall by the wayside. The extreme achievements of the one force the other into the opposite position. We see this mirrored globally. The wealthier and more overfed the prosperous Western nations become, the poorer are the Third World countries.

When does breakdown occur?

Breakdown occurs when we can no longer cope with ordinary life as we have known it. Most of us can recognise a personal 'breaking point'. Many of us, at some point in our lives, have felt as if we had come close to 'breaking down'. It might be an intolerable tension – as if we might literally explode or burst; we might feel as if one push would plunge us into the depths of an abyss; we might feel like a rat in a trap, caught alive, but doomed to chase our tail in a decreasing circle of exhausting effort. At the edge of breakdown we start to feel that we just cannot tolerate what is happening any longer, either

13

inside ourselves or outside in the world. We begin to look for a solution to our problem, using whatever resources have worked for us in the past or that are now available. Sometimes it is difficult to ask for help. Often we don't know what kind of help we need, so most of us struggle with our problems alone, making internal resolutions to 'be better', to be more in control or to 'pull ourselves together'. We make changes that we believe will make all the difference and we hope that by changing our circumstances we can change our feelings: 'If only the sun would come out' or 'If only I hadn't moved house'. When using familiar resources doesn't work, we begin to turn to more desperate measures, like alcohol or other forms of self punishment. Because we are increasingly isolated we suffer from withdrawal, negative, depressed or irrational thinking, and changes of mood; and alongside this our problems take on a physical component.

Because we are struggling to cope with what is happening to us and we have no map to guide us, we are making an enormous amount of effort every day just to keep going: even if we aren't doing much, just coping with the onslaught of depressed thinking and alien mood swings costs us heavily. We tend to sleep poorly, waking early and anxious. We eat oddly, choosing food which is easy, instant and often not nutritious; or no food at all. We may try to escape using tranquillisers or other drugs if we have been offered them. We find solace in television programmes and lying in bed curled up under the covers. We stop wanting to be seen, we begin to dislike ourselves, we begin to think of ways of putting out the agony of waiting for something to change. We have probably stopped some time ago believing that something will come along. We begin to lose hope.

Breakdown occurs in different ways

If we are unable to get the help we need, at some point along this journey we may develop symptoms.

Physical symptoms

We may develop digestive disorders, such as stomach or bowel inflammation, or ulcers; infections internally or externally, including boils, abscesses or fevers; hormonal disorders affecting menstruation and the reproductive system in women; disorders in the cardiovascular system, such as hyperventilation, angina, high blood pressure, coronary spasm, or worsening of existing chest problems such as asthma and bronchitis. We suffer a general weakening of the immune system to fight off colds and infection, and we become more prone to accidents, back troubles, migraine and headaches.

Depression

What may have started as depressed thinking for periods of time, traditionally weekends and evenings when we haven't much to do or are alone, can develop into more severe depression. This may stop us functioning altogether for a while. Symptoms include continual crying and extreme despair, not wanting to see anyone, to dress or get up, and withdrawal into oneself. In severe instances, the sufferer may become mute, unable to communicate at all, or catatonic, rigid and uncommunicative.

Anxiety and phobic disturbance

What may begin as a dislike or mild fear can progress into something we avoid at all costs and which becomes so fearful that physical symptoms such as sweating, diarrhoea, dizziness, fainting, palpitations and chest pain are involved, which compound the fear and contribute to the avoidance. This may take the form of agoraphohia, a fear of going outside; or anorexia or bulimia, severe forms of phobia about food and eating.

Loss of feelings

We may realise that we have gradually become 'numb' to people around us, that we don't feel anything any more. This sometimes happens after the shock of a crisis, or after a serious loss such as bereavement or marriage breakup. We are living as if we are suspended out of life. The state of numbness has its own terrors, and we may go to desperate lengths just to try and feel again, like harming ourselves.

Acting out

We might find ourselves doing unexpected things like shoplifting, driving off in the middle of the night, becoming violent and breaking things up or becoming abusive. We might take an overdose as a

15

desperate measure, forcing our internal crisis dramatically and desperately to the surface.

All of these may be symptoms that represent an attempt to find a way out of the dilemma we find ourselves in. We may not have been able to do it consciously, as few of us have the understanding, the words or the means to communicate at these times, so the unconscious acts for us, sending signals in the form of symptoms. They lead us to help because they bring to a head something of what may have been brewing inside us for years. They also tell the world 'All is not well with me. Help! I cannot tell it another way.'

WHAT MAKES US PRONE TO BREAK DOWN?

Our ability to weather a breaking point depends a great deal on our individual make up, the resources we can find inside ourselves and the resources or help we can find outside. Difficult or stressful periods seem to be best weathered by an ability to be flexible, philosophical and assertive, to know what we need to help us and to be able to find it. A sense of personal discipline, such as having small rituals which nourish and recharge worn out batteries throughout difficult days, for instance meditation, running, short sleeps or eating well, all seem to help protect people during personally stressful times. But when we have been unable to develop such skills, when we are more rigid, frightened of our own voice and needs, vulnerable to outside pressures and inner demands of how we should be or respond to others, we are much more vulnerable to break down under pressure.

Psychological lopsidedness and 'no go' areas

We all have 'no go' areas – places inside ourselves which frighten us and which we avoid. We may have built powerful control mechanisms or defences to guard against confronting those places. In this way we tend to get lopsided: the more accepted and controlled part of ourselves becomes much more developed than the 'no go' area which has been shut away. Anything which threatens the control of the area we are afraid of is rejected or pushed aside.

If our 'no go' area is to do with feelings we will avoid expressing feelings or being in situations or with people who make us react on a feeling level. We may decide unconsciously 'I will never let anyone get close to me', and we will tend to live at a distance from feelings, using rational thinking and logic with which to cope with our life.

If anything to do with the body or sexuality is our 'no go' area we will avoid anything physical or close, and tend to engage in activities that are remote, such as academic or business work. If our 'no go' area is thinking, organising or having to be logical we will tend to engage ourselves in activities which don't demand of us in this way – being at home or being involved in the arts, perhaps. We can manage quite well through avoiding the expressions which are least comfortable for us, and many would say that it is sensible to do so, but our avoidance may be based on fears which were powerful a long time ago and need not be so any more. We are living 'as if' it were still a bad or frightening thing to behave in a certain way, when this is no longer valid. Also, when we live lopsidedly for too long, we can get seriously out of balance psychologically, and the smallest thing can push us over. When something is inappropriately avoided for a long time, it becomes even more fearful and we can become phobic about it. It can get much more frightening than it really needs to be. What adds to the fear is that we get out of practice. For example, if we have decided not to express feelings because a long time ago our feelings were stamped upon, abused, ridiculed or misunderstood, the whole of our feeling

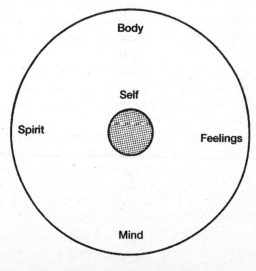

nature tends to remain at the stage when we put it away out of defence. So when feelings do come to the surface, as they always do eventually, they tend to come out in the childlike way that they went underground. This can frighten us even more and make us keep them more firmly under lock and key. Like anything kept in the dark for too long the hidden part of us festers and grows desperate for the light and recognition, for love and nurturance.

Where is my 'no go' area?

Exercise: Mind, body, feelings, spirit

Pause for a moment here and spend some time quietly by yourself and ask yourself the following: What is my personal 'no go' area? What situation am I most afraid of in my life?

A useful way of looking at ourselves as a whole is to look at the different parts of ourselves: **body**, mind, emotions and spirit. Spend some time with each of these four. With body, experience your body and note what this is like. How much do you normally use or value it? For **spirit**, feel into what spirit means to you. When are the times that you feel stirred by something spiritual or 'other' (this does not have to involve any creed or religion). Look at **emotion**: how do you express your feelings – love, affection, sadness, anger, passion – with other people or alone? Or are you unaware of what you feel much of the time? Consider **mind**. Does thinking – the logical, rational, approach – dominate your life? Do you like things to be rational and ordered or are you afraid of, or inexperienced in thinking, preferring the world of spirit and feelings?

Make a drawing for yourself showing how you imagine these four aspects of yourself to exist within the whole. Use different colours for each and write one or two words to describe them and how you feel about them. Use different shapes to depict each part. Is one part bigger or smaller than another? Which part do you use most, or least? Can you tell which is your personal 'no go' area?

'Seed' self and 'survival' self

'No go' areas seem to be formed because of our survival needs in early life. Anything which is taboo in our family will tend to become so for us too. If our family is afraid of anything to do with the body and avoids any kind of touching or physical contact we will be inexperienced in these matters. If certain subjects are never discussed, such as politics, religion, intimacy or feelings, we will be unlikely to feel comfortable about talking of these things. If there is a great deal of negative feeling associated with certain areas we are likely to avoid them like the plague, entertaining fantasies, images and wondrous thoughts about them, and associating them with much more potency than they really have. These matters tend to get adjusted to a certain degree when we leave home and make our own decisions about taboo subjects.

What is more difficult is when facets of our own self expression become taboo and we put away parts of ourselves because they are judged harshly and we take this judgement in, believing it as absolute. If we are naturally ebullient and creative, but are labelled 'show off' or 'big head' often enough in situations where it hurts, we will probably decide that our urge to express ourselves naturally in this way is wicked, bad and naughty. So we learn to put away our natural self, our 'seed' self, and to take up a 'survival' self, which copes and responds to what is expected and demanded of us.

The climate in which we spend our first few years of life sets up a framework of self-perception which governs how we see the world and how we believe the world sees us.

The framework consists of what we view to be our choices in terms of identity and what we come to believe our life is about. From this lens we begin, from the time of our birth, to form a set of skills and strategies for coping with things that happen to us, the thoughts we have, the feelings we have and evoke in others, and the life events we provoke or which are beyond our control. In Chapter 7 we will be looking at how faulty thinking about ourselves shapes patterns which become problematic: until they are challenged they govern our behaviour, our choices of career, partners, living, the ways in which we take care of ourselves or are self destructive. And it is from this state of faulty thinking that our 'nervousness' or illnesses of all kinds stem.

What happens to us early on is a mixture of who we are naturally (the seed) and our early environment (the soil). Some of us get planted in alkaline soil when our growth needs acid soil. Some have an apple pip inside us and get planted into an orange grove where more oranges are expected: every time we show some appleness of our own nature it is stamped upon because it is misunderstood. Most parents are new at parenting and do what they can, they love in the only way they know; some do seem more caught up in patterns that are harmful to their children, and some parents suffer from mental illness which affects their ability to be a good enough parent. Often we cannot see our parents freely until we have separated ourselves from the hold they have on us internally.

Every person I've met or worked with who has had a breakdown has felt that they didn't fit into their family. Several people have said 'I never felt I belonged' ... 'I was always wrong somehow' ... 'I didn't fit in' ... 'I always felt there was something wrong with me' ... 'I was a misfit' ... 'I was an oddity' ... 'My mother terrified me as a child. She was always waiting for me to make a mistake, spill my food, utter a blasphemy. I used to literally hold my breath after I'd done something waiting for the axe to fall. I feel her to be there still, in that way, but in reality she's a rather senile old lady, quite harmless and worried about the light bulbs and whether the dustbin men will come before the cats disturb her bin.'

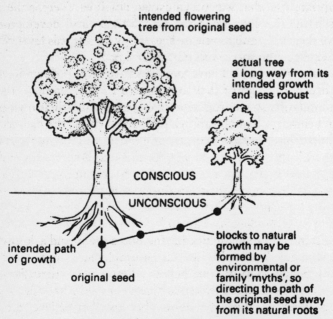

THE JOURNEY OF THE SEED

'The journey of the seed' shows what happens when we feel a misfit in our family and have to accommodate to an alien way in order to survive. We grow into adult life and into consciousness with something of a straggly growth, not as robust as we would if we had gone our natural course, and we are carrying a heavy load of conditioning and false ideas about ourselves without any kind of strength to help us fight them. We are living on our wits, and many people like this have literally brought themselves up by their own bootstraps. In some families individuals are actually rejected if their natural gifts or looks are a subject of envy, or rejected because they are feared and not understood. Parents who are themselves immature and unsure feel 'shown up' when their children shine in a way that confounds their understanding.

During the process of rebuilding after a breakdown there is an opportunity to reclaim the child in us that may never have been fully appreciated before, never loved and encouraged, never allowed to have the whole range of human, childlike emotions. This inner child can be held and given hope and a life, and allowed to mature in the appropriate way that was previously impossible. There is the chance to discharge the content of the blocks to natural development, to remove their hold and to release the energy held at this level. We may then begin to reconnect with our natural path.

Several of the people I have met who have broken down have done so in order to let go of their old pattern of development, their old accommodation to environment, in order to claim their own natural way of being. For example, if in a particular family, the men for many generations have become bankers or gone into the army there will be a powerful pull on a son to be likewise and develop his 'rational' masculine skills. His own seed self may have a more 'feeling' nature and would become an artist, write poetry, go into politics or into teaching. But early on in life the drive to survive – and for this we need love and a useful place in the family – is the most powerful; we bend and twist in order to be significant and find a useful and acknowledged place, whether this emphasises our natural being or not.

Many people who become depressed later on in their lives do so because they decided to please and placate and do what others wanted to the detriment of their own needs – because they believed what they really wanted was wrong and that they would be punished and rejected for being themselves. Many times in therapy I've commented on someone's natural ability which has been played down and hidden. Every time a person who has learned to hide who they are and what their natural gifts are will be surprised and at first ashamed about being noticed. Later there comes a realisation 'you mean it's all right to be like this? I am allowed?' Breakdown may be the only way we can break free of the 'false self' we've had to develop and claim our 'real self' or original seed.

Survival adaptations

We also have to adapt ourselves to our position in the families into which we are born. Oldest and only children have new, inexperienced parents and are special until another child comes along. They have to be helped to share. If there is no encouraging process for learning to share, they may feel that they have to strive constantly to achieve that special position later on in life, in order to feel good again, in the position they once knew as safe. They may feel they have no significance unless they are 'on top', the best, the only one. Middle children are always jockeying for position, trying to find a significant place, and can often feel 'pig in the middle' in later situations: frustrated, neither one thing nor the other, wanting a specific place. Sometimes middle children become the scapegoat. Youngest children are sometimes babied for too long, protected, taken for granted, forgotten, always trying to catch up. People born into very large families can sometimes feel as if they had no personal mothering or fathering, no special place of their own, and people brought up in institutions feel similarly but with a much greater sense of unrootedness, as if it were difficult to belong. Often what we miss out on in our family life we try to make up for later on, by deciding to have very different families.

These early adaptations can cause wounds, which we carry with us and which affect our later choices. We take up careers, lifestyles and marriages in the belief that we are as we've adapted ourselves. It isn't until we have some kind of crisis that we see that these choices do not necessarily reflect our real selves. This type of crisis always feels like a catastrophe but it is often an opportunity to sort out a way of life that is much better in the long term. For example, people who get married in order to get away from a difficult home situation often find that they have married into the same kind of situation, so rather than the marriage being a freedom, it is another trap. It is natural that we should be drawn to what is familiar, however destructive or bad for us it may be. It is what we know and, as we've seen, human beings are very good at survival and adaptation.

Sometimes people get very upset when they realise how much energy they've put into just surviving, and they wonder whether there is anything of their 'real' self left, or whether they are just very good accommodators, pleasers and adapters. However, it is important to realise that, although we may have stretched our ability to accommodate way beyond the appropriate point, this particular skill is one that we can take pride in. When we decide to use our gifts and energies in the service of our real self we then become connected to a much greater sense of purpose and meaning than before the crisis, when we were living lopsidedly, and cut off from a great wealth of energies inside ourselves. Often breakdown frees us into this, and allows us to claim our real self.

Adolescent or adult breakdowns have already happened in childhood

Without fail, a person who breaks down later on in life has suffered from some form of breakdown early on. If our attempts to communicate in childhood do not succeed we put the lid on and make a fixed decision about the way in which we should live. This means we start early on living lopsidedly, without the benefit of the fullness of our personality, and the original seed gets left far behind. We become brittle in the inner sense, cut off from our full resources, using up huge amounts of energy to keep down a whole host of feelings and images, thoughts and beliefs, that swirl like troubled mists inside us.

We know, from many professional studies, that early infant life is like a delicate keyboard: the note of the individual is there for the playing but the players are in charge of sounding the right tone, of laying an imprint and of unearthing that which is already imprinted. Our sense of safety, for example, is laid down according to our early bonding with whoever is mother for us. We know that very young children who are left for longer than a week can give up their search and longing for mother and appear not to know when she returns. This causes a wound but it can be healed. Sadly so often people interpret the crossness or withdrawal of a child as an attack against

23

them, expecting the more adult joy on reunion. They mistake the withdrawal for 'badness' when it is in fact a child's way of coping with impossible feelings.

Because few of us have many conscious memories of childhood and because the very early times are before words, what happens then is unknown in the conscious sense. It tends to get stored in the unconscious in the form of images or dreams or in the body as posture; smell, sound or touch may reawaken these memories. Sometimes when life pushes us into a situation in which we feel very small and dependent, like an infant, some of the fears we had when we were very young come to the surface. Early in life we defend ourselves against these fears because they feel so awful. Dr. Winnicot, an eminent child psychiatrist, used the term 'primitive agonies' to describe the kind of overpowering anxiety that fills a young infant who fears falling for ever, losing contact with his mother or someone close, or losing his sense of what is real to him, of disintegrating. The infant will find ways of defending himself against the unbearable; an autistic state is sometimes an extreme defence of this kind. Later on in life the person may find themselves living rigidly, in a limited, fragile way, as if the same fear were still in force.

In *Fear of Breakdown* Dr. Winnicot writes that some people carry a deep fear of breakdown all their lives, and this fear is, in fact, of the breakdown that has already occurred in early life. If we are able to realise this, to look at it, to share it as part of our journey, most effectively in a therapeutic situation, we are able to relieve some of the primitive agonies that dominate our lives. To reach breakthrough after breakdown, it is essential to reconnect with all the different facets of our early life, to discard those things that are no longer appropriate, to separate properly from the powerful adult figures who may still dominate our inner landscape and to reconnect with and build upon those aspects which haven't had much of a look in.

Exercise: Journey of your life

Here is a short questionnaire to help you piece together your early life and its patterning for yourself. Take lots of time and arm yourself with a notebook and pencil. If you have a good enough friend with whom you can share this exercise, take it in turns to ask each other the questions. Ask each question separately, so that you have time to feel its impact without the distraction of moving on to the next one. Alternatively you could write out each question on a different piece of card or paper, to free yourself to look only at one at a time. Browse, and let your memory or imagination supply you with any kind of answer, in whatever shape or form. Pictures or colours may appear; a memory may be triggered that seems unrelated; or an image of feeling may be stirred that has been forgotten and is not yet understood. Don't be put off, and don't be tempted to look at this section as you would a school book. You don't have to read every word. Just jot down what is interesting to you, what seems to click and what is useful for now. Any kind of drawing, sketch, pattern, jotting that you can make will help you put together a journal or description of your inner processes.

The exercise is best done lying down or half reclining: in bed or on the floor or sofa.

Imagine that your life is a journey ...

1 What kind of path do you feel you are on? Grainy, rocky, smooth, hard, short, long, wide, narrow or any other kind.
2 Is it your own path?
3 Or do you feel it belongs to someone else?
4 What kind of path do you feel you'd like to be on?
5 Imagine yourself on this very path and yourself travelling along it. What kind of clothes are you wearing, what are your surroundings like, what is the nature of your journey?
6 What would you most like to leave behind you?
7 What would you most like to take up and take with you? This can be anything: objects, animals, people, sound, plants, ideas, angels ...
8 What makes your heart sing?

With this image of yourself in mind cast yourself back now to the time of your early life.

1 What kind of family did you have ... brothers, sisters, father, mother, grandparents, housemother, fostermother? Make a family map for yourself picturing the time you were born: put in all the people who were around, give them colours and shapes. Put in other details such as people's occupations, their style according to mind, body, emotions, spirit. Describe one or two of their major qualities. Include family myths: for example, in our family, we always ... we never ...

Every family map tells a story. In this one, we can see a long line of strong women who had to be independent, and the effect this could have had on the children in the family: some of the men in the family became powerful themselves, such as the half brother, others had quieter, more withdrawn lives. There is also the fact of the deaths of the two firstborn children in each grandparent family, and the possible effect this had on the youngest child, particularly on the mother's side, as the dead 'lost' child was a girl. If the family map is worked in colours or shapes, using adjectives to describe each person, or particular sayings they had, we are able to see another kind of thread. There might be a long line of blue for example, or of women who suffered, or men who disliked their work. There will be a difference between town and country people, and in the type of education, religion, morals, ethics and habits.

2 Make a list of the main family mottoes or mores, the important messages you picked up about your family.

3 What was it like when you discovered you were a boy or a girl: was it a good thing to be your gender? How were boys and girls talked about? What ideas did you grow up with about the two sexes' roles in life?

4 What was it like during your early days at school? Were you prepared for school or was it a shock? Get in touch with some of your early memories of school and see what the picture is of the small boy or girl you were then. How do you feel about him or her now? What would you like to say to that child if he or she were here now, or if your he or she were your own child here and now (he or she actually is your own ... but so often we forget this, especially if our early times were painful).

5 What was your position in the family – eldest, middle, youngest, only – or were you passed from family to family? How did you cope with whatever position you had to take up? Looking back, what would you say you had to do for survival and love: did love come naturally or did you have to win or earn approval in order to feel loved?

6 What about sexuality, touching and matters to do with the body? How were these talked about,or were they not? What messages did you take in?

7 What were the religious views of the family? How many of these messages hold true for you now?

The aim of this questionnaire is to open up and amplify something of our past life and its influences upon us. The emphasis is always that *it is not what happens to us but what we make of what happens to us* that is important.

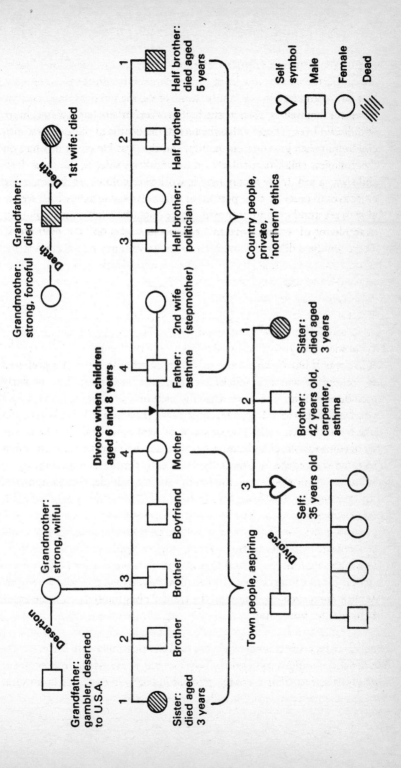

AN EXAMPLE OF A FAMILY MAP

Grandmother: strong, forceful

Grandfather: died

1st wife: died

Half brother: died aged 5 years

Half brother

Half brother: politician

2nd wife (stepmother)

Father: asthma

Country people, private, 'northern' ethics

Death

Death

1 2 3 4

Grandfather: gambler, deserted to U.S.A.

Grandmother: strong, wilful

Desertion

Sister: died aged 3 years

Brother

Brother

Boyfriend

Mother

1 2 3 4

Divorce when children aged 6 and 8 years

Sister: died aged 3 years

Brother: 42 years old, carpenter, asthma

Self: 35 years old

1 2 3

Town people, aspiring

Divorce

Self symbol ♡

Male ☐

Female ◯

Dead ▨

We may be extremely angry, and rightly and appropriately angry, for what we feel was done to us, and many of us seek to blame the perpetrators of what we see as injustice. However, what we have to do when we begin to look at our lives and take our development into our own hands, is to separate out what we want to let go of from what we want to keep, and get on with it. People who were deprived either emotionally or materially sometimes create an either/or split in their thinking. Their important relationships may become either idealised ('the one who's going to be everything I need') or rubbished ('he/she just has no idea, doesn't care and is hateful'). In this dichotomy we swing from idealisation and hope to despair and loss, without getting what we need, because there is no place where someone is 'good enough'. We cannot spend our lives looking for an idealised image of a mother and father we didn't have – what we need to find are people, places and experiences that are good for us and meet our needs.

THE STAGES OF BREAKDOWN

For most of us breakdown tends to happen when external events press us on internal places where we have few or poorly developed coping strategies. These external events may be extreme and totally out of our experience, for which nothing could have prepared us. They may be life events which challenge us in a new way and with which we cannot cope. Or we may have been becoming more and more vulnerable because of what we are feeling about ourselves: our self esteem may have become low or we may have been continually disappointed so that we begin to lose hope of change or of something new happening.

In the previous section we were looking at some of the reasons for breakdown in terms of our personal development and the values we grew up with. But we need a framework within which we can view what is happening to us that will allow us to extract as much as possible from the experience. We need to begin to develop some idea of the shape, time, stages and purpose of our breakdown. Even if it is just a thin thread, it will help us to hold on to something when we feel ourselves in danger and when we feel the criticism and judgements of others. Breakdowns are always difficult, painful, and turbulent experiences and not many people have patience for them. It is important to have some kind of light to find the way in such a dark place. We can hold on to this ourselves, or friends and family can hold it for us.

I see breakdown having the following five phases:

The onset of symptoms

Our symptoms may be physical, mental, emotional or have visionary, dream and fantasy components. Something in us is changing, although we may not notice it significantly at first because we try to carry on as best we can to overcome what we may see as a nuisance or a difficulty. Who we consult at this time will have a significant influence on how we approach our symptoms and how we take care of ourselves. When the message of the symptoms is not heard they tend to become more severe, they begin to have a firmer grip on our lives so that we are forced to consider them seriously. At this stage we may have very little idea of what they are trying to tell us, we just know that they are ever present and that we cannot ignore them.

'On the edge'

This is the stage when we begin to feel desperate because we can feel our symptoms taking over, and nothing we try works to relieve them. We can feel ourselves being pushed into a corner. We wonder when and where it will all end. The tension is appalling and exhausting. Because we are still trying to survive by the means we know, all our energy is used up and we have no time for pleasure, friends or relaxation, and comfort seems a long way away.

We may begin at this stage to think of forcing a way out of the intolerable tension: driving into a tree, walking in front of a train, taking a bottle of pills, getting on a bus and not getting off, drowning ourselves in alcohol or drugs, doing anything recklessly and desperately because we imagine anything is better than what we are feeling. We begin to worry that we are going mad, but we don't have the words to communicate our fears and it feels as if no one will really understand – we're not sure ourselves exactly what the trouble is. We may have made all kinds of external changes: house, job, hair, partner, to try to relieve our problems, but this still doesn't help. We may have dreams or fantasies about 'falling in', drowning, falling off the world, being in a lift which crashes, a train which comes off the rails or a ship that is sinking.

Crisis

This is where we hit rock bottom, we fall into the abyss or pit, we reach our 'no go' area or 'impasse' and we become helpless and out of control in varying degrees. Our conscious energy is given up and we enter an unknown, either semi-conscious time or are actually unconscious. In this place we face our personal ghosts or demons, everything we've feared about being out of control. We are vulnerable, we feel alone, we feel as if we have been stripped bare, forced out of protective covering, like the hermit crab who grows out of his shell and has to find another one. In this space we may need to be safe and protected, nurtured in the most basic of ways, allowed to take up what we are experiencing and not organised or interfered with in ways that jar or compromise us; we need time to heal the hurt of the crisis and of the exposure to intense fear.

Thawing out

We need time to recover from shock and re-enter life. This is a very painful time with many doubts and questions, many fears about the future and about who will help us and stay with us. We feel the painful return of circulation in the same way as when a limb has been frozen or numbed. We are like shell-shocked soldiers, nervous and apprehensive, wondering what it was all for.

Rebuilding

This is a very crucial time. As we begin to feel better we may be tempted to put a lid on the whole experience and try to forget it, carrying on as we did before. This is patching ourselves up too hastily. In this phase we have a chance to look and learn from what has happened, to process the experience, to grieve for what has been lost and heal the feeling of onslaught and attack. We are open still at this stage and vulnerable to forces around that are helpful and unhelpful. We are in a unique position to feel into which people or experiences are useful and valuable and which are not. We may not have been able to do this during the other four phases of our breakdown. This is an opportunity to learn new ways of experiencing and coping with life, to try to practise speaking out what we think or feel, being assertive, being objective, taking up our lives in a more positive way. We may here really let go of old defences and learn new skills.

Breakdown means something quite different to each person who goes on this journey as we will see from all the different stories of people who have had breakdowns, who have shared in the writing of this book. The timing of the breakdown is highly individual and the length of time it lasts varies from two years to nine years in terms of the five stages. The longest consecutive time spent in hospital was six weeks although I have met other people who have spent much longer than this and needed to have subsequent stays at other stages. Breakdown is a totally individual experience and one which means something to each individual in terms of their life and what they make of that life. There are as many breakdowns as people who break down.

How some breakdowns are experienced

Here are some of the ways in which people describe their experiences of breakdown:

It was like drowning.

I was on the edge of a precipice, about to fall in.

I felt again and again as if I was standing in a whirlpool, holding myself up by the collar of my shirt so that I wouldn't drown, my arms getting tireder and tireder.

I felt as if my skin would split.

If I cry I will never stop; if I speak I will cry; if I move I will shatter into a thousand pieces. If I smile, my face will crack in two. I am alone. No one knows, really knows, how I feel.

I cannot take any more of life. I cannot go on. I am numb.

If I stop I will die. If I don't stop I will die.

I felt all my nerves break ... my tummy blew out ... I was in agony and I didn't know what it was.

It was like a bomb going off, in a way. I just collapsed on the bed and couldn't stop crying.

I saw my teacher, a woman whom I greatly feared, coming up to the house where we lived and suddenly in front of my eyes she turned into the Devil. She was carrying these buckets that she'd been feeding the chickens with and she was looking very much her usual self and suddenly I felt this totally other thing, something completely evil, and I had the greatest feeling of terror I'd ever had in my life, and I gathered the few belongings in my rucksack, jumped on my bicycle as though all the evils of Hell were after me. I felt that my only hope was to go to Rome to the Inquisition, confess all and ask to be received into the Order.

Every one of these people had an individual journey to make, and their language gives us clues to the nature of that journey, their starting place. What does drowning mean to one person, for example? What figure does the Devil take in the shape of this man's life? At points of crisis people may not be able to respond to these kinds of questions, but later on, in a place of safety or containment such as in therapy or in reflection, they may come to understand the meaning of their personal imagery. This can help to put them in touch with the kind of journey they are embarking on. For example, Nadia had a breakdown soon after her first child was born and after a period of what is called post-natal depression. Her images and her dreams during her breakdown and just preceding it were of children, or of a foetus being ripped out: they both referred to her actual experience of childbirth and beyond this to her own unlived life, the child in her that had not been allowed to develop. This particular story is amplified in the section on birth trauma and post-natal depression.

So the individual journey and language comes first. But there are some common denominators among people's experiences of breakdown.

1 The feeling of being out of control and in alien territory with nothing previously 'known' to help cope.
2 The feeling of isolation, and at times, of alienation.
3 The struggle to keep going and to try to find a rational explanation.

4 The terror of going mad and of mental illness.
5 The power of the internal images and sometimes voices and messages. The demonic quality of the experience.
6 The feeling of shame, and of guilt.
7 Obsession with one thing as a solution, or with an event, perhaps a long time in the past, that comes to dominate all thinking and communication.
8 The sense of persecution, being 'got at', sometimes fear of crucifixion.
9 The loss of humour, light heartedness, sense of perception and insight, and an inability to be flexible, to adapt.
10 A difficulty, almost an inability, to express verbally what is happening.
11 A sense of hopelessness.
12 An intense suffering.

THE FORMS BREAKDOWN CAN TAKE

Breakdown may be experienced in a long drawn out way, taking months or years. This drawn out process may be contained, as it often is during analysis or therapy, or it may be allowed to happen spontaneously because an individual is in the right place for this: within a caring family, in a religious order or community, or with caring others who help look after but do not interfere. Breakdown may also appear in acute form, becoming a crisis for which professional help is needed in the form of hospitalisation, medication, safe containment and looking after. The long drawn out breakdown may include a period of acute breakdown.

Contained breakdown

Sometimes people know intuitively that they need a period of withdrawal from life in order to process something that is happening to them. Sometimes people get an urge to travel and during the journey they have a realisation that changes the way they approach things. Writers like Virginia Woolf and Rupert Brooke were able to contain their individual breakdowns in the form of poetry or the novel. One of the best documented contained breakdowns is that of C.G. Jung, who consciously decided to allow and explore what the unconscious offered him. In *Memories, Dreams, Reflections*, his autobiography, he writes 'I lived as if under constant inner pressure. At times this became so strong that I suspected there was some psychic disturbance in myself. Therefore, I twice went over all the details of my entire life, with particular attention to childhood memories, for I thought there might be something in my past which I could not see and which might possibly be the cause of the disturbance. But this retrospection led to nothing but a fresh acknowledgment of my own ignorance. Thereupon I said to myself "Since I know nothing at all I shall simply do whatever occurs to me". Thus I consciously submitted myself to the impulses of the unconscious.

'In order to grasp the fantasies which were stirring in me underground, I knew that I had to let myself plummet down into them, as it were. I felt not only violent resistance to this but a distinct fear. For I was afraid of losing command of myself and becoming prey to the fantasies – and as a psychiatrist I realised only too well what that meant. After prolonged hesitation however I saw that there was no other way out. I had to take the chance. I had to try and gain power over them. For I realised that if I did not do so, I ran the risk of their gaining power over me. A cogent motive for my making the attempt was the conviction that I could not expect of my patients something that I did not dare do for myself.

'The essential thing is to differentiate oneself from these unconscious contents by personifying them, and at the same time bring them into relationship with consciousness. That is the technique for stripping them of their power.

'It is, of course, ironical, that I, a psychiatrist, should at almost every step of my experiment have run into the same psychic material which is the stuff of psychosis and is found in the insane. This is the fund of unconscious images which fatally confuse the mental patient. But it is also the fund of mythopoetic imagination which has vanished from our rational age.'

During this period Jung kept a journal of his experiences, and painted the images that came to him. He created mandalas and built a stone city on the beach near Bollingen where he lived, so that his unconscious experience was contained and 'grounded' in this very special way. It is important that the powerful images from the unconscious are allowed time to meet with consciousness by asking, for example, 'What do you want of me? Who are you?' It is also important that these powerful images are validated by another person, so that the person experiencing them feels safe to tell of his images; otherwise they may be dismissed as 'only' fantasies of no use, or they may feel too terrifying to acknowledge. When these powerful images are accepted as offerings of a psyche that knows what it is doing, they can be seen as an aspect of the individual whose self image is undergoing great change or transformation. Although these powerful images may be labelled psychotic they often have visionary components but these are not able to be experienced as such and allowed and validated unless they are met by others who are prepared to offer this meeting.

Analysis or therapy offers one way in which a person may be able to share and process what is happening unconsciously as he journeys into frightening territory. Another example of a contained breakdown came from a woman I met who had struggled with a marriage break-up at the same time as keeping an extremely busy and demanding job where she was in sole command. She said, 'I realise now why I'm going back to live near my family in the USA. I feel I need to be allowed to be in a place where I can be looked after in some form if that becomes necessary. I know that they would support me, even take me in. Here I've no-one like this.

'I suppose I feel I need to be allowed to break down if this were necessary. Here I can't do this, I have to keep going and inevitably if I carry on as I am doing, in a few years – maybe sooner – it is all going to crash in on me, and I will probably have a more severe breakdown than if I put myself in a safe place and allow myself to experience whatever it is I need to. I just know I am sitting on a volcano which has to erupt at some time. I would rather allow for the eruption, than be taken over destructively.'

Such experiences are perhaps rare. They tend not to have specific labels because they are allowed to become part of the stuff of life itself, they are contained amongst the ordinariness of life. Many contained breakdowns are therefore hidden, perhaps written about in journals or woven into the fabric of novels, becoming a personal journey, a rite of passage, an experience of self. Social differences play a large part in the ease with which breakdown is allowed. It is perhaps easier to be a little odd in the country, if you are self-employed or if your job description is 'arty'. It is much more difficult in high profile city life and in traditional professions such as banking and accountancy where a high degree of control and regularity is expected. It is hard for people in the caring professions such as doctors and nurses to break down or to show signs of needing help and, because of this, they are actually the most vulnerable of all. Many people impose limits on themselves: they are frightened of how they feel because there are no maps for it in their experience and they are afraid of being dismissed as 'loopy'. They may not therefore, allow themselves to break down unless it becomes forced upon them.

Acute breakdown

When long drawn out symptoms become a crisis and we lose control completely, we enter a phase of acute breakdown. This may appear to be sudden but with hindsight there are always signs or clues. During this period we may become mute – unable to speak or acknowledge contact; we may become catatonic – rigid and staring in one position; we may curl up in a ball, in a foetal position with our thumb in our mouth, perhaps just able to rock to and fro. We may not be able to stop crying. Sometimes we have hallucinations, visions, hear voices ordering us to do things, driving us on. We may become fixed on one idea or thought.

Tom told me 'I had this religious thing. It all had to do with the life and death of Jesus. Friday was the day I would be crucified. The days leading up to Friday were awful: all I could think about was how I would deal with Friday'.

Kathleen said 'I knew I was extremely tired and anxious and depressed but it was like a bomb going off in a way. I mean I just collapsed completely on the bed and couldn't stop crying'.

Margaret described her experience: 'It was as though I had suddenly found some kind of energy which I experienced as a voice at times, anyway an impulse, which was all hostile or mocking and which was stripping down all the ideas I had about myself. This stripping process seemed to take them right down to the bare bones, and the bare bones of me felt extremely inadequate, small, extremely defenceless and vulnerable. The idea of betrayal was such a strong feeling – why should it happen to me? It was the first question that came to me. It actually incapacitated me, the attacking voices. I had to give up work and went into hospital'.

Prolonged breakdown

But the most common form of breakdown is prolonged – long and drawn out. Sometimes the pressure of this forces people into a state of collapse, and they may spend a period of time being looked after in a hospital or nursing home. However, most people I met or who wrote to me soldier on alone, being supported by family and the friends who are allowed to know, or fighting their experience completely alone, unable to communicate to anyone, unable to ask, suffering from people's rejection of them because of the perceived stigma of mental illness. What was undoubtedly a crisis extended sometimes into years.

Fiona wrote to me: 'The first symptom was that my brain slowed down – I became unable to digest information or absorb the written word. I got mental blocks at work and because my job involved plenty of brain power I got word-dazzle and could no longer comprehend what was going on. Fear set in, and panic. I felt sure that I was cracking up. Help me! I was in need of Samaritans, but my pride would not allow me to involve anyone else. I relate here the words I wrote at a critical time:

It is Sunday 16th May and for 13 days now I have felt like a zombie. Just in case it is the onset of a mental breakdown (as I fear) then just in case I snap, I would like to record how I felt leading up to this state. It all began with an anxiety state during a love affair with a married man, which ended so sharply, and then a period of total apathy and then deep depression, the last stage where I am physically coping but mentally numb and psychologically dead. I have got to a stage where I cannot hold a reasonable conversation and when somebody talks to me, little sinks in. To read is a daze. To sort out sense from what I'm reading is almost impossible. I don't hear all my children say to me when they speak. I am short-tempered and trembling some of the time. My eyes don't always feel they are focusing. Each day is a little worse to bear. I've been to the doctor who because I had headaches said it was a sinus infection and gave me penicillin. Should I ask to see a psychiatrist, will it hinder or help? At all times I must be in control of my life. I fear for my kids if I can't look after them. Is there a preventative step I should be taking? Should I give in; should I fight it? Is it just mental exhaustion? Have I already stopped functioning?

Help! I am trying really hard but nothing works. Will I be any better tomorrow?

Fiona experienced all the dilemmas produced by her 'new' state – what should she do? how should she cope? who would help? what did it mean? As her symptoms – being unable to concentrate on people speaking to her or on written words, trembling and headaches – became more frequent she tried to deal with them by a series of questions, grasping at external concepts, at explanations for her state and so perhaps for a solution.

Other common feelings during prolonged breakdowns include feeling depressed and anxious for no apparent reason; living daily with an exhausting emotional turmoil, interspersed with manic, excited periods; or saying things which don't make sense to anyone. Some people cannot stop crying, especially when on their own, and several people reported making rocking movements, as they sat in a chair weeping through most of their days. The feeling is of having nowhere to go – that there is no future or hope – only an increasingly despairing landscape. Other symptoms include strange dreams and fantasies, being fixed on a particular theme or image, becoming obsessed with a particular person or situation that may be present or have passed, or becoming obsessed with work or tasks.

2
The individual language of breakdown

Between seed and survival self there are often gaps, when neither self is in operation. In these gaps we are vulnerable to anxiety, depression, fears and phobias of all kinds. Often these gaps are experienced more profoundly when a major life event, crisis or loss has occurred and we are thrown off course or are in a new position and uncertain how to be. If these gaps are prolonged we develop symptoms.

These symptoms contain the essence of our dilemma and they are the link between survival self and seed self. They often contain, in metaphor and symbol, something of what the seed is trying to communicate but has no language for as yet. We can learn to read these symptoms as attempts of the psyche to restore balance or as an indication that the survival self is no longer needed. Symptoms are signalling devices aimed to help us get in touch with parts of ourselves we've forgotten or pushed aside, and which have been excluded from our consciousness. They can link us with the depths of our inner world. Their presence means that something is happening: we are not static machines but living, learning, growing human individuals. As long as we are alive to these processes we are alive to the possibility of change and to fulfilling what we come to find our life is about.

We are all familiar with the heroic quests of the Gods and Goddesses from Greek and Roman mythology and from fairy tales from all lands. Many breakdowns have the same heroic flavour: journeying in the dark, meeting terrifying figures and monsters, overcoming obstacles and climbing out from the abyss. By reaching into our symptoms with purpose and exploring them with meaning we are claiming the right to journey in our own myth or story and we deepen our experience. Not all breakdowns are vivid mythic experiences but if the opportunity to view breakdowns in this way is denied the alternative is to become a passive patient taken up by a system that would medicalise symptoms or cut them out, reduce imaginative experiences to meaningless madness and leave us stuck in a limbo between psychological life and death.

STRESS, FATIGUE AND EXHAUSTION

Some form of stress is necessary for all movement and is therefore an important part of ordinary life. The kind of stress people mostly talk about today is unhealthy stress. This is usually caused by situations in which the demands on us are far greater than the effort we feel able to make. Everyone has their individual stressors: what to one person is easy and taken for granted (flying an aeroplane or driving a car, for example) is to another intolerable. Likewise some people seem able to survive many serious life events such as bereavement, numerous moves, marriage break-ups, illnesses and other deprivations with little ill effect, whilst others find one act of effort, for example making and sustaining relationships, extremely difficult and painful and are under constant stress from this worry. Stress is not something that is always obvious. Loneliness and depression are stressful, and so are anxiety, mood swings and all phobias. Everyone who suffers emotionally in this way brings to the things they do in life an added burden.

The Rahe scale of stress indicates points for stressful life events. If we have scored over 150 points in the last six months we are under stress.

Although this stress scale is a useful indicator for assessing the kind of stress we are under from external matters, assessing how much stress we are under from internal conflicts is a very individual concern. Each person will bring to the evaluation of their score on the Rahe scale whatever are their own inner conflicts and problems. The death of a close friend, for example, will be far more stressful to someone for whom this friend was the only friend, than for someone who has many friends. Change in work status might also carry the burden of defeat, or the anxiety of finding ourselves in a job we feel unsure about doing.

40

It is useful to make an individual map of our internal stressful burdens to go alongside the Rahe scale. One way to do this is to make a list of all the things you find fearful. Then list whether you encounter these fearful things daily or have to find strategies to avoid what you fear. Sometimes we don't actually know what we find fearful because we have overriden it by pushing the feeling down. What happens in our bodies is an indication of the level of fear or stress we are under. If you have difficulty making the list of your fears, make a note, for one week, of the times you notice that you are clenching your fists or raising your shoulders without realising it, or that your pulse is raised while you are talking to someone or doing something you find difficult. Stomach churning, frequent swallowing, headaches, nausea, dry mouth, fast-beating heart or having to go to the lavatory more than usual, are all also bodily responses to fear. As you look at the scale below, make your own individual ratings (1–5 top end) on top of the Rahe scale.

The Rahe Scale of Stress

Event	Scale of Impact	Event	Scale of Impact
Death of spouse	100	Change in work status	29
Divorce	73	Son/daughter leaves home	29
Marital separation	65	Trouble with in-laws	29
Jail term	63	Major personal achievement	28
Death of close family member	63	Change in spouse's work	26
Personal injury or illness	53	Starting or leaving school	26
Marriage	50	Change in living conditions	25
Loss of job	47	Revision of personal habits	24
Marital reconciliation	45	Trouble with boss	23
Retirement	45	Change of work hours	20
Health problems in family	44	Change in residence	20
Pregnancy	40	Change in schools	20
Sexual difficulties	39	Change in recreation	19
Gain of new family member	39	Change in church activities	19
Business re-adjustment	39	Change in social activities	18
Change in finances	38	Small mortgage taken out	17
Death of a close friend	37	Change in sleeping habits	16
Change in line of work	36	Change in family reunions	15
Argument with spouse	35	Change in eating habits	15
Large mortgage taken out	31	Vacation	13
Foreclosure of mortgage	30	Christmas	12
		Minor violations of the law	11

Serious fatigue

When we are overstressed in whatever way this happens for us (this can vary during different periods of our lifespan) and we have to keep going through the stressful period, we use 'reserve energy' or willpower in order to manage the situation. We usually get more stressed when we feel we have few options in choosing how to cope with something. Sometimes these periods of being overstressed are unavoidable, as when a close family member is ill and has to be looked after while we keep up our full time job at the same time. If we are able to ask for the help we need and get some support for the tasks we have to do, our burden will be shared and the effect of the stress much less. Sometimes this is impossible; sometimes we feel that we cannot ask for the help we need, take time off to rest when we have been overstressed for long periods or lessen what we do in order to accommodate the new situation we find ourselves in. If we feel that we must meet any demands made of us in whatever way we can, we are steered into the path of ill health rather than recovering naturally from a period of unhealthy stress.

If we feel like this, we justify it by telling ourselves that we must be stoic, be brave, keep a stiff upper lip and go it all alone; or we may be extremely frightened of being disadvantaged if we ask for help or advice or if we are seen not to cope; or we may be terrified of seeming 'lazy', 'needy' or 'underactive'. Many of the people I see who suffer from unhealthy stress do not know when they are tired; they do not know how much work is enough, how much is too little or too much; something inside them drives them on to go go go, to work work work, and never to be seen as weak, wanting or vulnerable. When these demanding inner figures take over, our life is at their mercy.

When the stress we are under has pushed us into serious fatigue we begin to manifest symptoms of different kinds. When we wake in the mornings, even if we have slept all night, we still feel tired. Our sleep may become disturbed, we may have difficulty in going to sleep, or wake early, at three or four in the morning and not go back to sleep. There may be other, added reasons for sleep disturbance, such as depression and anxiety, but fatigue itself can produce difficulties in sleeping. After a weekend break we may also still feel tired and wonder how we will get through the week ahead. When we are seriously fatigued we do no more than is absolutely essential and, because we are so tired, we tend to take longer to do what we have to do.

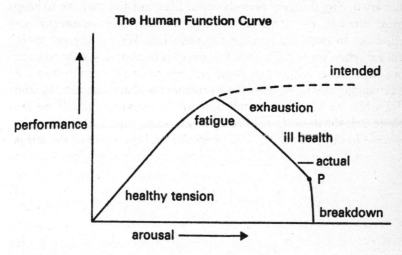

The Human Function Curve

P = The point at which even minimal arousal may precipitate a breakdown

The Human Function Curve

The Human Function Curve, invented by Dr. Peter Nixon at Charing Cross Hospital, London, describes what happens to us when we go 'over the hump' into exhaustion. Rather than stop when we are extremely tired, some of us press on, trying to make up for what we feel we lack. We work harder, longer, sometimes through flu, colds, even pneumonia and broken bones, in order to try to meet the gap between what we intend to achieve and what we are actually achieving. Because we are getting exhausted our performance is actually dropping, causing us more and more anxiety. After a while we lose all sense of reason and judgement, we are unable to listen to people who try to help us and we become fixated with the job we feel we must accomplish at all costs.

At these times we are functioning only from our *left brain* – the part of the brain responsible for the right side of the body and for the more focused, goal-orientated, rigid activities. We are not in touch with our *right brain* which directs our ability to relax, have pleasure and take in love and affection. We sleep poorly and feel guilty for sleeping or

43

EXHAUSTION

I'm tired

From inside out
my spirit craves for
crumbs of comfort anywhere.

A body lost at sea
I sink in hopeless search
for your attention.

I'm almost proud of
my exhaustion
I wear it like a medal
to prove 'she tried'.

But now's the time
to say 'I quit'
and let the pain begin.

Fatigue and pain must
fade away
through ticking minutes
of my alarm

and only then will I become
more than I was before.

stopping at all. Long ago we gave up enjoying ourselves or taking relaxing breaks, being sensitive to our needs. In this state, which can go on for as long as two years, it takes just one incident, in itself not significant, to push us into breakdown and collapse.

Exhaustion

When we put ourselves under prolonged stress and suffer for a long time from serious fatigue we become exhausted. Exhaustion is a catabolic state in which our whole system is highly active or aroused and it can produce serious physical symptoms which may be confused with organic illness. Our hormone balance becomes lopsided and we produce too much adrenalin, affecting the kidneys, heart and reproductive systems. When we are exhausted we tend to hyperventilate (breathe shallowly from the upper chest with occasional deep sighs). Hyperventilation can bring on symptoms such as dizziness, pins and needles in the hands and feet, coldness in the limbs and chest pain. When we are exhausted we are very fixed and blinkered, so we tend to appear highly obsessional and even paranoid; the highly aroused state of exhaustion with its accompanying feelings of entrapment, frustration and fury can sometimes give the appearance of a psychotic state and be confused with this. Sometimes only an enforced sleep of at least six days can help people to get out of these highly charged and dangerous situations. It is easy to see how exhaustion and breakdown can be interlinked.

CHARLOTTE

Charlotte, a beautiful young actress whose professional life demanded several public appearances, came from a family that were never allowed to stop. Their motto was 'I work, work, work'.

> In my family you were never allowed to stop. Being ill was the only way to stop: you didn't get pampered but it was an excuse to stop. It was a form of communication – illness they could talk about, they couldn't talk about anything else. It became a false kind of communication. My mother died when I was seven. We weren't allowed to mourn her, we weren't allowed to be vulnerable. When I

started having anxiety attacks, a friend said I should talk to someone, but I said 'Absolute rubbish'. One didn't talk about these things because the family said 'Put your head down, wait, keep quiet until it goes away, or you die'. No one was to know. All this stress was on myself I now realise.

Her breakdown started when she was about 25 but she didn't know it.

I think it showed itself first as hypochondria. I had constant illnesses – tonsillitis, respiratory infections – I had a totally unnecessary lymph gland biopsy. I turned a muscle in my knee and couldn't walk for months. I got strange viruses that would last forever and leave me totally drained and energyless. Then I got pneumonia and bronchitis. I had some very important work which I went on and did. I had no sense of decision any more, no sense of being able to withdraw or choose. I just had to keep going. Of course it was bad artistic judgment, but I think I was losing all sense of judgment.

Over the next four years Charlotte struggled to keep going.

I was in enormous distress inside but I didn't know what it was. I was blinkered, out of touch with everything that was to do with inside me. The man I was living with was all driving energy and drove me on too. Then we were evicted from our flat with a lot of huge old furniture and nowhere to go. At the same time my parents moved from the house where I'd been brought up. Everything became terribly cut off. We had no money so I started sewing dresses but immediately my right hand collapsed. We were drinking an enormous amount of whisky. Michael was rehearsing his part nine hours a day, but I had no shape to my life: I'd lost my voice, and I had all this work coming up. I'd be trying to learn my part with no voice, feeling terribly ill, no money coming in, in a state of complete panic, never knowing what would happen next.

I couldn't go out of the house, couldn't bear to see anybody, be with anybody. The thing that finally broke me was that I got paranoid. I thought 'They're out there not valuing my wonderful art. They have no sense.' I was being persecuted. Then I went blind in an anxiety attack. I couldn't see. I lay there terrified. I was completely out of my head with it.

At the time I was terrified anyone in my profession would find out. I would cut myself off from professional colleagues. I had no telephone. I could disappear but I couldn't be seen to be ill. I had to be seen without any vulnerability. If I had been seen to have any vulnerability someone would threaten, would kick it immediately – that was the fear. I had to be in control all the time. I continued working, coming back to our one room, sleeping on the floor and seeing no one but my boyfriend at the time. I needed him desperately to be with me all the time. I remember giving him all my books saying 'You use them, you're the brilliant one'. I felt as if I had lost everything, my identity, everything. And when this relationship broke up – a friend told me Michael had been having an affair with someone else – the betrayal, what I'd always feared would happen, what I always almost expected would happen, took me as low as I could possibly get, because it was the one thing I was expecting all my life. Almost always that was what people did. Now Michael had gone, I was in disarray ... no meaning at all.

During this time, Charlotte stayed in her room for a year with the television on most of the time. Her GP came and visited her and they became good friends. She started counselling twice a week. It was the only time she went out, and she remembers crying most of the time.

I was really at rock bottom, in the pit, the abyss. I did venture out once I remember. I forced, drove myself to a recording studio but I couldn't say anything. It was unthinkable to cancel it as people would know. It was the only time in my career that I let anyone down – that was my nadir. I couldn't make the journey home. I remember there was no one and it's the only time in my life I thought about a way out. I saw a bus coming and I thought without passion of any kind – 'I wonder what it's like?'

I think that the turning point for all this was a wonderful dream I had, from which I woke in deep, deep sobs – but somehow everything was different for me than anything that had gone before. In the dream, it was completely black, pitch, nothing and then I saw the figure of Christ in Gethsemane and He said 'I'm here with you and I've been there before you.' It was wonderful. I reckon I was cured (whatever that means). The depression went on but nothing was ever the same.

I feel that I broke down because I was in the wrong place doing the wrong things and one day something snapped. I was in the wrong kind of pot, in my family, and out of extreme sensitivity I joined in, aided and abetted as far as I could. My brothers and sisters are all severely damaged but I was the only one that broke down. I feel now that I am somebody – before I had these swings of feeling I was nothing – nothing whilst I was in the grip of my critical monster driving me on never to stop and nothing if I stopped and was ill. I had no sense of my real self. I only realised recently that I never took a holiday. And what perpetuated the drive to go on was the way I jeopardised my chances. I would work very hard and do a good performance and get lots of offers and every time I would muck up the next offer. So the cycle would have to start all over again and the drive would have to begin all over again.

I've been to the place I most feared ... total vulnerability. I don't think I'll ever feel that vulnerable again. I'm bigger, freer from what I've learned and I don't believe I could have learned it any other way, and I've found something which gives me a true sense of love and oneness.

For the second edition of this book, several years later, Charlotte adds:

The wounding is fresher than ever, and when triggered, more open and fluent. What is different is that I am increasingly more connected to and aware of the triggers, those events which will sting the wound into bleeding. The wounding was to me, as a child. Over the last twelve years my inner parent, connected to my own adult, has come into being. She works to take care of the (inner) child at these times, and makes sure that the child's needs get heard, and if possible attended to enough, for the inner child to survive the pain.

The pain is different in that it is no longer a symptomatic pain, a depression, paranoia or emptiness, developed to alert me to the deeper, hidden unhappiness and bewilderment. When it comes it is the overwhelming and shattering pain of loss followed by a sense of isolation and fear of the tribe. But now at last the pain receives a loving response.

Having received from my mind and body the urgent message to pay attention – presented as breakdown – I have learned to face my fears, instead of pretending they weren't there. In doing this, largely through continuing therapy, I have discovered a courage and resource in myself, stronger year by year. I have contacted my own depths and power, and touched an understanding of the unity of all things. And I have learned that fear can be transformed only if you do not run from it. The alchemy is created by spending time with the fear in oneself; there is nothing to do *to* it.

I have learned to confer with others rather than to defer to them It truly was Breakdown to Breakthrough.

I would like to say to anyone going through the worst stages of breakdown, something that may not be able to be heard, but can be seeded: 'you are not alone in this experience, others have walked this way and come through it. However hard it is, make marks on paper – words, colours, drawings, whole sheets if necessary, but begin to encourage what is inside to come outside. I am reminded of an art student who, in despair, went to his tutor and said 'I can only draw horrible angels, there is nothing else'. The tutor wisely said 'then draw them until they stop. Then there will be room for something else to appear.'

In looking back I realise that I was looking for the blueprint of how a human should be, the map, the rules of how you did this thing called living. (With a frequently absent mother from $3^1/2$ years old and an emotionally absent father, it wasn't surprising that I didn't have much of a clue!). I felt that everyone else knew, and I had to be careful not to let them know I didn't, or I would die. I never did find the blueprint. I've since discovered there isn't one. I can make up my own life. It is such a relief! Now I can have joy in it as I want to!

The kind of messages that drive us on until we lose judgment, sense, value and proportion could be:

1 I must never stop because to stop, take a rest, take a holiday, relax, take up a hobby or to play, means nothingness. My dilemma becomes: either I am constantly driving myself, developing tasks all the time, building business, work, doing things for other people, or I am nothing. In this dilemma there is no place to be real, myself. It is as if our real natural self, the person we find we are in between the driven monsters, is not allowed to exist.

2 If I stop I will fall off the end of the earth, be swallowed in the abyss, kicked to death, annihilated, exposed, devoured, eaten up, left on a bare mountain, be the last person left on the earth.
3 No one will love/want/admire me unless I am constantly striving and achieving.

Sometimes this idea about how we must conduct ourselves comes from an early role model – parents or family. One parent may be admired and the other seen as weak and vulnerable. If mother was strong, dominant, pushing and striving, and father was weak, absent, indecisive or alcoholic, the mother's qualities will be identified as the better ones to strive for. If father was a traditional breadwinner and mother stayed at home and had a negative self image, a daughter who wants a career for herself may identify more with father and put down the feminine side of her being, associating it with negativity and vulnerability. Finding a middle place, a place where we can begin to trust that there is something inside us that is truly ours, that comes spontaneously out of us and can be strengthened, so that just *being* is safe and happily creative is what our journey is about.

ANNA

Anna had a breakdown six months after completing a very difficult year of hard work. During this year she did not feel stressed and her previously high blood pressure stayed low.

> I felt more fulfilled that year than I have ever done in my life. I felt incredibly strong, the days were full and so much was happening. I was working for the Peace movement on the perimeter of a missile base and we lived in pretty awful conditions, freezing cold and living rough. There was a lot of pain and upset but we all felt that we were doing something concrete on an issue we felt strongly about. There was a lot of external stress: it was a very bad winter and we had to walk four miles for water; and then there was seeing what for defence the Ministry were doing to the land; and having 500 policemen hovering round 150 of us when they put the fence up. But in spite of the difficulties and personal discomfort it didn't feel hard. For me – I'm really quite a conventional person and people who normally do these things are not conventional – it was a big thing to do. I put my

whole self into it and really felt that we were achieving something important in terms of communication with the police and MOD – all the uniformed people – because we made tea and talked a lot to them and they sat by our fire and we kept a prayer vigil. I think we broke a lot of stereotypes: they saw us as real people and we saw them as people not uniforms.

But when we got home after that year everything changed. To begin with it was lovely, all mod cons again, and we started to write a book about our experiences. But I began to get very emotional for no reason at all: bursting into tears, not nice to my husband, my moods kept changing. I was in terrible conflict with myself. I wasn't sleeping. One of the doctors in the practice suggested it was the Change which was awful. I was only 47, so I half hoped I might be pregnant rather than being 'over the hill'. I thought perhaps it was all to do with hormones and I must live with it, feeling ghastly inside. I couldn't do any of the things I wanted: I was at home, trying to do some things but at the last moment I'd get panicky, afraid I'd cry if someone spoke to me, so I opted out and felt very guilty ... a catch 22 situation. Then I got very bad, very irrational; not myself, not sleeping, I couldn't switch my head off.

Finally I saw my own doctor who I like and he said he thought it was a lot of stress that hadn't come out the year before – all the living at such a pitch that suddenly my body said 'Enough is enough' and that was the sort of reaction to it, he thought. He gave me anti-depressants but I only took them for two weeks. I have been feeling OK since but through July and August I was feeling I was going to have to be sent to hospital – a terrible fear. I recognise now I've got to know my limitations and allow myself space for doing things for me.

The year away any kind of personal enjoyment got sacrificed ... it was very difficult to fit it in. As well as this when you are involved with something like the Peace movement and you are dedicated you do feel very guilty a lot of the time, especially if you have a slap-up meal and you think of those who haven't anything. A lot of me says I'd like a super holiday but I know I couldn't do it. I know it doesn't do much good for me to go without my tea but if I'm more fortunate I can't say 'I don't care'. The other thing is that when I'm doing something I get right into it. I don't hold back, I completely give all and I don't realise how tired I am until it's too late. Then I'm so knocked out mentally I can't do the things I want and everything is racing, like being on a 'high'. I think that's my nature really, all black and white. I can't say 'no'. Perhaps some of this comes from my parents who never praised us, only criticised us for what we did wrong. We were always aware we'd got to do better and better and one day we might do something right.

As well as having to keep on working hard in order to receive affection and praise, Anna felt very alone during her childhood. She spent most of her time alone and got used to doing things for herself. She was born late on in her parents' marriage, long after the other two children. She was referred to as a 'mistake'. Thinking that she was a mistake made her feel 'awful ... that you're not wanted'. She also married a man for whom she has to be strong. 'My husband doesn't like it, can't take it when I'm depressed or unwell'. Each of these ingredients possibly harnessed Anna's energies to work hard, mostly alone, and not to ask for help or support. She might also have felt that she had to make up for her existence, as she was told she was a mistake, by giving selflessly to others who were less fortunate than herself, and in fact negating her own individual life in the process.

I've learned a lot from my breakdown. I feel as if I've come through a very dark tunnel and come out the other end. I feel very different from having been through. I've had periods of depression before, usually lasting two or three days maximum, but this was different, so very frightening, and frightening because I wasn't in control. It lasted two months and it was terrifying. I wanted to escape: I had fantasies of booking myself into a hotel and being anonymous, sitting by the sea and reading, watching mindless television programmes. It was wanting to end it all – what was going on in my head – and not being able to do things and feeling so unstable. At times I wanted, not exactly suicide, but to be somewhere where no one knew me or expected anything ... just be myself without any pressure. I wanted to build a hole and retire from the world. I've learned that I need to do the things I want to do as well as things for other people. I'm not going to be always available for everyone. I've had a fright. I was frightened because it went on for such a long time. I tried to understand when people said 'you can't have the vision without the pain'. But I understand what it was about now: about not living enough of a personal life but thinking I had to save the world. I realise that individual, ordinary life is just as important.

Several years later, for the new edition of this book, Anna provided the following update:

> I am very happy to share how my experience of breakdown has changed the way I lead my life. For me that time of 'not being in control' has helped me to learn to live my life a different way. At the time I was feeling 'lost', I had an overwhelming urge to right all the wrongs in the world. I couldn't seem to live with the injustices around me and not *do* something about them. I didn't think about 'me' and my own needs at all. When I came out of that miserable state of indecision and uncertainty I decided to apply to go on a three year counselling course. I wanted to learn more about myself and explore what has made me who I am and then to possibly use my training in some relevant work.
>
> The course proved to be invaluable. I believe that I have changed a great deal. I can take time out for myself now with no guilt feelings at all. I go very much with my feelings. I try to only commit myself to what I feel able to cope with. I have no difficulty in saying 'no' which was something that I used to find very difficult. The memory of what happened when I 'overloaded' myself is still not very far away and there is no way I will let myself get into a similar situation again.
>
> I try to make sure that my life is 'balanced', that there is work, play, relaxation and spiritual awareness in equal parts. It really does work! Recently I asked for 'time out' from a voluntary organisation I am involved with. This was not easy but I knew that for me it was the right thing to do. Without doubt the experience of breakdown has made a complete difference to my life. I am in control of it now, I understand myself and my own needs and dare I say it, I actually like myself – wow!
>
> I am very happy with my life as I feel I have choices, the world is out there for me to do what I want or nothing, it's my decision. I am working as a counsellor in a G.P.'s practice two days a week. I am very happily married and am an adoring grandmother of a three-year-old granddaughter.
>
> I would say to anyone who finds themselves experiencing

symptoms of breakdown to try and use the experience positively. Accept the time you are unable to do the things you usually do with grace. Don't feel ashamed or pressured by anyone to do anything you don't feel like doing. Just allow yourself to '*be*'.

Burnout

Possibly because our culture admires hard work and success, research into these areas of stress has tended to be quantitative rather than qualitative, and has concentrated on externals such as stressful events, stress-producing factors in offices and factories, in everyday life and in the chemical properties of food. Little qualitative research has been published on what is inside people who drive themselves into unhealthy stress, into exhaustion and into what is called 'burnout'. Dr. Harvey Fischer writes in *A Psychoanalytic View of Burnout*: 'Burnout is not a general phenomenon specific to any particular setting so the sufficient cause must be sought among the personal psychological factors'. Burnout is described as a state of chronic energy-depletion including emotional exhaustion, depression and depersonalisation. In her study on the *Psychological Preconditions of Burnout*, Dr. A. M. Garden's findings were that the factors that made people most prone to burnout were as follows:

1 Guilt if not involved in work.
2 Difficulty with 'boundaries' between work and other activities. People prone to burnout stay in their work environment longer, including weekends and evenings, and some feel they can't leave the work situation at all.
3 Very few leisure pursuits were followed by those at risk, even pursuits that had in the past sustained them.
4 A low capacity for self monitoring: an inability to sense their limits even with body cues such as bloodshot eyes or a two-week headache.
5 A compulsive need to finish something, and even when finished, a feeling that things were not quite right, and a resentment that they were not working; an inability to get involved in other activities.
6 A constant need for challenge to feel worthwhile. A need to test out personal resources ('let's see what I'm really made of') by pushing

themselves to the limit. A tendency to be always alert, ticking over, and to feel that if there is not a struggle, they are short changed.

A driving parent as a role model or perfectionist parents may make us strive for self worth through effort, feel that we haven't done it right unless we are thanked, feel that we have to be successful, central stage, special because only then do we feel we will be loved and valued – all these things we learn early on and inform our working lives. When they begin to work against us our health breaks down and we suffer heart attacks, infections or gynaecological problems (the hormone system is affected by constant fatigue and pushing against the body.) Many so-called nervous breakdowns are in fact burnout. One woman said to me about her husband who had just died from a heart attack: 'He behaved as though he could run past death itself'.Nervous Breakdown

Exercise: Stress evaluation

If any of this section is familiar to you ask yourself 'why do I exhaust myself?'
   Is it because:

1   What I do is never good enough ? If the answer is yes, which voice in you decides what is good and bad? Stop and listen to the tone of that inner voice that drives you on when there are signals to stop. Whose voice is it? Give it a name, a shape or image.
2   Do I believe I have to be infallible, never be seen other than coping, doing well, invulnerable? What do I fear will happen if I am seen as failing in any way?
3   Do I believe my life should be sacrificed to some collective project, whether religious, ideal, community or for those in need more than I? Where has this idea come from? Is it really true that I am worthless unless engaged in a cause?
4   How long is it since I touched another human being, held them fondly, got up close? How long since I enjoyed anything to do with my body: taking a bath, walking in long grass, breathing in the scent of a rose, running to the pace of my own breathing, eating a meal I had chosen for taste and real hunger?
5   Do I feel bad if I get angry and cross? If yes, what do you tend to do with these two feelings, badness and crossness? Make a note of times when you

feel angry, either express it or not and then feel bad. Do this for a week. See what pattern you make: the times, people, situations that make you angry, what you do about it, what you are left with and how you cope. If you find difficulty in being appropriately angry when something angers you, and bottle it all up inside festering resentment, turn to Chapter 7 when we look at ways to change what we call 'unwanted' behaviour.

6 If I have a surprising collection of 'yesses' in this section, where do these constraints come from? Name the voices, thoughts and constraining figures. Every day score from 1 to 10 (10 being the highest) for how much your behaviour is dominated by this constraining presence. After one week evaluate what this means.

How to recognise fatigue and exhaustion

I wonder how many of us take real tiredness seriously: the prolonged, miserable kind of tiredness that isn't relieved by a night's sleep, a weekend break or a holiday. It's the kind of tiredness that won't go away, that forms itself like a fog around us so that we cannot move, we cannot go forward and we cannot stop, nor can we see what's happening to us. We all get tired: at best healthily tired after a day's work or a long stretch of activity. In a person whose body is working well, this tiredness will be relieved by sleep or time away. And, in the same way, tired spirits will be lifted by a good laugh with friends, a letter from someone we've missed or by happy news, and the melancholy felt before will go. But if nothing of this kind relieves your tiredness; if in fact, good things such as laughter, beauty, the warmth of companionship or a deep reviving night's sleep pass you by or do not even exist, then it is likely that you are on the downslope of the Human Function Curve. This means that you have moved from ordinary tiredness into fatigue and the next stage after prolonged fatigue is exhaustion. When we push on through fatigue and exhaustion, trying increasingly hard to make up for our dwindling performance, gathering frustration, a sense of hopelessness, despair and fury at our not accomplishing what we feel we ought, we are pushing against our bodies. This path leads to physical illness and ultimately physical crisis and breakdown.

Knowing the ways in which fatigue often shows itself will help you to recognise whether or not this is a danger for you or those close to you. The signs of prolonged fatigue register as follows:

A gradual lessening of pleasure

Food becomes rather tasteless and after we have eaten, we still feel unsatisfied. Our appetite for sex diminishes: we can't be bothered or put it off until tomorrow until we can't remember when we last experienced sex or thought about it, and it feels a remote event in the past. These things tend not to bother us because all our energy is taken up with keeping going with what we feel we 'have' to do. Enjoyment of simple things – a walk in the country, a warm bath, the smile of a friend- passes us by. We may not notice this until someone points it out to us and even then this may feel like yet another nag when our life feels already full of nagging.

Sometimes it may dawn on us early in the morning when we can't sleep that a major event such as the death of a close person, the birth of a child, a major world news item, has actually left us with very little feeling. We have not been really moved. And if we are not naturally cold, this is a horrible shock. We might think 'is this really me?' but not know what to do about it. It is as if we have put our feelings and sensations away somewhere while we 'get on' with what we have unconsciously decided must be done at all costs.

What happens when we are not in touch with our feelings and sensations is that when they come to the surface they do so unexpectedly and with the force of a volcanic eruption. We experience unexplained bursts of temper or crying but, above all, a deep longing for something nice to happen that will make us feel better, which is not met.

Indecisiveness

Not being able to make up our minds within reasonable time and taking much longer than usual about decisions, often on a very mundane and ordinary level, is another sign of prolonged fatigue. For the three years preceding my husband's heart attack, he had only black ties and the same identical shoes so that he wouldn't have to decide which to wear in the mornings. Now he enjoys choosing from a range of colourful ties and takes his time with pleasure. During a period of acute tiredness myself, I wore the same two skirts and sweaters for over a month when I had quite a variety of clothes to choose from but not the inclination. I've seen people so torn between choices and so afraid of not choosing rightly, that they cannot choose at all and spend their time in a frustrating and anxiety-making funk, feeling worse at not being able to go forward with one choice or the other. Much of the reason for this goes back to the previous section on pleasure. When we are out of touch with our feelings and sensations, we don't know what will be nice any more so we have a hard time deciding what to do.

Increase in smoking, drinking, eating and spending money

Because our ability to choose well and to be 'at ease' with ourselves has gone into eclipse, we tend to be more obsessive about drink, food, smoking and buying things. They are all attempts to try to feel better, to erase that awful hunger and longing that lies within anyone who suffers from the deprivation which comes from being permanently fatigued with no view of a way out. Unfortunately, in this state we are drawn to instant or fast junk foods full of salt and additives that increase our craving, drive us on to want more and do nothing to diminish our real hunger. Likewise with cigarette smoking, we are unable to have a pleasurable long smoke with a satisfied feel, but tend instead to light up one after another desperately. Smoking becomes ritualistic and manic, as if in a symbolic way we are keeping ourselves together – without it, we would just crumble. And whether we have money or not, we find ourselves spending money in that same desperate way. The feeling behind it is: 'If I buy this dress, house, car, carpet, vase (or nowadays) jogging machine, course of vitamins or special health food for reviving tired muscles, I will feel better, I will be relieved of my exhaustion'. A number of the people I have seen over the years have indeed gone the route of buying expensive health cures, health shop remedies or equipment designed to make us fitter, healthier, more relaxed. There are whole new industries which have grown up around this need. But if you are exhausted, a new health cure won't help nor will moving house (moving is high on the Rahe scale of stress), a new dress or perfume. When you are well, these may be just what you need if you can afford them but, for the exhausted person, it's like pouring expensive champagne into a starving baby.

Mood Changes

We may experience extremes of feeling and 'mood'. On the one hand, we may feel a heightened, tense, manic kind of excitement in which we make all kinds of plans, get fixated on certain ideas, rush around gathering people in to support us, only to forget or move on to another idea the next day; on the other hand, we may experience deep depressions which are black and desperate, tinged with cynicism, anger, impotence and self-loathing. Then there are days of nothingness, bland, grey, stuck and monotonous when the whole point of living is lost and a banal 'sameness' covers everything we do. Sometimes we develop paranoia, we feel persecuted by someone or everyone, we feel there are villains everywhere. In extreme cases, exhausted people have been diagnosed as having paranoid illnesses and may be prescribed psychotropic drugs. I have seen patients come into hospital carrying just this label who, when slept and rested, are receptive to the idea of rehabilitation and lose all signs of paranoia. What is probably true is that the tendencies of characteristics that are unique to each of us become exacerbated by exhaustion as they do by alcohol. Someone who feels a little suspicious normally may be pushed into more severe displays of this tendency under the pressure of fatigue.

Feeling trapped

We may feel trapped in several different ways – an unhappy marriage, a difficult job, stuck with an unwanted invalid or the physical trap of overwork and fatigue. When we realise we are trapped, we may fight to get out and to resolve our predicament. If this fails, and we can't get out or go back to where we started, we feel frightened, furious, despairing, impotent and helpless. People react in different ways according to their personalities and upbringing. Some people accept their situation with saintly resignation, 'there's nothing I can do'. But the despair and anger seethe away inside, not always consciously. Others feel resentment and anger which becomes disabling and turns inward against themselves, creating a despairing bitterness which makes others shun them and send their sympathies elsewhere. Some people assume a martyrish role, submerging themselves and their needs in an increasingly tyrannical fashion, unaware of the ways they are using their energy, but often projecting their anger and helplessness onto others, producing a great deal of guilty feelings. But overall, feeling trapped makes us try to work harder to get out and, if we are blinded by fatigue and some of the feelings described above, we can fight against ourselves trying to fly away and crash, like Icarus, broken winged, exhausted and defeated.

Depression

Clinical depression and fatigue have very similar symptoms and are often impossible to separate because they are so often intertwined. My work is to look at both issues and try to determine what are the triggering factors that lead people into a depressed and exhausted state. Some people get depressed because of their predicament which may be outlined by any of the states described above. Some people may be exhausted by their depression, by a constant anxiety state, a lack of assertiveness, a vulnerable personality, weak ego structure, poor background, lack of confidence or lack of bonding with another person. It is the part of them which is struggling to be free of their exhaustive and depressed trap which needs to be held and helped to channel itself creatively, so that the results are more encouraging, more positive. When people know that being exhausted exacerbates their depressed feelings, they feel less trapped by the depression itself and, in particular, any psychiatric label they may have been given. Understanding about lifestyle and habits, breaking down just where areas of difficulty lie, where the lack of assertiveness presents itself, looking at just how the person manages his or her life and difficulties, can give an exhausted and depressed person something more to go on than looking only at the four walls of his or her trap or psychiatric label. Many people in this state tend to look at huge issues, they look at the whole week ahead and fear getting through it, rather than what they need to do in the next hour, which is much more manageable. The important issue to focus on is that it is not the *whole* of us which gets stuck, exhausted, depressed, psychotic, it is a *part* of us that has for some reason been driven that way. Seeing this as a part allows us to examine that part and to recognise it when we see it taking over. Knowing this also means we have it, rather than it having us!

Situations likely to lead to fatigue and exhaustion

Although the inner dynamics of each person's psyche determine how vulnerable they are to breakdown, there are some situations and attitudes that commonly precipitate crisis. Knowing what these are may help you to avoid them.

Difficult Relationships

We all know about 'Who's afraid of Virginia Woolf' type relationships, couples who are locked together in an invisible web of love and hate, with more expression of the hate and loathing than the love. Sometimes hate is a more powerful bond than love and people stay together for years for what would seem the flimsiest of reasons. 'I wouldn't let him get away with divorce after the way he's been', one woman said to me of her husband's infidelities. 'We've got to stay together because of the children' is a very frequent assumption, even when children have said they would prefer the couple to separate because of the awful situation at home. Evidence from studies of divorced families suggest that, in some very destructive situations, children are happier and develop better when their parents have separated and are leading more normal and relaxed lives. Many people find themselves left looking after a relative or difficult old parent and wonder how it all happened, they feel caught out of duty and often love but do not feel free to talk about their difficulties or get too tired to seek or ask for help. Some people blame themselves for getting into relationships that no longer work and leaving is not an option they feel they have because of religious or moral views, fears of the partner they would be leaving, loss of social position, money, prestige, friends, security and often one thing – a favourite pet, the garden shed, an aged relative – keep people in relationships that have become destructive.

Our emotional reactions to those we are intimately involved with, even if destructively, have a powerful effect upon our body and, in particular, our hearts. You only have to look at a patient's blood pressure chart at visiting time. Some charts are raised by twenty points due to the stress of the visit and the pressure the patient is put under. Some people seem to be addicted to each other; they haven't a good word to say about the other person but they can't leave them alone. It seems as if they need this daily dose of adrenaline, fury, blood

61

boiling, bile spitting and venom and both people are caught in it. These types of relationships come to a head when one person becomes ill. Their illness may be used as a weapon; or the other partner may not be able to stop themselves acting as before, only now with more guilt and more internalised anger. The partner's resentment at the other person who is ill and getting attention may push them further apart at the same time as the new situation, the current ill health, forces them together. This can become a locked situation where counselling can help. There may be no answer to many life problems and no clear way out but outside resources can often be found to offer support and understanding, even if there is no possibility for change.

Poor sleeping habits

Worry may cause poor sleeping habits. And there may be times when our sleep is interrupted: after a baby is born, for example, or during illness or when looking after a sick relative or child who needs our attention in the night. When our sleep is broken several times during the night, for whatever reason, we don't get our proper, deep sleep and, although we may be able to carry on in this way for some time, we are running ourselves on reserve tanks of energy which soon get used up. It may be true also that poor sleep itself worries us, that we begin to fear going to sleep in case we don't sleep properly and that the fear of not sleeping itself may contribute to keeping us awake.

If you have a period of worry or have to take charge of someone who is ill and needs you in the night, try to plan it all as you would an expedition. Know that you are carrying this added burden and accept it as such. Know that in your current situation you are going to feel tired and must take this into account. Know this when you are offered invitations or plan travelling or outings, accept visitors or take on an extra little job. Make the burden an 'event', something tangible, rather than trying to run along without noticing it or as if it didn't matter. It does matter: not sleeping takes away the stores of energy we need for a day. Take any chance you can of resting and sleeping at different times. On the bus, sitting waiting, even in queues you can close your eyes for a minute or two. It's as if you are saying to your body: 'Here you are, here's a chance for some refuelling'. Ask for help from people, someone to take turns to help look after the person who may be ill, someone to share your worry with. It always helps to talk over a problem with someone else or to write it all down so that you can get some focus on it, so you can get things into proportion. It may be that you need medical help from a doctor when poor sleeping becomes a problem. Even if you don't like taking drugs, it may be worth taking medication for a week to get your body properly rested and out of a bad sleeping cycle. You may also be helped by taking herbal teas.

Lack of self esteem

Behind our tiredness and exhaustion may lie a lack of self esteem. As well as carrying out our daily tasks, we carry the extra load of fear and worry that we might make a mistake, that anything that goes wrong will be our fault or that we will lose our job if we put but a foot wrong. We may have difficulty sustaining relationships, we may never be assertive or like to ask for anything for ourselves because we feel we are not worth it and that no one will care for us anyway. Lack of self esteem then undercurrents everything that we do, and can make life very much more difficult for us, giving us a feeling that we are walking uphill all the time. If you feel you suffer from lack of self esteem, you may be helped by Chapter 6 of this book, by finding out for yourself just where your poor self esteem is located, where it comes from and what you might do about improving the situation.

Overpowering work ethic

If we suffer from an overpowering work ethic we have often inherited it from our family. Work is the big God and success at work comes before anything else; the more personal, feeling side of our life gets pushed into second place. We start out early on the treadmill, expecting a great deal from ourselves and from others and suffer impatience when things go wrong or don't come up to scratch. We may naturally be hard workers but if you feel that your work ethic is ruling your life and your body, driving you into exhaustion, it might help you to recognise this and examine it more closely. Chapter 7 looks at this situation in more detail.

Breathing and hyperventilation

We take breathing for granted and until something goes wrong, we tend not to think about it much. Breathlessness is something that people are universally afraid of. Shortness of breath, difficulty in getting enough air, pain upon breathing, tightness in the chest or windpipe all have the same effect: they make us panic. The more we fear not getting enough air or get frightened by constricting feelings, the more a panic reaction sets in and the more the symptoms develop, as we gulp and gasp at the in-breath and almost forget to allow a proper out-breath. The result is 'overbreathing' or hyperventilation. We take in too much oxygen and not enough carbon dioxide. Hyperventilation actually makes us feel worse, it increases pain and tightness in the chest, coldness in the hands and feet, tingling sensations in the arms and legs, lightheadedness, dizziness and headaches, and can bring on a faster pulse rate, indigestion and chest pain. Habitual hyperventilation can be the root cause of sleep disturbance, exhaustion, anxiety, cramps and palpitations and, in extreme cases, prolonged habitual hyperventilation can cause coronary spasm.

Some doctors and researchers believe that hyperventilation or faulty breathing becomes a habit and is the prime cause of the symptoms mentioned above. One study showed that the correction of faulty breathing habits brought about a permanent cure, both of physical symptoms and the anxiety and psychological disturbances. Others conclude that anxiety is usually the cause of the hyperventilation syndrome. Whatever the original cause, faulty breathing becomes a habit of which we are not aware and just as we can be addicted to cigarettes and alcohol, sugar or caffeine, so we can to faulty breathing. Tests show that as we get used to quick, shallow, short in-breaths, so our haemoglobin (red blood cells) gets used to frequent oxygen bursts and gives oxygen up less easily, reducing its availability to other cells around the body.

How to recognise hyperventilation

If we hyperventilate, we breath shallowly from the upper part of the chest so that the muscles of the diaphragm are used only to push the lungs upwards. If you put one hand on your diaphragm (the lower part of your hand should be over the navel) you will be able to feel the diaphragm moving up and down. Put the other hand on your chest and feel this moving up and down. This position, one hand on the diaphragm and one on the chest, is one to keep up when you are relearning to breathe properly. Imagine that your breathing capacity is like a balloon and your task is to get the air into the end of the balloon first. Posture makes a great deal of difference in breathing. If we sit hunched over, air can't get to the end of that balloon properly. If we thrust our chests out – many men do this to look big and brave – the diaphragm is too stretched and we breathe shallowly. Both ways force us from time to time to take in great gulps of air because what we feel all the time is that we aren't getting enough air in and we want to make up for it.

The things to look for if you suspect that you suffer from the habit of faulty breathing, either in yourself or in someone close to you, are:

● poor posture
● shallow, upper chest breathing
● frequent big sighs
● too much concentration on the in-breath and not enough on the out-breath. The out-breath should be the longest breath and is, in fact, almost more important than the in-breath.

Learning how to breathe properly

The best way to learn to breathe properly (or what is frequently called abdominal breathing) is to learn from a trained occupational therapist, a yoga teacher who understands this technique, a singing teacher or someone experienced with singing or from a physiotherapist who understands how to teach this method. You may also find it helpful to use the breathing exercise on page 216.

PROLONGED DEPRESSION

Depression has many different colours, mainly shades of grey. In looking at an artist's palette after she's been painting a winter sky we may see mixtures of different greys: shades of slate, dove, charcoal, blue; greys that are tinged with a faint yellow or mauve or pink; there are greys that have silvery threads, so fine that you only see them when you really concentrate; there is a grey that has a lot of white in it, seems watery, opaque, ever-yawning; and there is a grey that slides into a deep dense black, the black that is purple or tinged with blood red. And there is the black of the black hole.

Depression cannot be quantified, it is individual and different in every case. There are some common metaphors: feeling 'down', blue' or that it is 'a grey day'. Other common feelings include helplessness, hopelessness and despair; a feeling of not wanting to bother with anything, not wanting to make any effort; there are the tears, the heaviness, the longing for it to end, the wondering if it will ever end. In depression we often don't want to see anyone, we lose interest in people and in life and in ourselves. We slide into negativity and become inward-looking, pessimistic. This may be what we feel inside but we don't always communicate it to others. We may mask our depression by a wide forced smile, attempts at heartiness, being jolly, busy, rushing around, piling ourselves with commitments and jobs, being needed by others. We may return to our inner feelings when we are alone, at such times as weekends, especially Sundays, and on holidays.

When depression becomes serious it takes on a physical component, we suffer loss of appetite and tend to wake early in the morning, at about three or four o'clock. We stop being able to do our usual tasks and stay indoors in a kind of 'no man's land'; we perhaps begin to have thoughts of ending it all by taking our life. Our isolation may be interspersed by tears or bouts of uncontrolled weeping; we may shake, be unable to move, or become mute, without words. If our situation becomes severe and life threatening we need medical help in the form of anti-depressant medication and we need to be taken care of.

Different types of depression

Depression is not an illness unless it becomes a clinical problem for the reasons stated above. Most depression however is a reaction to a significant event or loss, or the depression caused by depressed or negative thinking. Depression is sometimes thought to be endogenous because it seems to come from within the person, and can be linked to a family history of depressive illness. It is then viewed as a specific illness with its course to run.

DEPRESSION

Though cracks there be, and mortar falls,
The wall of bricks, of fears and prides,
. Of locked resentments, oughts and shoulds
– I cannot tear it down.

I planted ivy either side; its fingers
Creep between the jaundiced blocks –
The words of wiser women than I
Their tender tendrils crumbling touch.

How long is time? And does it curb
Or merely bind the walls ...?
Iron bands of habit hide my heart
Which longs to show it hurts.

To break the seeming power of Fate
I bring my will to bear,
And hammer strong against the bricks
What power have earth and straw?

Long years of unspent anger
In destructive power beat on
The striking workmen in my head
Shout out, while rebel

Blackleg! Blackleg!

Manic depression

This is a difficult illness where the person swings from being manic (overactive and out of control) to being severely depressed.

Reactive depression

When our lives are shattered by the death of someone we love or any other major event that has profound implications for our own life, we naturally react by withdrawing. We need time and space to recover from shock, we need care and protection because we are so vulnerable, we need to be allowed to be inside ourselves while time goes by for us to heal our wounds and adjust to our change in circumstances. Depression can follow disappointment, not getting a job we want, seeing a friend depart for another town or losing a pet. Depression can also build up gradually, almost without our realising it. A significant event or realisation may be 'dealt with' by carrying on as normal, seeming to cope, but underneath thoughts or ideas are gathering that are depressive, such as: 'I'm not very successful', 'I'm never going to manage to finish this job', 'I never seem to do anything well' or 'I don't seem to be able to get on with anyone'.

Depressed thinking

If all our actions are undermined with phrases like 'I'm not going to be able to do this', 'He's going to hate my shyness' or 'They're all watching me and waiting for me to make a mistake', we are suffering from negative thinking which produces a negative result and makes us feel depressed. We may not be aware of how much a pessimistic view of ourselves is buried somewhere inside us, until we begin to pay attention to what kind of thoughts we have about ourselves. There may be general thoughts about ourselves and life that subtly inform the way we go about our days. If we feel we are basically bad inside we will tend to look for confirmation of that from others, we will feel guilty for enjoying ourselves, we will not believe it when someone likes us ('ah', say the inner voices, 'they're just humouring me.')

This is a very depressing place to be in. These false beliefs have a hold on us because we have been operating out of our survival self and not our seed self. When we reach our seed self and allow it to express its way it has a life of its own which is real, which we can come to believe in and which is beyond the judgment of others. It is when we are caught up in our survival self that we are more tender to other people's views because that self, as we said in Chapter 1, is only a tiny fraction of our whole being, and it is sensitive and vulnerable because it is not in touch with its proper roots.

In her excellent book called *Depression, a way out of your prison* Dorothy Rowe writes:

> If you want to build for yourself the prison of depression this is what you must do. Hold as if they were Real, Absolute and Immutable Truths the six following opinions:
> 1 No matter how good and nice I appear to be, I am really bad, evil, valueless, unacceptable to myself and other people.
> 2 Other people are such that I must fear, hate and envy them.
> 3 Life is terrible and death is worse.
> 4 Only bad things happened to me in the past and only bad things will happen to me in the future.
> 5 It is wrong to get angry.
> 6 I must never forgive anyone, least of all myself.

Holding ideas such as these and living by them in a fixed way can wear us out and bring us to the edge of breakdown and into the chasm itself. Likewise reactive depression, if not lifted after the passage of time, can begin to undermine our existence to the point of breakdown. In each case there is something in us that has been allowed to become so powerful that it takes over our life. We may carry on under its influence for a long time, suffering daily from the pressure and exhaustion of battling with it. During the breakdown we may feel ourselves to be taken over by the blackness, the shroud, the dark enveloping cape of depression which is what we've been fighting.

KATHLEEN

Kathleen had a breakdown in her mid forties after years of struggling with depression and anxiety. From an early age she had been encouraged to be a 'little mother', to be capable, responsible and grown up before her time. Because of this her more vulnerable, childlike needs had been left behind, unmet, and the only way she could identify herself was as the very efficient coper, always on top and doing everything herself.

> My background is pretty stiff upper lip: you soldier on, not showing your feelings, you don't cry. If you give up you have a sense of failure. I was the first girl after Mum's three boys and she leaned on me quite a bit, to do things and be a little mother about the house. I didn't feel then that I was having too much responsibility. I remember when I was about eight my little brother was born. My father came to fetch me home from school to go and cook the dinner. That was lovely, I felt ever so important.

Having this important role in the family and being valued for her efficient skills, it was very hard for Kathleen to show any of her more childlike side. Another event in her early life had a profound effect on her in an unconscious way.

> Before my little brother was born, my eldest brother, who I hardly remember – he was twelve at the time and I was three- he was found hung. I was hardly aware of what was happening. We took flowers to the grave, mother, grandmother, me and my sister, but nothing was ever said. Later on a girl at school said 'your brother killed himself didn't he?' We were told it was an accident ... and I started to think, was it an accident? He was alone playing with a rope. He was in conflict with my parents. He had been awarded a scholarship to a public school, just a country boy. Mum wanted him to board; Dad didn't. The psychiatrist at the time of my breakdown said it was very unusual for a child that age to commit suicide. When my breakdown occurred I fixed on that boy's death. It was like a catalyst. It wasn't the cause, but I fixed on it. I was obsessed with him dying and actually wanted to be with him.

Sometimes sensitive children take 'magical' responsibility for things that go wrong in their early lives. They blame themselves and feel inside that they are bad and then carry around a burden of guilt for events which actually have nothing to do with them whatsoever. It is possible that Kathleen, naturally an alert and caring child, felt guilty in a 'magical' way about her brother's unexplained death. Such misunderstandings early on can often be avoided if children are talked to about what has happened and if matters are explained clearly. When things are kept secret or talked about only in whispers sensitive children can believe that the secret is something to do with them and carry this around for the rest of their lives. The fact that Kathleen's family did not talk about or express feelings meant that there was no chance for clarification and so her fears were buried, possibly undermining her own life in the form of depression, or in the negation of the value of her own life. Kathleen went into a profession, nursing, that valued her coping, hard working and caring side, and she married a man who expected the same. Because she was always giving out, her own unmet needs expressed themselves in the form of anxieties and in depression.

> I've known for years that I'm a bit depressive and anxious, but I've usually overcome it with medication and a stiff upper lip. I started taking anti-depressants when I was 26. I was in a new place for my husband's job, I'd left a job I loved and I suddenly went to pieces. My GP put me on Benzodiazepine straight away and said for me to get a job. I got on with this and felt better. I went back on the Benzodiazepine again six months after my first child because I was anxious again.
>
> Then in 1969 we moved North. I couldn't settle. I had two babies and did part time work. I was totally depressed, got flu and bronchitis. I think my anxiety and depression have always run hand in hand. Then in 1972 we moved again to another part of the country. I got over-tired, we were short of money, relations with my husband weren't easy. The worst came after we had pooled our resources and started a joint venture: my husband had got fed up with his job, I worked day and night and after a month I collapsed. It was like I got obsessed. I went to hospital, the doctor said 'You really must have some time off and get away'. I said 'I can't ... my husband and four children rely on me. I have to get back.' It was a mistake. About two months later the breakdown came.

Kathleen felt that she was worthless unless she kept going all the time, giving out and looking after everyone else. Her depression was trying to draw her attention to some other language within herself but she was unable to listen. The very demanding 'inner figure' that insisted on her feeling a failure unless she met the impossible standards she constantly set up, dominated her view of herself. 'I had no choice, the standards set for what I was doing were so very high, and I wanted to be the best around.' Kathleen felt that she had to do everything on her own and found she couldn't talk to anyone about her problems. She felt she shouldn't have any, the demands on herself were so strong.

There was no solution to any of my problems. Things started to go wrong again in March, three months after leaving hospital. I was entirely depressed. I heard my husband shouting at the youngest boy, 'why can't you grow up' at the top of his voice. I thought, I'm going to do myself in. I'll go down to Norfolk. I don't give a monkey's. I got in the car and drove off. As I drove my little one's face came in front of me again, my little one, smiling. I thought, this will kill my parents if I go and do this now. I'd bought myself a bottle of Paracetamol at the chemist's and a bottle of fizzy lemonade to wash it down with. I drove to my parents' house and said 'I'm really terribly ill. I think you'd better get the doctor. I'm at the end.'

I was thoroughly miserable, I couldn't sleep, I couldn't eat. I heard the church bell ring every hour through the night: it was like the bell of Doom. I lost everything. I stayed with my parents for six months, and when I went back home I could only stand it for a couple of months. I did try and make a go of it with my husband but he didn't really want me. He had no more interest in the marriage.

My breakdown was a catalyst. I was brought face to face with myself and as a result I've decided to preserve my health and myself. But I've lost my family home, marriage and business. When you feel as trapped as I did you have to do something extreme. My husband refused to compromise. I would have liked to try to sell out and get a place where we could all be together. He could only blame me for not keeping up as I always had done. My family have rallied round. I felt shame and failure but my mother came to see me and didn't show any of this. She gave me her mother's engagement ring and said 'wear this, it will help'. It was very touching and extraordinary, a kind and thoughtful thing to do. My friends and family, my present employer have been wonderful. And within myself I have allowed the person I am rather than the superhuman I thought I was before. Allowing weaknesses. It's all right. I've started praying again and if there's a God there he'll be listening. I've come back to God in a small way. It's very pleasant to be self-indulgent and talk about oneself once in a while.

In your mid-forties you take stock. Things build up over the years. I do think my brother's death had a hidden impact on me somehow. Also I had this tradition of always coping: people came to me and expected it and I obliged. I thought of dependency as a weakness. I married a rather cold man who couldn't show his feelings rather like my family and I felt I had to make up for it. I wish I'd had more fun earlier on. But I've learned a lot about myself. I'm also aware that nothing's ever final. Although this may be a difficult time for the children and me we're not arrested in time. We all continue to grow and develop. My life has taken a quite different direction but it need not be miserable or sad. It's actually quite positive.

Kathleen has provided the following update for the second edition of this book:

The eight years since my breakdown have been full of growth and achievement. I think recovery from breakdown is ongoing. The initial stage probably took 2–3 years. Myself and two younger children lived with my parents for a year and then I rented a cottage nearby, which was when I was first interviewed for this book. Fairly suddenly after the initial interview I decided it might be OK to return to the family home in the north of England (one earlier attempt had proved abortive). But right from the initial breakdown my husband had had no wish to resume the marriage. Now we meet at work and his attitude is of one of indifference or hostility. I am sorry that I could not handle this relationship better.

I have opened up emotionally, allowing repressed feelings, anger in particular, to come to the surface. A better awareness of my particular anxiety/depressive cycle has been invaluable. It is allowable, it is manageable. I can cope without too much adrenaline being wasted. It is wonderful to give myself permission to be ill (hardly ever), to rest and to have time for myself. I am also able to help and counsel others who may be in trouble. I enjoy my nursing work and interaction with all grades of colleagues is very satisfying. I have several loyal long term friends and a varied social life.

I have seen my daughter happily married and all the children are very loving. My eldest son had a traumatic adolescence (before, during and after my breakdown) and is still not settled in his mid twenties. I suspect heredity has a bit to answer for. I still take Anafranil at night, just half my prescribed dose. I discontinued this recently on my own initiative and was fine for about six weeks. Then I became irritable, my personality felt fragile and I was aware of sliding into depression. Back on the tablets my spirits lifted within ten days. I am unsure whether I need antidepressants like a diabetic needs insulin or whether in coming off I will have to endure withdrawal symptoms for a while and need to be prepared and helped with this. It was not a chance I was prepared to take on my own. I am exploring different views on this.

My hobbies are my animals (dogs, cats and chickens) and a large garden and orchard. I now look forward to the future and to retirement on a smallholding with animals and books.

THE 'VOID' EXPERIENCE

We can also become depressed because we feel empty inside, because we cannot feel close to anyone or anything. I call this place the 'void'. The void is a very painful place. Most of us experience it at some point in our lives and some suffer from it more than others. The void is what we feel when we are unable to get close to another person, to be intimate, to give out love, inspire love and to receive love. It is a hungry place, out of which comes a deep longing to be met by another in an important way. Often we struggle to try and fill this spot by a supreme effort of will, and by supplying what we have learned will gain attention from others. Many people carry around this sense of void and have very successful external lives, they appear to 'have everything' in terms of material possessions, looks, gifts and talents, and are often great performers – the life and soul of the party, the proponents of excellence. Sometimes achievements of this kind are attempts to find something meaningful. If we have learned early on that academic or financial success, looking slim or beautiful or taking care of others is what gets us affection or admiration, we may believe that we actually 'are' our performance, so that when we are not performing or fulfilling the desired standard we do not exist. At these times we get very depressed and fall into the void. Alice Miller writes:

For the majority of sensitive people, the true self remains deeply and thoroughly hidden. But how can you love something you do not know, something that has never been loved? So it is that many a gifted person lives without any notion of his or her true self. Such people are enamoured of an idealised, conforming false self. They will shun their hidden and lost true self, unless depression makes them aware of its loss or psychosis confronts them harshly with that true self, whom they now have to face and to whom they are delivered up, helplessly, as to a threatening stranger.

If, in the passage to breakdown, we suffer from a sense of void inside ourselves, we tend to try many different experiences that we imagine will be the 'right' one. As we are often a long way off centre, a long way from living out of our own seed, the people we get caught up with and our work or achievements tend to mirror what we believe, falsely, to be our own worth. A very common dilemma at this stage is: everything I do must be perfect or it is the opposite, it is rubbish. This drive to over-achieve leads us to bash ourselves against the rocks of presumed excellence, striving for the most difficult, the most ambitious, the most perfectionist tasks; and for the most inaccessible men and women, the cleverest, most attractive, daring or magical person. On this journey we may get pulled into disastrous relationships with others who are charmed by our admiration and adoration, as if caught up in a spell, but who abandon us when we begin to behave like an ordinary human being and thus show need or vulnerability. Thus is the drama of early life repeated. The consequence of this rejection is that the person believes they must try or work harder, look prettier, become more macho or more successful.

Another route we may take is to be seduced or absorbed into the charisma of a guru movement, something so intense and enveloping that we sink into its foundation with a feeling that here at last we have come home. Sometimes this works. Sometimes it is felt to be another trick.

Yet another route is the using and abusing of self and others in relationships where there is no means of discriminating between exploitation and genuine loving. Women who interpret any attention as caring will be taken in by men who are only looking for sexual partners. Men who feel they are only worthy because of their worldly achievements will be taken advantage of by women who want to live through a man's money, status and fame.

Relationships are also sometimes only possible in the form of fantasy, not experienced but seen from afar: this painful journey through repeated unsatisfactory relationships, using exhausting bouts of energy, can cause bitterness, cynicism, resentment and disillusionment as it becomes more and more obvious that something is not working, and often ends in some form of breakdown. The self cannot live under this kind of pressure and so often extreme measures have to be taken by the psyche so that we may be helped to live again in a more realistic way and find the beginnings of our true seed.

This picture should not be all negative. Painful though this journey is and serious the breakdown, when we begin to experience our real selves we are able to use our gifts more fully. The fact that we have in the past used our gifts in the pursuit of love and affection does not mean they are invalid or suspect: and we can use them now in the service of our true seed self. Sometimes people feel aggressive about the efforts they have made when they realise what it is they were striving for without realising it, as if the underlying longing made it false. In reality, we need only to realign ourselves: when we know a little more of who we are we can make a choice about how we use our talents and know when we run the risk of getting caught up in old ways.

The other important factor is the amazing capacity of the human beings to restore themselves even when they have had very little real affection early in life. Helen Plaut, a Jungian analyst says:

> I am constantly surprised what people can come back from – the capacity to get interested in things, the courage, hopefulness, a wonderful renewable curiosity about things tinged with hope that something good will turn up. If people have a poor early start in terms of mothering ... even from inside the womb they feel they were a negative and distracting thing in mother's life, a pest, spoiling her life – they arrive on this earth with no welcoming look. After the frightening journey of birth there is no enfolding presence, just cut-offness, blank. Babies need a mother's welcoming face. They are naturally so in love with their mothers and inclined to find her beautiful. If they don't get this experience there is an eternally

VOID

You cannot make the poem come
The unconscious you cannot drive
You cannot force the real self
To rise and shout 'Survive!'

He, she, it will not be grasped
Though desperate be the hands
That, nails torn, fight the well-built walls
The conscious mannered lands.

But fall confused, a crumpled heap
And every pore unknowing
Lose every grain of fighting heart;
The embattled spirit is growing.

Allow yourself to sit and cup
Your tossed, distorted soul
In peaceful hands – there is no shame
But *drink* – for no one else will.

unreachable beauty they feel they cannot reach. A kind of unrequited
love for their whole life plus a fear of life. But serious wounds can
be restored by other people ... there might have been a nice auntie
or someone with whom there were good times together and people
can realise they were mothered in this way.

MATTHEW

Matthew started to be aware of the 'void' inside himself in his mid
teens. He would stand on the edge of a group of boys, not feeling a
part of the group and unable to make any contact with girls.

After school and at weekends I would walk about with one or two
people. We would look in shop windows, buy chips, and stand
about. If girls came out with us they would be in one group and boys
in another and we would generally ignore each other. I was just a
sheep. I remember little about our life at home. I do not remember
any love or affection, physical or otherwise, from my parents. I once
remember being cuddled and kissed by my aunt. That was probably
when I was about ten.

I clowned about a lot and was generally thought of as a pest. One
of the teachers would make an example of me by asking why my hair
was not brushed or tidy. My neck and ears were always dirty and he
would question me in front of other children. I was made to wash in
the disinfectant dip before going into the swimming pool. We had no
bathroom at home and my parents rarely bought us clothes. When
I went to secondary school I was made fun of as I didn't know how
to use a knife. We didn't talk at home and we never had people
round.

After leaving school Matthew became more and more withdrawn
and cut off from ordinary contact with people. He had a good job
working with computers, and he would joke and clown about as he
had at school, as a way of coping with desperate shyness and
uncertainty about how to behave. By the time he reached his mid
twenties he was suffering from very depressed thoughts and feelings
and thought frequently about suicide. He had managed to buy his own
home and had moved out of the family house without speaking to his

parents. He had not spoken to his sister for four years. He had believed that when he moved into his own house and had his own life, completely separate from and in quite a different style from his parents, he would find friends and feel much happier. He had set about attending to all the things his parents had neglected: he had been to a dentist for the first time, made sure he had a bath every day and tried to organise a proper life, cooking meals regularly and keeping neat and tidy.

When this did not bring him into contact with other people, his hopes were crushed, and his feelings of isolation increased. He found travelling unbearable because he felt that everyone was looking at him and finding him 'odd', and he became phobic about going into shops in case someone spoke to him and he made a fool of himself. He began to think that death was the only way out of his dilemma and began telephoning the Samaritans for help.

Matthew was befriended by the Samaritans and then sought some counselling. He sat very still and asked me to sit at the side so that I could not see his face. He held himself stiffly as if hanging on by sheer will. He was terrified of being on his own with another person, especially a woman, and he was terrified of all the confusion of feelings inside him that had never been allowed to be expressed and made safe or normal. For the next three years he lived on the edge of breakdown in a world of extreme isolation.

Born as a bright, sensitive, intelligent boy into a family who never communicated, he had learned, for survival, to defend his sensitive feelings by withdrawing into himself. This place was 'safe' because he could feel pain less, but it was also isolated and cut off and he kept people out in this way. At the same time he was longing for contact and kindness, for feeling and closeness, but this meant danger and panic. Outwardly he kept himself in isolation and inwardly he fantasised about a fast racy life with cars and women in which he was famous.

Matthew came regularly for counselling and kept up his contact with the Samaritans by telephone. These were the only times he had anyone to talk to and outside this his life was extremely isolated and lonely and his unhappy distressed feelings remained constant. As therapy moved into its second year he became very worried about getting attached to me. His instinctual feelings came nearer to the surface and frightened him. He became afraid that he was dangerous, that he was going to crack up. He began drinking more excessively to blot out the pain of these 'new' feelings, especially at weekends. He felt he would rather be at home and drunk than suffer the pain of therapy and the raising of feelings he didn't know what to do with and which frightened him. These feelings were primitive, instinctual and largely to do with his early life: they were feelings that had never been made safe for him, never allowed or 'held'. They had to do with envy, rage and murderous intent on one hand, and with a desperate need for contact and gratification on the other hand. He felt an overpowering neediness which terrified him. He had survived through his own efforts but his bid for independence was at the cost of his rejected need which he experienced as overpowering and at times violent. He got to a point where he couldn't withstand the tension of what was happening to him and the conflicts the therapy was bringing to the surface. He cut off all contact and disappeared. He put an advertisement in his local paper to meet someone. He met several women, had his first sexual experience and made friends with two of the people he met.

After six months silence, Matthew decided to make contact again and he settled down into weekly therapy and began to experience himself as more confident, more outgoing. During these sessions he was able to look at me in the face and was much less self-conscious than before. After about ten months he experienced another swing of feelings and was distressed at their negative quality. He had been able to express a lot of affection for the women he had met and for myself and had been able to engage in conversations with feeling and some depth. He felt much more reachable and talkative, much more able to trust his self expression and the things he wanted to do or say. When these good feelings swung to the opposite, to feeling bad about people and about me, he experienced a great deal of hate. He was unable to express it with me but he wrote about it in letters. He was able to withstand the pressure and terror of these strong feelings long enough for us both to make sense of them and to put them together. Love and hate are very close. Unfortunately what so often happens in early life is that they get split off from each other. The love becomes idealised and the 'only place to long to be', and the hate gets split off on to other people, who become hateful. Matthew had been expressing a lot of his hate in his desire to kill himself, he had turned it against himself. Being able to project it on someone with whom he also experienced some love meant that at last it was safer.

Since finishing therapy, Matthew has kept in touch occasionally by letter and visited me before Christmas 1986 sporting a fine beard, very smart clothes and a new car. He had passed his driving test during therapy. He was enjoying voluntary work and had joined the local church. He had friends of all ages and was able to spend time with children. His warmth, his wonderful smile and his humour moved me to marvel at the kind of hellish journey he had been on and come part way through. Life is still very difficult for him: he is lonely and has to work hard to be with people on a regular basis. Close contact frightens him very much and he gets very depressed when he feels the void again. His enormous efforts to make a life for himself, to build a home and a lifestyle out of nothing, are remarkable but he does not always see this as a worthy achievement from his seed self.

Although there is an improvement in his life, he does often long to be held close with another human being or with something of real meaning where he believes in himself, where he believes that he has a place, a rightness and a being for no other purpose than just to be.

What can I do?

Counselling and therapy are an essential part of beginning to enter into and heal a void part of oneself. The actual intimate sharing of a relationship with another person in the safe professional premises of a well-trained therapist is the main kind of healing for this problem. In no other setting – except for a close caring relationship with another – can one learn to trust and stretch out the part of oneself that has been 'on hold' since early life. This meeting with another in depth can act as a restorative rebalancing middle ground to the extremes that living around a void can present.

SEVERE ANXIETY, PANIC ATTACKS AND PHOBIAS

When we are anxious it is as if our life is 'on hold'. We feel sick and apprehensive. Every time our mind brings us back to the thought, collection of thoughts, event or object that we are anxious about, our body seems to lurch, and we feel taken over by this mysterious process called anxiety. We may focus on one thing that makes us anxious, or

ANXIETY

My life stopped for a while not even a smile
Could I manage without a tear,
What is this feeling I don't understand
Someone said this feeling's called fear,
Fear of what I don't know when I walk I walk slow
My head feels like it's tightening
I don't understand this tight tight band
This is what makes it frightening,
I must try to forget what I've been through and yet
It's a warning to me that others you see
      can hurt me and then just forget,
I will get better I know I will walk as though nothing
      has ever happened,
It built up inside me my mind in a whirl
It's over now the end of the curl,
Life's for living and enjoying each hour,
God's there if you ask just pray if you think
It's your turn for life to turn sour.

we may suffer from what is called 'free floating' anxiety which seems to have no particular pattern to it, but just hits us at different times.

Anxiety can be useful in that it keeps us alert and vigilant to what is going on, it makes us aware of important issues and it makes us take action. Anxiety uses up a lot of energy, and in its most positive form can mobilise and use all kinds of stresses and external stimuli. People who work as actors or performers report acute anxiety states before they go on stage or give a speech, and generally maintain that this anxiety forces them to be alert, to prepare thoroughly, to perfect their art. Writers, poets, artists report the same finding. This creative use of anxiety need not be limited to people who work in professions of this kind. I have found in my work that the use of guided imagery, guided fantasy and day-dreams, and the use of imaging techniques and drawing, have helped people to get hold of their anxieties, sometimes even severe anxiety, and be able to get alongside it well enough to handle it in their everyday lives.

'Anxious' personality

Some of us have a high level of anxiety for most of our lives and have to learn to make allowances for ourselves when we do challenging or anxiety-making things. An example of this is a guided fantasy I once did with a young woman who was suffering from a duodenal ulcer. She described herself as being in a constant state of anxiety, always fearful, apprehensive and expecting the worst. She had just come through several years of difficult life events – a broken marriage, having to bring up and support four children on her own and cope with the serious illness of her son. But she realised that she had always felt anxious, since about the age of ten when she went to boarding school. There were a number of issues which we looked at together in counselling, but early on we took the guided fantasy down into her stomach and duodenum. In the stomach she came immediately to figures that were clear and dominant. One was a roaring lion and the other was a terrified cringing mouse, cowering in a corner. The mouse she identified immediately as her anxious part. It took some time before she realised that the roaring lion represented her driving, demanding, more fierce side, the part of her she'd had to use a great deal of in order to survive her difficult situation. We asked each animal to talk to the other and ask what they needed of each other. The lion asked not to have to roar so much, or to be exercised so frequently; the mouse asked to have some more space and not be threatened by the lion.

This exercise meant a great deal to this woman. Naturally an introverted, quiet reflective person she had had to become more extrovert, aggressive, and pushing than her seed self found comfortable. At school during her first term people used to say to her 'What, has the cat got your tongue?' or 'You poor frightened little mouse, you'. She had been teased about her spectacles, her seriousness and her shyness. When her marriage broke up, she again experienced being left in an alien world where she had to make new moves, in the same way as she had at school. Through the imagery she learnt to be able to tell when the lion was roaring too much, crashing around on overdrive and pushing the mouse into the corner; and she learnt to value the more introverted, inquisitive, neat little mouse who enjoyed peace and contemplation.

Severe anxiety and panic

Anxiety can become so severe that we begin to panic. Panic by itself can have frightening physical components such as sweating, palpitations, very fast heart rate, dizziness, wobbly legs, dry throat, speechlessness, blackout or fainting. The frightening psychological components are depersonalisation, feeling as if we are no one in a no man's land or feeling as if we are the last person on earth with no one else around. If our severe anxiety or panic is triggered by particular things and this situation persists without relief or help it can develop into an obsessional or phobic disorder. For example, if we find ourselves panicking before going to sleep at night we could get phobic about sleep; if we get panicky when in a queue at the post office, we may later on perhaps decide not to go outside the house at all. Our intense fear then becomes attached to a place, event or thing. Panic and anxiety are extremely tiring and also limit our lives tremendously. The limitation and pressure may force us to break down. Any severe phobia can be seen as a long drawn out breakdown in itself.

Why?

We are again up against a 'gap' in ourselves between our seed and our survival self which is being filled with anxiety. We need to ask 'What is the current anxiety in our life?' and 'What is the underlying anxiety that goes back a long way?' We need to be able to monitor our anxious or phobic states in terms of when they happen and what was happening immediately prior to the panic: the place, people around and, most importantly, thoughts. In this way we get hold of the times when our anxiety is at its worst, and we may be able to separate out some of the current fears and lead back to the deeper, underlying anxieties.

PETER

Peter was 24 years old when he started having panic attacks. A year later he began to suffer from chest pain which brought him into hospital as an emergency. He was extremely anxious and tended to hold his breath, as if waiting for a blow. His life was certainly 'on hold'. He was unable to work because of how he felt and although he kept applying for jobs and going for interviews, his anxiety was such that sometimes he didn't manage to get there. He had a good relationship with his girlfriend with whom he lived, and his interest in keeping fit and healthy meant that he went running twice a day with his dog.

After he had been examined and investigated medically and was cleared of any physical problems he came to see me for some counselling. During the first week he kept a diary of the times when his anxiety was at its worst, at panic level, and what was happening prior to and at those times. This revealed that the anxiety was worst when he felt he might be angry with someone. This enabled us to explore the whole area of anger and his feelings about it. His other anxiety, of which he was conscious, was about death and dying. He was obsessed with the afterlife, with finding out about it and whether there really was such a thing. This obsession had two implications. The first was that it formed one of the poles of the dilemma which dominated his life. His fear of anger seemed to come from the collective 'macho' image of Northern working class men with whom he could not identify; and also from a scene the night before his mother died from a heart attack when he, aged 11, witnessed his father throw a chair at his mother and hit her legs. His dilemma became formed in this way: 'Either I'm murderously angry like father or I'm non-existent, dead, like mother'.

Being caught in this dilemma he could have no life at all. He couldn't manage to be assertive over everyday matters because any action of this kind he associated with murderously negative feelings. The fact that this way of seeing things had begun at the age of 11, just before adolescence when he was having to make up his mind about how to be a man, made the dilemma a very powerful one and well embedded. In counselling he began to learn about his own levels of assertion and anger, to relieve himself from the burden he was carrying which contained this false belief about himself. He also learned to separate out assertion from aggression.

On a deeper level his anxiety was linked to his mother's death. Sudden death is always a breathtaking, awesome, almost magical happening. Peter's almost phobic preoccupation with the after life came to be seen as his attempt to find and communicate with his mother, after her 'magical' disappearance. Because of the macho demands of his background, grieving and mourning were seen as soppy, and there had been no place for him to go after his mother had died where he could talk about her and how he felt. He was able to do this during counselling and on one visit back home to the North he looked out some photographs of her and talked to his aunt about her. In this way his phobic attention to death and the after life could be relinquished as he had made its purpose conscious. He forged a new, conscious, heart-based link with her memory and no longer needed the phobia and anxiety to remind him that this matter was still unfinished.

Two levels of viewing anxiety, panic and phobia

The first level is one of management, because anxiety and phobia are frightening and people feel taken over by them. Management by self-monitoring or by behavioural techniques worked out by someone experienced in this approach, are effective at coping and gradually desensitising the individual from the grip of the problem. When we have some hold on the problem we feel more able to look at the underlying causes, which is essential if the problem is not to be directed elsewhere.

The second level therefore is understanding what the anxiety or phobia is about. Exploring closely with another person, especially an experienced counsellor or therapist, is of enormous value here. There are many different objects upon which anxiety fastens itself in a phobic way. The object itself can sometimes give a clue, because of the nature of its symbolic form, about what we are up against inside.

Exercise: What am I afraid of?

1 **Claustrophobia:** fear of small spaces. What is it we fear in a small space? Suffocation, being trapped, being wiped out, snuffed out? What are the body feelings during this panic? Have there been other times when we felt this way earlier on in life? What do these feelings remind us of? What element, or person, in our current life could 'snuff us out' or 'suffocate' us if we're not careful?

2 **Agoraphobia:** fear of going out, into the world. What is it we fear people will see if we go out? What part of us might 'take over' or surface that we are afraid of or find unacceptable? If we feel we are up against exposure, what is it in us, or in our life, that we do not want exposed? Is there something unknown and frightening that we fear losing control over? What is it we feel we must be in control of and have to go to the lengths of staying in to protect?

3 **Arachnaphobia:** fear of spiders. What is the spider like? What is its type, shape, size? What are his or her qualities? Where are we when we think of spiders? What is the spider doing or what are we afraid it will do? What do spiders remind us of with their particular qualities? Is it the web they make that we feel caught up in? Is this a form of suffocation or of being tantalised, caught up in someone's web? Is there someone in our life that is affecting us in this way?

4 **Acrophobia:** fear of heights. What is it about being high up that affects us? Is it that we get too far from our roots, we feel cut off from our seed self or from an important part of ourselves that we tend to underestimate? Does the 'high up' relate to our getting on in the world, our ambition? Do we feel we've been pushed too far, got too high for our needs or that we've been forced to become what we're not in terms of achievement at the expense of our seed self?

5 **Pathophobia:** fear of contamination by bugs or infection. What part of us feels 'bad'? Are we feeling guilty for something? Are we carrying a sense of sin? What is the sin – is it the thoughts we have, ideas we have, the desires we have?

6 **Monophobia:** fear of being alone. What happens when we are alone? Do we feel in the 'void', the nowhere place? Or do unwanted ideas and thoughts come crashing in? What does this remind us of?

7 **Checking rituals** can be seen as a way of protecting anxiety through obsessionally attending to certain aspects in our everyday life. Checking taps and gas, electricity and pipes could be a signal to alert our fear of flooding or contamination, or being taken over. Checking envelopes for their 'hidden' content, the boot of the car for 'forgotten' and sometimes neglected objects brings us in touch with whatever that object or substance means to us. We could ask, 'What part of myself is neglected or forgotten? What am I afraid will "take me" if I'm not very careful?'

PAM

Pam began to suffer from anxiety in May 1982. She had been feeling depressed since March and started to take anti-depressants, but her anxious feelings became worse and by May she was unable to leave her flat. She felt dizzy with a heavy head, sick and trembling, confused. When we first met in the Outpatients Department she said 'I feel as if I'm someone else' … 'the world is going on in front of me'. She had lost two stone in weight, lost interest in herself and her appearance, was unable to go to work and felt no pleasure in anything at all. Her brother-in-law used to bring her to hospital in his mini-cab and wait for her and take her home again, even though she lived very nearby. She was very proud of her home and had enjoyed looking after it until she felt it to be a prison around her. She had become agoraphobic, gloomy and was also afraid of being alone in the house. She found she couldn't concentrate, couldn't do her knitting or watch television. She said 'It's like being drunk: I've given up and my body has taken over'. Pam had been given tranquillisers and anti-depressants and also a programme of going out a little more each day to help her to get used to the outside world. But she found it extremely difficult as her terror was so strong. She liked to wait until night time and go down the steps of the flat and round the block just once. We also made a chart of her terrors: when they were worst and when they were least bad, and a list in terms of importance of the worst things she felt up against and the least bad, so that each day she could make small gains in terms of overcoming her fears. Pam had insight as to why she thought she had her worst fear.

I think it was everyone leaving and suddenly I had nothing, no control. My youngest daughter went to school in January and my middle daughter started work; my eldest, she got married just before Christmas and my grandson was born in March, only I was too ill, too depressed to be any help. I feel bad about that. But the worst thing really is with my husband. He left me six years ago for another woman; my youngest was only a few months old. I knew he had been seeing this woman and I thought it was best he went in the end. It meant he was very nice to me, out of guilt I suppose.

Pam felt she had control. During this time she became pregnant with her fifth daughter, who only lived 12 days.

I've never been to the cemetery I feel if I go I'll never come back. I love children, I like it when they're little. It's a blow when they don't need you. Even after this little one my husband went on with this woman. But he did go on paying for things. Then suddenly at my eldest's wedding he came back: he just stayed, he never asked if he could come back. I was strong when he was away, I coped because of the children, but now I can't cope with anything. I've just gone to pieces. I think he's getting the message of what I've been through, but married people – they don't talk do they? When you go down the club you can always tell the married ones: they're the ones never talking.

By August Pam was going out of the house regularly, mostly in the evenings, but she had been to her husband's club and out in a car to the end of her road. She was becoming clearer about the struggles she was facing inside and could understand how difficult it was for her to express herself; she could see how her phobia was doing it for her. She wrote this:

I know my problem lies within my insecurity, I think this can be a turnabout situation. When my husband left I adjusted better than I thought. I was very contented, relaxed and, unbeknown to myself, independent. Finance was my biggest problem, I was totally dependent on him to pay for everything. My attitude was he left, he pays. It does not work. When he came back he brought the tension, the domination I now know I was free of.

Once when Pam was feeling many of the physical symptoms of agoraphobia I asked her to find an image of how she felt. Immediately she said 'It's like a blooming great elephant'. Her first thought had been to view the phobia as a useless, awful problem to get rid of as soon as possible. But by recognising Flossie, as she called this elephant, as a symbol for 'blowing her own trumpet' she could see that the phobia was her way of trying to get across all the frustration, fury, helplessness, dependence and lack of power and control that her husband's unasked-for return had signified. Because there was a long pattern of not trusting or talking to men in her family, and because she felt she had no say in the matter, she couldn't express herself consciously.

I wrote to Pam while preparing for this book and asked her if I could include her story. She wrote to me in her letter:

> I would like you to use the circumstances which caused my problems as the truth from someone else's experience helps a great deal. I remember you talked about some lady who had agoraphobia and I kept asking you if she returned to work and you told me in time she did. I could never believe that at the time. But it is true. I have worked for two years now. It was the turning point in my phobic days: a terrible feeling at first and I thought I wouldn't last, but I have.' I work in the local pub as a cleaner and my employer has asked me to do catering and lots of other chores in her home. I love the work and have made many friends. I must add that my daughters have been wonderful. They got me out and about in the beginning and gradually my confidence came back. My husband and I are fine, I don't think we will ever be a hundred per cent but it is just a way of life to us. My girls are well and I have two more grandchildren.

DAVID

David wrote to me when he heard I was researching for this book and offered to tell his story. He was unsure how 'useful' it would be and was anxious about this, but he wanted to contribute. He described himself as still being very afraid and anxious, not quite out of his breakdown state, but prepared to talk about what happened to him. He was extremely anxious about his identity and about the recording but insisted upon it going ahead. When I played back the tape to transcribe it I found that not a word of our conversation could be heard, so indirectly his desire for no record had been granted. I also felt that somehow this was a significant event. I did make a few notes however and can reconstruct some of what was said.

David was a successful banker, married with three children. An attractive man with boyish good looks and a charming manner, well dressed and spoken, he began our meeting by saying shyly 'I've been a bad boy'. Soon after this he said, as he was trying to find words for what had happened to him, 'You see, I like women a lot', as if this were a bad thing, or something to be ashamed of. Three years ago, after what he called an encounter with a prostitute, he became terrified of having Aids. In 1985 there was much less information about Aids than there is now, and when he went to his GP his anxiety was seen as irrational, and he was treated with anti-depressant drugs. He feels now that if his anxiety had surfaced a couple of years later he might have been taken more seriously and not been projected into the psychiatric route.

During the first year of his phobia about Aids he had three inpatient stays in psychiatric hospitals, spent a lot of money and took a lot of medication, some of which had unpleasant side effects of which he was not warned. His terror of Aids was not reduced by either the negative test results for Aids nor by his hospitalisation, and his obsession seemed to become more fixed. He carried on working in between each period of hospitalisation, under great strain and worry about having the disease. It was as if the part of him that felt bad, diseased and contaminated totally dominated the rest of him. Nothing could convince him that he didn't have or would contract Aids.

I suggested that we look at Aids as a symbol of some part of himself he felt to be contaminating. He found this made no sense to him. He was convinced that he could be a danger to the species, that he had let down his wife and family and he needed to go over and over it, checking it out all the time, but never convincing himself that he did not have Aids. He said he was 'just about convinced now, after a third test' that he didn't have Aids, but he still felt pretty awful, and was gloomy about his job prospects. He felt that he 'was unpromotable'.

It felt as if he were still in the 'dethawing stage' of his breakdown only just emerging. It also felt that any insight, or what he saw as the perhaps invasive or probing aspects of therapy were too frightening to him, because he discounted any effort of others to reach him or help him understand what had happened to him.

He told me that his brother had committed suicide when he was 20 and David 18 years old. One month after this David had his first sexual experience with a much older woman which left him feeling extremely guilty and anxious. It is possible to hypothesise that he had taken magical guilt for these two events, with the deduction that his sexuality meant destruction, which could be the underlying deep anxiety beneath his current preoccupation with Aids. But when we met he was not ready to look at things in this way. It was not appropriate for him at this particular time. Perhaps when he feels more stable, has recovered from the effects of a very heavy and unsuitable combination of drugs, he will be more open to receiving some exploration of his inner world which could relieve him of this burden. He may also have a way of coping with what happened to him that is his own and which needs to be respected as such.

PERSISTENT PHYSICAL ILLNESSES

People sometimes break down under the pressure of a long term recurrent illness. Pain is extremely tiring and draining, and at times seems to be merciless, so it can make us feel persecuted, got at and trampled on, using up all our reserves of strength and hardiness, leaving us feeling ground down by what we consider a hopeless situation. The pain of arthritis, rheumatism, head or backache, old surgical scars and old wounds, seems to get exacerbated as we get older, or when there are fewer and fewer people around with whom to share what we feel and be comforted. To have to cope with disabling pain and illness as we get older, frailer and more alone, and can only see more pain and hardship ahead, is frightening and debilitating.

It is not surprising that sometimes we break down under this kind of strain. When this happens we need to be taken care of, looked after and helped. Many people soldier on way beyond any reasonable stopping point until they have to give in and get some help. People in pain with disabling illnesses need all the help they can get, from doctors, nurses, the community and relations, and from painkillers, dietary help, relaxation, meditation or special exercises. The encouragement of a friendly voice or smile or the caring concern of someone with time to spend is a tonic in itself. Fear and loneliness can make pain worse, as can anxiety and panic. We need to help each other with this: to visit, comfort and support anyone we know who suffers in this way. Nothing prepares us for old age wracked by pain and loneliness.

Physical pain can express psychic pain

There are other illnesses that seem to form part of the journey of breakdown. Sometimes people are unable to express what they feel, they become cut off from their feelings, and the contents of their feelings are taken into their bodies. Instead of expressing fear, anger or loss, the body itself develops a pain. What is psychic pain becomes physical pain; Freud first described this as hysterical conversion. It is a very hard thing for us to take this on board and understand it. Some people come to see me and say 'My doc. says it's all up here' and point to their heads. I really feel for them because what they are feeling in their bodies is real wracking pain and it shows on their faces, their sweating and inability to sit still; but the inference from their doctors is that it isn't real.

FRANCES

A young woman called Frances came to see me suffering from pain in her right side from a gall bladder operation. Every day she doubled up with pain and was unable to move. She had been to doctors and specialists who could find nothing wrong with the scar, although after a year of visits they had removed a neuroma from the scar site, but this had given her no relief. She was a bright, intelligent young woman with a young baby, a very responsible job and was the sole breadwinner for her family.

She had a long history of visits to doctors which had unpleasant consequences; and as a child she had been burned twice in two separate scalding accidents. These events were important in terms of how she dealt with the 'pain' of feeling. Frances was one of a very large family and her mother was always busy; Frances described her as a 'long-suffering sort of person, loving, capable, never complaining'.

When Frances saw her mother's long-suffering face when she saw her little daughter's scalded shoulders, she decided she mustn't make a fuss or she would add to her mother's already heavy burden. She admired her mother and wanted to be like her. What her own feelings were about being scalded in the bath were impossible to decipher, to get in touch with.

She became seriously ill during her first career as a seamstress when she lost her sight temporarily and had to give up the work she loved. She retrained herself for another career in her mid twenties. Her father, whom she also admired, worked very hard to build up his own business, so she too became a hard worker and a perfectionist. During this time she had a knee injury which never seemed to get better despite frequent trips to specialists. Her pain was not taken seriously until her fiancé intervened and came with her to visit her doctor; after this, a cartilage operation was performed. As she told me these stories she showed no emotion. Partly this was because she was on a high dose of anti-depressants when she first visited me, but partly this was the way she dealt with her life: no fuss, no complaints, no feeling.

She was already depleted of energy when she started her first pregnancy after fears that she would be unable to conceive. The pregnancy was the beginning of the process of gradual breakdown which brought her to the hands of the psychiatrist and myself. It was a complicated pregnancy, she was ill and unaccustomed to not being completely in control. At six months she had an emergency abdominal operation which began labour. She was extremely frightened and quite hysterical, but the labour stopped and she went on to deliver naturally a healthy son who is a great joy to her.

After this difficult time, lying in bed for most of her pregnancy, it is easy to understand how she would have ambivalent feelings towards her son. Her exhaustion, together with a loss of self esteem because she was not totally in control of everything, led her to withdraw, become depressed and not know how to cope or who to turn to. She was struggling on, not realising what was happening to her until her mother mentioned that she thought she was depressed and went with her to her GP. She was suffering pain from her operation and from the birth. Her back hurt and the old scar on her knee hurt. She was depressed and was given tranquillisers and anti-depressants. She had returned to work, dragging herself out on to the Underground every morning hardly able to open her eyes, suffused with guilt about leaving her baby, but trying to support her husband and his own developing business which needed income.

After a year she collapsed exhausted and was admitted to a private hospital and looked after for three weeks. Much of her experience then was cathartic: she remembered all that had happened during the pregnancy, and all her feelings about herself, her baby, her husband and her fears of what might have happened to her came pouring out to the surface. She has very little memory of this time.

After her discharge she went back to work again, slightly refreshed, but what I would call 'patched up' to carry on, rather than with any kind of understanding about what was happening to her and without insight into the deeper, psychological cause of her struggle. Sometimes it is very difficult to work with someone therapeutically when they are on high doses of anti-depressant drugs. My belief is that somewhere in the person a part of them that wishes to get well is listening and receiving. I was worried about Frances, however, and about how I could communicate with her in a meaningful way when she was so exhausted, only just coping and when she was clearly suffering so acutely from pain. She came for her weekly visits to me, the dark circles under her eyes deepening.

At the same time she was seeing a pain specialist, acupuncturist, relaxation and Alexander teacher and she had four consultant specialists. It was exhausting just keeping up with her appointments, let alone keeping a demanding full time job and looking after a year-old baby. I knew that part of her was desperately looking for answers, but that she was at risk of being deflected into looking for solutions in drugs, operations and hospitals.

Then her back seized up totally and she couldn't move. Her husband became more actively involved in her struggles. He had begun to realise that the pain she felt in her body was a kind of 'roving' pain, which moved around her body, and he felt instinctively that it represented or symbolised something, but wasn't sure what. They were both having to make a decision about whether she should have an operation on her back, quite a serious operation to fuse two vertebrae together, and Frances herself was in so much pain that an operation was all she could think of. This was a very difficult time for everyone involved. But with the help of her GP, the psychiatrist involved, her husband and myself, Frances spent the time in hospital being looked after and the pain controlled as much as possible, and in time she gave up the idea of an operation.

She was gently directed to work therapeutically on what was happening to her, although at first her dilemmas about pain, control, her job and her family often meant that she could only focus on these immediate demands. Some very simple monitoring of mood, pain and negative thinking helped her to feel more in control. Slowly she realised how awful it was for her not to be in control whether this was of a strange thought, strong feelings, or actions of others she perceived as controlling or demanding. She had never learned to be assertive and to express her feelings. When she felt frightened or helpless, for example, she pushed the feeling aside in hyperactivity. She worried about upsetting people, feeling she had to give in and do what they wanted or hold back silently, feeling guilty and frustrated.

Slowly she came to realise the kind of blueprint she had made for herself out of her early experiences and examples. She felt she had to be like her mother – long-suffering, never complaining – and also like her father– hardworking and perfectionist. This combination formed her survival self, and her seed self got left behind, expressing itself occasionally through her creative work – cooking, sewing or creating home and family – although even these were sacrificed to her survival needs.

Her body forced her to stop and re-evaluate. She learned she had a right to be, and could be, assertive, and that she could stand up for herself when other people seemed demanding – that becoming ill was not the only way of coping with impossible demands. She began to incorporate much more of a life for herself – friends, leisure time, family, all of which had become sacrificed to her survival self. She learnt to be able to relax and allow relaxation. After a year she one day said, naturally and of her own accord, 'It feels as if I've been using pain as a desperate measure to cope with feelings of helplessness and needfulness.' At the time of writing she has been off all medication for a year, is well, has learned a lot about how to manage her inner and outer life and she has not had to undergo further operations.

Medical treatment

This is an example of breakdown which presents itself through illness with a happy outcome. Unfortunately there are people who undergo quite unnecessary operations to remove pain, complicated and invasive medical tests to find out what is wrong with them, and all kinds of antibiotic or other medication in an attempt to treat just the body and what it presents. If the body presents us with a symptom then of course it would be negligent and foolish not to look at the physical process, but the person's lifestyle, their habits and their attitude to life also have an important impact on the development of symptoms. As medicine in the West incorporates many 'alternative' or complementary ideas from the fields of homeopathy, acupuncture and herbalism, it becomes naturally 'holistic'. Some GPs are already practising this approach in their work, and if they have been in practice for some time and have got to know the families of their patients, they are able to tell immediately what is going on in the patient's life.

The term 'illness behaviour' has always seemed to me to be somewhat derogatory, and people who suffer illness as the only way they can ask for help, ask to be cared for or to express their helpless and needful side (we all have this) often get short shrift from the medical profession. 'Malingerers', 'pretenders', 'only wanting attention' are terms I have heard used. There is also a considerable amount of anger when people who are caught in this kind of trap don't get well, but sprout another symptom in another part of the body. 'Difficult' cases demand a lot of thought and attention, and someone who is consistently ill can be seen as a challenge to each new practitioner who is approached: 'Perhaps I can be the one to cure her or him'. This desire to save or cure can falsely raise the hopes of the ill person who feels at last maybe they've found someone who knows what they need. The complicating factor is that when we are under a great deal of pressure inside and this gets located in one part of the body we do indeed manifest all the symptoms of an organic illness. The bowel can be more restricted for example, periods can be more painful and difficult, eating may become disordered and cause other problems such as an ulcerated stomach, and hyperventilation can lead to all kinds of heart ailments, as we have seen. The many tests now available will show up our body to be in certain distress on one day but may not show up anything the next day.

Do I need a hysterectomy?

An outstanding example of this is a number of hysterectomies performed on women who suffer pain and excessive bleeding where

97

there are no other symptoms. If what the patient is trying to convey, but knows no other way, is something to do with her emotional life, her mid life point, her dilemmas about identity, her desire for more babies, more sex, more affection; if the crisis reflects her unexpressed creativity, her need to feel full and satisfied, then an operation to remove her most potent and important organ can be seen as the ultimate cruelty. In some cases I have shared, it does seem intended as a revenge upon her for being needy and female in the first place. If on the other hand she is able to explore what is happening to her by listening to the language of her body, by actually feeling into her womb, her most intimate parts; if she can take an imaginative journey to this place and let the language of the unconscious speak out and let her know what else is at stake for her within her body's symptoms, she can move towards the help and support she needs appropriately. For she may also choose surgery, but she does it consciously, knowing why, and offering up this part of her to the surgeon's knife as a positive 'rite of passage' and sacrifice.

Martha had fibroids and endometriosis and was bleeding excessively every month, often missing meetings because the bleeding got so bad she had to lie down. She had very ambivalent feelings about hysterectomy and she wanted to be really sure before she had the operation. What came up very soon was her desire to have another child, which she found odd and impractical. She was forty, had three children and one step-child, and 'logically' didn't want any more. But something in her was pulling that way. The symbol of the child stayed with her and when we explored what this would mean she said rather dreamily and leaning back in her chair, 'Oh I could just wheel the pram out into the sunshine and play for a bit.' The image of having the child was for this woman permission to 'be', to play, to have fun, to stop being so deeply involved in her career which demanded a great deal of her more masculine directing and rational side. She started to think of ways in which she could actualise the desire to play a bit more, to take time for herself, to balance a very frantic working life. In doing so she became less stressed and her symptoms became not quite so severe. When she decided to go ahead with the operation it was gladly, freely and without the bitterness that I have seen in women who had their operations without questioning what it was all for. 'I did all my thinking afterwards' said one woman, still struggling with the unfinished business.

If we start to break down in our bodies with symptoms that don't seem to have an organic cause, it is a message to us from the unconscious that we need to be taken into areas we have not yet explored or made conscious. We really need to listen because there are times when the body is wiser than we are, and it becomes the vehicle through which we become conscious. If we only look at our bodies and symptoms mechanistically we run the risk of unnecessary treatment of every sort.

Heart surgery

The coronary artery bypass graft is another example of an operation that may be performed unnecessarily. During periods of difficulty and anxiety we tend to sleep poorly, hyperventilate, eat at odd times, and feel swamped by our moods or events in our life. We may embark on a path of constant fatigue and over-compensation through alcohol and overwork. We may have a persistent emotional problem or problems at work which don't go away. If this leads to chest pain, and we have arteriography or an angiogram, our coronary arteries may well show up to be narrowed and our blood pressure may have shot up. If these symptoms are not relieved by rest and sleep, then we may have rigid narrowings which do need an operation. If on the other hand we have dynamic narrowings, which are removed by rest and sleep, we can be helped to sort out our situation by looking at what's going on in our life and how we can cope. If these dynamic narrowings are subjected to an operation and we are then put back into the same stressful situation that led up to the physicalisation of our problem, we are in a worse state than before. How awful to have had a major operation when the problem was really an unhappy relationship!

The language of symptoms

Modern medical technology is magnificent. What needs to be developed in an equally magnificent way is the art of listening to the language of symptoms. We need to ask: How does it feel? Does it burn, sting, clench, pull, tighten, throb, pulsate? And how does it communicate itself to us? Does it creep slowly or suddenly appear? Does it spread, inch, manoeuvre? What is it like in graphic terms? Is there a shape, colour, form or image of it? (Some of the expressions

I've heard are 'stretched elastic', 'flooded basement', 'piece of meat on a butcher's slab', 'steam iron out of control', 'a herd of elephants'. Where is it in my body – head, heart, lungs, back, leg? What are my associations with that part of me, what does it mean to me? We can go deeper: stay with the feeling and your image of it in the body and ask yourself, does this remind me of anything?

In this way we open ourselves up to what has possibly been unconsciously stored in our body during the past. The body remembers everything that happens to it: the way it was held, stroked or not stroked, handled, thrown about, smacked or caressed, and the body stores feelings that cannot go anywhere else during our early years of life. If we are terrified that someone will not come and feed us when we are hungry as a baby we have no way of communicating this except by our cry. If no one comes our cry gets louder and enraged. All we know then is that we're hungry and it's intolerable not to be gratified because without that life is unthinkable. If there aren't enough good feelings alongside the bad feelings early in life so that we have a healthy mixture of good and bad together, bad feelings get split off either on to others ('The Wicked Witch'), or internalised inside ourselves. The body can be one of the places these feelings go.

At other times in life, when something awful happens ... Mum and Dad split up, someone we love dies ... what we feel about it may have no words, no language. It gets stored within the body as 'body armour' which protects us from powerful feelings we just don't know what to do with. We can often see some of this 'armouring' in the way we sit, stand or hold ourselves, particularly when talking or getting in touch with something painful and difficult. Staying with that can help us to unlock some of the past memories that are ready to be made conscious.

Georg Groddeck, born 1866, had a clinic in Switzerland at the turn of the century for people who could find no help in other places.

He was a general practitioner who was also interested in social problems and his main thesis was that 'Man's true profession is to become a human being'. Groddeck was using the idea of an 'it' before Freud's discovery of the unconscious. He was keen on showing that there was no basic difference between organic and mental illness and is today hailed as the founder of psychosomatic medicine. His ideas stemmed from his belief in the 'it' and the way it communicated itself. The 'it' drives us and moves us in ways 'it' decides. His idea was that illness was useful to us, enabling us to understand or express ourselves.

He wrote in *The Meaning of Illness* 'We have become very careless in our use of the label neurosis and have completely lost sight of the fact that illness is not an evil in itself but always a meaningful process and not infrequently brings out forces which are only effective within the context of being ill.'

Groddeck's 'it' is a similar concept to what Jung called the 'collective unconscious'. Both contain forces or 'archetypes' which become constellated in our being at times of our life when we need to integrate some aspect of ourselves. This process has nothing to do with conscious will or the logic of the ego. I said in the introduction to this book that breakdowns can be triggered by unconscious forces which we cannot control. They seem to ask us to surrender our ego control and enter a different experience. When we do this we open our life to a greater sense of meaning, deeper and wider than we can 'know' consciously. And in doing so we link ourselves with a collective process and to the possibility that we are not really alone. Other souls have trod the path that we are wearily contemplating. All of us can be together in this soulful process.

The mysterious viral infections, multiple and crippling allergies, and the recent discovery of myalgic encephalomyelitis (postviral fatigue syndrome) seem to be a response to a form of medicine that has become over-rational and technological, and which seeks to give a label and a cure to every ailment that comes its way. Perhaps this is our 'collective' answer to medicine when doctors begin to believe that health is never having any illness. Illness is part of life. It can help to keep us 'whole'.

EATING DISORDERS

Eating disorders can be a symptom of the unhappiness and despair that leads to breakdown. I see anorexia nervosa and bulimia nervosa as a form of breakdown in themselves, whether or not the people concerned are admitted to hospital or have any medical care. Usually the prolonged crisis becomes acute because biological functioning of the body is seriously impaired and medical help becomes essential. But I believe the breakdown state begins far earlier than this point. It begins when a man or woman (statistics show that eating disorders are much more common in women) begins to be phobic about food.

Food then takes on an almost magical quality, seen to have potencies that can assume demonic proportions. Food becomes either 'bad' food or 'good' food, and this split into good and bad seems to symbolise the split inside the individual and the identity they are struggling to assume.

Food phobias often accompany transition periods when we look ahead and question our identities. What is it we may or may not become? What is it that is, or is not, within our grasp? What may we do freely, what is taboo? What is expected of us, wanted or needed from us? How should I look? Should I be slim, slimmer than I am? As a woman, what is my life to be like – who am I?

In an eating disorder food ceases to be just what it is: necessary nourishment for life, which we eat when hungry and finish when satisfied. People with eating disorders often do not know when they are hungry in the usual sense. They are in fact starving all of the time. The anorectic is literally starving; the bulimic gets rid of food as soon as it enters the stomach and before it can be processed; the compulsive eater eats obsessively, compulsively, usually any food that is on hand, bulk food that will fill her up until she is satisfied and cannot move, until she hates herself so much she is sick, but inside she is still hungry.

The wear and tear of an eating disorder is tremendous. It is exhausting to battle every day with food: to wake in the morning and worry about what foods you had yesterday that you shouldn't have had, and whether today you will be able to stay in control or not. Sometimes the craving for food is so strong that people steal it and line their cupboards with it. The anorectic cannot and does not eat any of it: it sits there tantalising her all the time. The bulimic may plan a binge and lead up to it all day, but as soon as it is completed she will make herself sick into buckets kept under the bed; or she will take doses of laxatives between each mouthful. The compulsive eater binges and lives with her bloated, overstuffed desperate feelings of aloneness, sadness and need, and her increasing selfloathing and self-disgust. As her body swells so does her desperation: she longs for real comfort, and real nourishment inside herself, but in actuality her increased body size often shuts people out.

We suffer eating disorders silently and alone. We feel bad. We feel out of control and can't tell anyone. We fear more punishment.

Punishment for the compulsive eater who is overweight comes in

NIGHTMARE

Terror arrived in the night
    and forced open my eyes
And showed me its moving shape
    and altering size
And pressed close to me
    and hurt 'till I called out the name
Of someone I love.

the form of a diet, which makes the split between good and bad even more extreme, and misses the point about what it is the person with an eating problem is trying to do. The anorectic is punished by a medical system that force-feeds her against her will, and makes worse her fear of being fat by filling her full of food. All people suffering from severe eating disorders are punished by their bodies, which start to break down under the strain. The throats of bulimics are permanently sore from the stomach acids in their vomit. The bulimics who take laxatives lose the elasticity of their intestines and cannot excrete without help. The seriously overweight compulsive eater has all the problems associated with overweight: swollen legs, breathlessness and a tendency to hyperglycaemia, diabetes, hypertension and varicose veins, as well as the social pressures of rebuke and ridicule. And in all this people rarely ask: What is it people with eating problems are trying to tell us? What are they signalling via their symptoms that they cannot do in any other way? What is it we should be looking for? How can we help them?

Food as symbol

The language of food and eating is what the individual has had to use to express her underlying struggles. She may be trying to express an issue for her whole family, acting as the scapegoat for them all. Or the eating disorder may be a way of coping with feelings that are too disturbing, like anger and pain, hate and desire, feelings which have not been expressed or become safe because they are unacceptable to the family. Food may be seen as a comfort for anxiety, worry or feelings of emptiness and aloneness; or it may be used to stuff down anger and frustration which has no outlet. Alternatively, food may be denied because of what it represents: perhaps desire, fullness or being out of control; or it may have an association with womanhood that is unacceptable.

In all eating disorders food represents an inner split. Good food is slimming food, lettuce, low calorie, calorie-controlled, non-fattening, light, cold, grilled, ungarnished and unsauced. A good person is slim, successful, thin, attractive, asexual, bony, androgyne, nonfleshy, in control, lean, spare, pure, unneedy, fit, active, starving, empty. Bad food is starch and stodge, fries, sauces, taste, fix, high-calorie, thick, creamy, hot, spicy, luscious, appetising and desirable. A bad person

104

is fat, out of control, unsuccessful, undesirable, fleshy, full, sexual, needy, greedy, hungry, desiring and longing.

The fear is always of being bad or of appearing all that is associated with bad and therefore being rejected and abandoned. The person who takes the anorectic position has an active, aggressive, outward view of the world, and the person who takes the obese position has a more passive, depressed, inward view of the world. She puts things inside whilst the anorectic shoves them out. Both are a statement of helplessness and need: the anorectic becomes dependent on her control mechanisms and feels they are all she has between herself and collapse; the obese person is driven by her compulsive, insatiable appetite which she cannot control. Both are slaves to the ravages of appetite and the feelings it brings in tidal waves. Both are searching for something that will give peace to the inner turmoil.

Eating disorders and women

All eating and food in this context takes on a symbolic and magical significance. Many women who suffer from eating problems are reacting to a confusion and ambivalence about their role as women in the extraordinary times in which we live. The split between good and bad is perpetuated by a society that seems not to enable women to have much control and choice over what they do or how they are presented, or to have time to find what they are best at.

A successful woman insurance underwriter suffering from bulimia said to me:

> From early on, little girls get the message that if they're not attractive they won't get a man, and although 'men are awful' as mother made clear and so did her mother, you need one because society isn't as nice to you if you don't have one. So be pretty and play your cards right, eat your low-calorie food and exercise and wear all the cute clothes and you'll be OK. But there's another thing – it's OK to be clever now and women can do well in the world if they work really hard. They must be careful not to be too pushy and upset men or they won't get on. And they must be careful to make sure all is well on the home front – you're not a proper woman unless you have a successful sex life, multiple orgasms, a harmonious partnership and happy children, at the same time as

organising cordon bleu dinners and a colour coordinated home. It's impossible odds women are up against. If you're bright and ambitious you have to go along with trying to stay on top, you have to take control and do it. But at what a price – we can't afford to have any feelings about the amount we're supposed to do. And there's something about being successful that makes me feel guilty, as if I'm taking from others and shouldn't have it.

There seems to be a collective conspiracy to offer women a little more equality on the one hand only to take it away with the other. Women are allowed to achieve in some new areas but they are not yet freed from the image of woman as object. Although they seem at opposite ends of the spectrum, the super-achieving, active 'Superwoman' with bulimia and the terrified agoraphobic housewife, unable to go out, are both living statements of the ambivalent social position of women today.

On one hand, modern women are expected to be independent and emotionally self-sufficient, and on the other hand, their appearance is still one of the key ways in which they are judged. So it is not surprising that some women come to believe that changing their appearance will satisfy their emotional needs. Men and women are both in the conspiracy: men by setting the scene and women by going along with it. Into the gap fall the women who object and cannot oblige but can only show it by their protest with food.

WINIFRED

Winifred grew up feeling that it was 'bad' to be attractive, sexy and desirable because her father interfered with her and abused her sexually during the time her mother was in a mental hospital. She was frightened by the power she seemed to have with her father, and attracted to it at the same time, because it gave her a little something in the family landscape that was very bleak. When her father finally left and her mother had a breakdown, Winifred convinced herself that it was all her fault. She took 'magical' responsibility and therefore felt guilty for her mother's shattered life (see Chapter 7).

At the same time she grew to be more intensely terrified and fascinated by her attractiveness to men. She desperately wanted men to like her and find her attractive. But because she felt so guilty about it, she made a subconscious decision that she would only allow herself unpleasant men or men she didn't like. This way she would be punished, which she believed she deserved. She was a very bright girl with a good job which she did well, and she longed for praise and confirmation that she was good at her work. At work she was in control, did well and was successful. Underneath she was hungry, empty and only allowed herself to choose men who would beat her up or be unpleasant to her. If men were adoring she would soon come to despise them so that she could keep control. Either way she was getting no emotional satisfaction.

All these conflicts were expressed through her bulimic or anorectic phases which were what brought her to the hospital and to an attempt to get appropriate help. When she had allowed herself to enjoy something or to listen to something nice someone had to say, she felt she had to destroy it, either before it destroyed her or before she tainted it with her badness. She would be anorectic for several months and feel very good. When difficult feelings began to surface, to force through the control, she would start bingeing and vomiting. She felt good during the anorectic period but would be fearful the good would not last. She would become anxious and would eat to cope with the anxiety, vomiting after the binge because she couldn't bear any comfort or fullness inside her as it made her feel so bad and had to be immediately rejected.

Winifred had no concept of herself as a person with a set of rights, values and sensitivities, but saw herself as an object. She was either 'very good, controlled, doing good work and getting praised' or she was lazy, bad, selfish and too fat: she was a slim girl but thought of herself as fat and on 'bad' days came to the clinic in a huge overcoat whatever the weather. Once she began to realise all this – how she saw herself and why she saw herself like this – she began to feel she had a choice. She realised that she could now change the way she thought about herself, that it need not be limited to the way she had come to think of herself in the unhappy climate of her early life: she could give up the faulty thinking of her survival self and experience taking in something potentially 'good enough'. She started by letting herself experience difficult feelings for as long as she could tolerate without using food to cope. She formed a friendship with a man at work who had seen her efficient 'good' side but who she gradually allowed to see her 'bad' or unhappy, needy, fearful, anxious and sometimes desperate side. She allowed him to meet her mother, who was by now very disturbed, which was important as he was the first boyfriend of hers to do so. She began to heal the split in her thinking and feeling, and in her perception of herself and her symptoms became less severe.

MELANIE

Melanie, a beautiful American girl in her mid-twenties, broke down when her eating problems and their associated terror and pain invaded her with a constant feeling of depersonalisation.

> I used to take the dog out at 9 am and watch all the people going to work. I thought 'I'll never be like that'. I'd get back and have two crispbreads and one cup of black coffee. I'd then go back to bed. At 3 pm I'd take the dog out again and then go back to bed again till 5 or 6 pm. Then I would prepare food for my mother and stepfather who came in at 7.30 pm. I never ate with them. I never slept at night. No one ever noticed anything, even though I never ate with them and looked awful. The doctor I saw eventually said that I did look awful and yet no one noticed or said anything.
>
> I was never taught how to cope with anything. I grew up with my father and step-mother in America and we had a very well-to-do-life. No one ever told me I would have to work. It never occurred to me that I would ever be on my own. My step-mother never really liked me. She used to say 'You're sick, and we're going to have you put away,' and all that stuff. I never learned to be my own person. It was all 'Don't think, Don't do that, You're crazy, Don't do that.' No one ever said 'Oh, you do that rather well, why don't you think of doing that as a course at school?' or whatever.
>
> I honestly don't think I was prepared for anything at all. My mom and my father said I was such a lovely little girl. I was really happy. I was bright. Look at this (she shows me a photograph), this was taken when I was four or five years old. I'm posing in the doorway like a model. I need to have that picture wherever I live. I need to look at that. I wonder what I would have looked like, what I would have been like if things had been just that little bit different. I just

wish I'd had the opportunity to go on being that person. I have this feeling that there was never anyone to protect me and I think that's left a lasting mark on me – whether for the rest of my life or not I don't know. If I think that I may as well give up now. I'm trying hard to say, 'OK I'm bulimic. I had a difficult childhood.' I don't seem to get much further than that.

I have so much bad feeling. When I get angry I scare myself. I fear being pushed too far. My father had an appalling temper. He would go berserk, hell for leather, hit out at us. I wanted to see the marks on me. My step-mother, who hated me as I've said, she was an alcoholic ... she would encourage him to hit us. There was one time when I'd been sarcastic and he was furious that I'd been rude to her. She just sat at the counter (bar) with her drink in her hand and she said 'I don't think she understands: she needs to be hit again.' And he did. And I left next day. That was when I was seventeen and I left his house for ever. He broke a cheese board on my brother's backside, all the while telling us, 'Be honest, use your effort, be neat and clean.' I hate the expression of anger like that, yet I do it. What's worse than that? There's a boy at work and I scream at him. He doesn't deserve it and afterwards I'm so tired, so exhausted, and I get depressed. Any expression of any feeling with me leaves me just ravished, so tired.

Melanie was caught in a terrible trap. In order to survive in her family she had to adhere to rules which were impossible: to be blonde (she is very dark); to be an 'angel' (she felt a 'horrifying' girl when she burst out in protest at her situation); to be good, neat and in control when her father with whom she needed to communicate because he was her only 'real' parent, was furiously angry and punishing. To cope, she took comfort in food which forced her up against another family rule for acceptance, to be slim and beautiful. 'Beauty in my family was, and is, a big deal: it's the only thing that you have to be in my family.'

Melanie started bingeing and taking laxatives around the age of 14, when her body naturally started to change shape. At the same time, she was struggling with the difficult mood swings of adolescence. Her step-mother found out that she raided the fridge from time to time and put a padlock on it, telling everyone what Melanie had done and making her feel guilty and very bad.

I did everything I was supposed to, I tried to be what they wanted. I don't recall being depressed then. No one told me how to be sad. I don't remember spending a lot of time crying, but I did ask 'Why?' a lot. I asked my step-mother once why no one talked to me and she said it was because I wasn't beautiful, because I was ugly and fat, and because I wasn't blonde – all her children were blonde. I believed her. All the children belonged in the house except for me. I really did try but I wasn't a saint and sometimes I could be horrifying. I don't remember much about the bingeing: just that I did it and felt awful and took laxatives because I was terrified of getting fat. I didn't know what I was doing had a special name.

My crisis really started when I was 22 and living in New York, doing a stupid job earning very little money, living in a studio flat with two other girls, one of whom was a model and everything I'd always wanted to be – tall, blonde, very beautiful and everyone loved her – people used to stop her in the street. The other girl worked in an advertising agency and knew hundreds of people. I worked in an office with just five other people and I got fired from that. These two room-mates and I met at a place called 'Thin For Ever', which was about how not to over-eat. They weren't as fat as I was! I think they took pity on me. We did do a lot of things together. I took a lot of drugs. I wanted to be thin and I didn't care how I did it. It didn't bother me at all, and also there it was very accepted. I took a lot of drugs and speed and I was never hungry. I wouldn't eat. When I was thin people always wanted to be with me: I was pretty, I looked good – I didn't get gross like a lot of people who take drugs. I didn't look bad. I was a lot of fun, was very popular and went to all the dinners, parties, everything like that and everything that everyone does and for a year I had a great deal of fun.

The effect of drugs, little food and little sleep took its toll on Melanie. She became very depressed and when she did sleep she had nightmares. To keep up the drug habit she took two jobs, night and day, and she moved 11 times in two years. A particular television programme on teenage suicides brought many of her feelings into consciousness.

I identified with it so strongly it completely knocked me for six. I didn't get up for three days after that. I just … it took everything from me ... all of a sudden I understood why it was that people found it possible to kill themselves, easy to kill themselves. And it felt not such a bad thing to do.

The impact of this programme in which Melanie identified herself heralded the beginning of a new phase. Now that she had made conscious some of her inner difficulties she was more in touch with her feelings about them. Her instinct was to be drawn to food, but this had been forbidden as a resource by her weight- and beauty-conscious family. She kept on with the drugs until they ran out, desperately hoping that someone would notice, hoping that something would happen to release her from her trapped state. At Christmas that year she visited her mother and step-father in England and returned to New York full of resolutions to go to night school and to improve herself but also aware of a deep sadness, the sadness she mentioned earlier that she had never been given permission to experience. She was beginning to allow her feelings to surface, to be able to experience the depth of all the feelings that had been denied her and that were hidden within her eating problem.

Later that year she felt able to go to England and be with her mother and step-father, a necessary reconnection and possibly a safe place for her to be if she had a breakdown. She did not know this at the time and seemed surprised when I suggested that this might be a positive move on the part of her psyche. Symptoms take a long time to build up and the crisis which the symptoms ultimately create often comes at a time when it is safe: people can hold on for a long time under disastrous circumstances. Her first few months in England were very painful. She was withdrawing from her drug habit, was unable to get a job and had no friends. She felt alienated from everyone. This was the impasse experience of her breakdown.

> I had no reason to be. I couldn't think of one good reason to be, to get up and do anything or just open my eyes. I would sit at home and hear everyone going to the pub on Friday and Saturday nights, having such a good time. I felt no association with that at all. I wanted to but I couldn't and I didn't think I ever would. I didn't feel that I belonged walking round in this world, I really didn't; I lived in complete fantasy. I was sad. I hurt badly. Real, painful, physical hurt right here.

She holds her chest as she sits on the floor, rocking slightly.

Then I got hold of a book – I don't remember the name of it – but it was about bulimia and eating problems. I read it and I thought, this is me, this is what I've been doing for years and yet I'd never thought of it as a 'thing', a something with a name and an identity. Here were people writing about what to me had been a shameful secret, something I hid as a matter of course. I took it for granted that it was bad and undesirable to be fat and that no one would like me and that was the basis of everything. I hadn't really thought of it as a problem. Of course I felt bad, I knew I felt awfully bad, but no one else noticed so I thought perhaps this is how I ought to feel. But this book started me thinking that there were other people out there who felt the same way. I did ring up one person who I thought would know about these things and told her and then I felt as if someone had reached out a hand to help. I finally had a hold on something and I had talked to someone who didn't think I was insane or making a fuss about nothing. Her reaction wasn't 'Oh God, how awful, don't tell anyone' but 'Let's think about what to do'. This help made me feel better, as though there was something could be done about it, and that it was OK to feel awful and that I might get better.

Melanie did receive help: she joined a group for eating disorders run by a psychiatrist and took a course of anti-depressants. When we met she was off all medication and had stopped taking laxatives. She still worried about eating and wanted to lose weight but was not obsessed by eating to the point that her whole self image and life was dominated by it. She is still struggling with the 'good or bad' and 'love or hate' issues and is gradually finding out more about herself through individual therapy. She has now thawed out from the impasse stage of her breakdown during which she experienced all the hate and fury she had denied while it was still unsafe, and she is now rebuilding.

I have tried so hard, awfully hard. I feel I deserve to be a little bit free. I do it all to myself, I know that. I end up hating everyone: they do something and I choose to hit upon it and end up hating them. I have to remove myself from them: I can't see them or talk to them. I don't get over it easily.

112

You can see how Melanie's world was divided by polarities. The words she uses illustrate this: beautiful or gross; a saint or horrifying; really listen or ignore; good or bad; love or hate; real or false. These describe her inner landscape, the all or nothing feelings and swings of mood she has. There is no 'middle' or 'good enough' place from which she can feel comfortable to experience love and hate, depression and happiness, good and bad.

The bad feelings seem synonymous with bad food and fat and are equally desirable and terrifying. She acknowledges she has a lot of anger but the expression of it depletes her and leaves her exhausted and 'ravished', like the aftermath of a huge meal which she has to get rid of. She associates anger with her father, who she sees as destructive. There must also be a great deal of deep-seated anger about the value put on her appearance. She feels depersonalised, having grown up feeling like an object that is only acceptable if it is pretty and thin. Once she is free of this – and she is fighting to be free of it – she will be able to use her considerable intelligence and energy in more useful and fulfilling directions.

When she lived on drugs she could feel good but at cost to herself. Her idealisation of good means that it feels constantly out of reach, exacerbating her feelings that she is bad. Melanie's perception of herself seems to be 'If I'm thin, people will love me. If I'm fat people will find me gross and reject me'. She has either to be thin, in control, remote, safe and busy, with no strong feelings; or fat, the object of everyone's lasciviousness and hate, a gross failure. Either way she is not claiming the lively girl in the photograph.

Five years after first being interviewed, Melanie updates us on her situation:

I no longer take drugs or laxatives to maintain or lose weight. I have tried various diet pills which do work, but the price I have to pay is now too great. All my anger, depression and paranoia return and I become so self involved that I cannot cope with the smallest details of ordinary life. I am a very different person now. When I re-read the previous section about how I was feeling in 1987 I thought 'that's not me'. I cried at how low I had allowed myself to go. It brought back all the pain and despair I had felt then, which went on for some time afterwards. For a long time my appearance was the only thing I cared about. All my family required of me was to look beautiful. The person I am inside or what I feel counts for nothing.

I am much stronger spiritually, have a stronger belief in myself as a person, regardless of how I look. I no longer feel negated by not being judged beautiful in other people's eyes. I have my ups and downs but the ups last longer. I don't try to change myself to suit whoever I am with, so I am not so confused about who I am, because I am always the same person. I have had several different kinds of therapy. Some were good, some not. I have now taken the responsibility for my own actions, not blaming a bad childhood or bulimia for my difficulties. I used to think that when I was 'cured' I would begin my life, but I cannot wait to begin my own life which is now half way over. A cure cannot begin my life, I must do that. So, I am not very beautiful anymore, I am very heavy, I still wish I was thinner, but not all the time. I still have bouts of depression but not the depth of the past, and I'm not dragged down. I get through the down times. I take anti-depressants, and I am able to see life, if not through rose-coloured glasses, through realistic glasses or no glasses at all. I sleep now, and do not often have nightmares.

I don't want to be looked after and admired like a little girl any more. For the first time I have a 'womanly confidence' and it works! I live in a lovely apartment and have started my own business. I could become a hermit, but I make myself go out and don't refuse invitations just because I am not thin and beautiful. I have friends I can count on, who like or love me for whom I am, not what I look like. I have come to be comfortable with myself. And I am finally making some good relationships with my family, on my own terms this time!

Exercise: Fat or thin, good or bad?

1 Make a diagram like this:

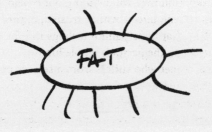

Write into the spaces all the words you associate with fatness in two minutes.

2 With this diagram, write in all the words you associate with thinness.

Spend some time after you have completed each diagram pondering the words you have chosen. Each one may have its own particular history or story. Examine where each word comes from in your life and how often the word chosen comes from premises that need no longer apply. Explore how much your inner world is divided into the two categories of fat and thin.

Many people with eating disorders have no real perception about their body shape because they project on to their bodies what they feel inside about themselves. Most people suffering from anorexia feel they are fat and do not want to be seen. Most people who are obese try to present themselves as slimmer than they are. Both are constantly vigilant to any sign from others that draws attention to their bodies. Both feel extremely self-conscious all the time.

This very negative self image often makes it difficult for people with an eating problem to ask for help. They are afraid of being rejected because of being 'found out' for what they feel they are. Being in therapy or counselling also involves closeness. Many people with problems around eating and body shape are terrified of the vulnerability associated with closeness, and the feeling that in this situation they will be more out of control than ever. This is their 'no go' area. Going into it with a trusted, experienced professional person is the only way that these painful feelings may be understood, made safe and incorporated into the person's whole life.

Everyone I have ever met who suffers from a serious problem with eating is struggling with much more than the confines of their own body. They are caught up in a collective confusion of the Western world about what is feminine and what is masculine and how these qualities are to be incorporated within the changing roles of men and women. Inside the individual troubled body there is always a very angry, active, protesting, intelligent and talented person just fighting to get out.

ADDICTION TO TRANQUILLISERS

Tranquillisers and other sedative drugs may be used to suppress the symptoms of breakdown. They may also cause problems or exacerbate existing difficulties. The case history that follows shows how they may become an important part of an individual's breakdown.

CLAIRE

At a difficult period in Claire's life when she was far away from her family, when her husband was away much of the time and there was no one to talk to, Claire consulted her GP about poor sleeping.

1979 was a difficult year. I have two small children plus I was looking after a friend's little boy in hospital. We were building our own house and had been spending all our spare time at the building site. My husband had the kind of job that took him away a lot and even when he was home he was busy with paperwork for so long that I often had to cope with things on my own. I felt run down, I wasn't sleeping. I was very tense. I knew I should have had more patience with the children and my husband so I went to the doctor thinking some sleeping pills might help. He prescribed Benzodiazepine – a tranquilliser I didn't know anything about – so I went home and took them. Within half an hour or so of taking them I felt better and I slept well so I took them again. I had enough to last about three months. In September I began to notice, just before my tablet was due, that I had some strange feelings. However, once the tablet was taken, the feeling went away.

We moved into our house in January 1980. I decided there and then that I was not going to ask for any more tablets so the evening we moved in I threw them down the toilet. That was the beginning of four nightmare years. The next morning I felt as I had never felt before. My joints were all swollen and my limbs stiff. I had dreadful

116

palpitations and I was trembling. I couldn't concentrate on doing the most simple of things, like making a cup of tea. I felt I was on automatic robot, as though everything was unreal. I was very emotional, depressed, crying. I had no interest in what normally I would have loved doing, which was getting my new house straight. I had feelings of pressure in my head like a tight band round it. Also I felt as if a dark cloud was sitting just above me. I was frightened to leave the house. I couldn't drive my car. I didn't want to answer the telephone or even pay the milkman. Every task became a major problem. Shopping was a nightmare, even writing a cheque. My husband realised I was really ill when I couldn't stand being in Marks and Spencers as before I had spent hours browsing about. He insisted I went to the doctor. My first visit to him was awful. Most of the time I cried. He had not met me before so I couldn't blame him for thinking I was yet another neurotic woman. He prescribed some drugs as he said I was suffering from anxiety depression.

I went home and took the drug and felt worse. After two days I phoned him and he prescribed the drugs I'd had before. Within a short time I felt fine, almost back to normal. I stayed on them for a month or so but I began to worry that I had become dependent on them. After a while I began to cut the dose down, leaving out the midday tablet.

Almost at once the symptoms returned. I was very frightened that I might have a brain tumour or even multiple sclerosis. The symptoms I was having were very similar. My personality had changed, I had been a very cheerful outgoing person, always having people in for meals and doing ten different things at the same time. Now I had to force myself to get out and do the basic things in life. Maybe if it wasn't for my daughters I wouldn't have had the incentive to do anything. I had lost a stone in weight, my skin looked sallow, I had no confidence in myself and when the children wanted friends in to tea, I would set the table and have to go and lie down because I couldn't stand the noise. Everything became larger and louder than life. Every now and then I would go back to the right dose of tablets and feel better, at least until the tablets wore off. When I went back to my doctor he felt I was just suffering from anxiety depression. I couldn't believe I would be having so many physical symptoms. The months went by and if I kept to the full dose of tablets a day the symptoms felt better, but still there. In my heart of hearts I didn't want to rely on drugs so I was continually trying not to take the full dose. My poor husband and family could not understand what had happened to me. I was a stranger to them, always feeling ill and depressed, not wanting to do things I'd always enjoyed.

About this time I went to my doctor and said I wanted a full check-up, and an appointment was made for two months later. I saw a physician at the hospital and he said there was nothing wrong with me physically and prescribed another tranquilliser and some anti-depressants. For a while things improved. I had to go back to him in six weeks: when I went back I had stopped taking the anti-depressants because I didn't want to take any more pills. He was cross with me, and said I should see a psychiatrist. While I was waiting to see the psychiatrist I decided to try alternative medicine. I tried a chiropractor and eventually an acupuncturist. He said he could help. Within three months I was not taking any pills. I was being treated twice a day, five times a week and certainly I felt better. However, I was still feeling giddy. It felt as though I had got the wrong glasses on, and when walking I seemed to be dragging myself to one side of the street. He didn't seem to be able to solve this and mentioned it might be a sinus problem. I went back to my own doctor and he treated me for sinus. After six weeks things were no better, I felt continually as if I were going to one side and being pulled over. In the end I went privately to have my sinuses X-rayed. They were clear. The ENT specialist said my problems were probably hyperventilation (breathing too fast). I asked how to solve it and he suggested a muscle relaxant. When I looked at the prescription it was for the same drug I had been trying to come off. I felt so low that I decided to take them again and when my appointment with the psychiatrist came round he said that taking tranquillisers was no more harmful than drinking a cup of tea. Eighteen or so months went by and I took them regularly and although I did have some symptoms from time to time, I lived with them.

Then I watched a programme on television one day about people who wanted to come off drugs and the problems they were having. They said to send for a list of people who were having the same kind of problem so that we could contact one another. When my list arrived I phoned everyone in my area and suggested a coffee evening at my home. About twenty people came with husbands and wives. We all started to talk and found we all had the same kind of symptoms, when we tried to stop taking the tablets. Also that all of the doctors had refused to admit that you could become physically addicted to them. We agreed it would be helpful to cut down slowly and to support each other through the bad times. The relief to know that other people were having the same symptoms was enormous. It was helpful to partners, too, to know they were not the only ones. We met once a fortnight and found out that a charity called 'Release' knew about our problem and one evening a lady from there came to talk to us and to show the powerful advertising doctors are subjected to, encouraging them to prescribe these drugs and telling them how wonderful these drugs are. She also told us how millions of pounds of profits are made by this company.

I heard also from Release that the Maudsley Hospital in London was researching into the problems of tranquilliser withdrawal. I wrote directly to them and had an interview with them. decided that I was probably someone who could cope with my life without pills and I began to go to them as an outpatient once a week for ten weeks, while they monitored my reaction to the drug withdrawals. I had blood tests, ECG, tests for memory and the time it took for me to react to certain things; I filled in forms and had urine tests. The most helpful thing about this was that there was a doctor at the other side of the desk who believed in what I was saying. He was able to reassure me that other people had the same problems. Then I was on my own for ten weeks when I had managed to come off and stay off. The same old symptoms came back. Now that I knew what was causing them I coped better. I was determined to win this time, I had a life waiting for me out there and I was determined to live it.

It was six months before I felt any better and ten months before I had any good days. Progress was very slow and maybe if I had known how long it was going to take me at the beginning, I wouldn't have been able to face it. It was about two years before I felt really well again. The spring this year has been especially good because you lose so much when you take pills that the feeling of changing seasons doesn't exist. I think the saddest part of this for me was that when the drugs were first prescribed for me my children were small; now, five years later, they have grown up and I feel I have missed those years together. My husband has been very supportive and I now spend a lot of time helping others with the same problem. You have to have been there yourself first before you can really understand how awful it is.

If I had gone to a GP who had suggested going to a counsellor I would have gone because I would have thought that anything was better than nothing. I've always had a thing about not using pills and chemicals unless it was really necessary. Having said all that and gone through it all I think it's made me much more a cold person than I was before. It's a very painful way to go.

It is difficult to ascertain whether Claire would have had some kind of breakdown even without the effect of tranquillisers with all the difficulties in her life.

What I know is that the anxiety I experienced when I wasn't taking the pills, during the withdrawal period, was fifty times worse than the anxiety I had experienced at my worst before I started taking them. It would have been far more comfortable to have been helped to cope with the first anxiety and not the pill-induced one.

I do know that I have the typical British stiff upper lip attitude: that you keep going no matter what. I would have considered whatever I was going through a weakness, that I ought to be able to cope and that you keep trying to do things you were able to do no matter what is happening in your life, or you're a failure.

So certainly a lot of it was perhaps aiming at perfection which I thought, at that time in my life, I thought existed ... which I know now is fantasy land.

I suppose this contributed to my not being able to talk to anyone: it was, now I think of it, hard for me to acknowledge to myself that I was allowed to. I felt as if I was on a ship without anyone to captain me. I was being set adrift. I didn't have much say in what was happening to me, my life was being taken out of my hands. The decisions my husband was making at this time were affecting me and my young children and I wasn't able to have much to say about it. I felt very powerless. I had to relinquish all my own feelings and thoughts to somebody else and that's a pretty unpleasant experience.

Many women share Claire's experience with her GP who made her feel very helpless: 'Just another neurotic woman'.

All women have the same story: they are given far more tranquillisers than men, to sort of shut them up. I see it again and again in the counselling service in which I now work: the women get tarred with the same brush, and I'm aware that my job can be so limited. It's such a short time and the drugs themselves mask who the person really is and what they're struggling with.

Claire now helps other people to get off tranquillisers and was trained by the Westminster Advisory Centre on Alcoholism who help people with all addictions.

What would be so important is to have a counsellor or helpful person as part of a GP practice, so the GP could say 'it feels as though things in your life are in a bit of a turmoil and this could be contributing to your sleeplessness' or whatever. Then the person could stay within the safety of the practice, it would not be unusual for the patients and it would take the pressure off the doctors. So many families have relationships that are going wrong and if you can just take a step back and look at yourself with fresh eyes, it makes such a difference. I think the younger doctors are taking an interest in not prescribing drugs in the beginning but many of the older doctors I've met won't believe that there is a problem with tranquillisers: it's going to take years before we change doctors' attitudes. One of the doctors I went to brought out his own supply and said 'I've been taking them for years'. If the doctors are on them what hope is there?

3
Events which can trigger a breakdown process

In Chapter 1 we saw that catastrophic events, for which nothing could possibly prepare us, such as earthquake, murder, violent rape or muggings can cause us to break down. There may be other events which are not in themselves enough to cause breakdown but which may be powerful enough to challenge us in our most vulnerable spot, and may so precipitate breakdown. Our 'no go' area may be entered by what we experience emotionally during or after these times.

MEANINGFUL LOSS

We may lose something specific, like a loved person or animal, or we may lose an ideal or a purpose in life, such as a religious belief or faith in something or someone. Sometimes when we lose a job or move house, a friend moves away or we give up a course which hasn't seemed to mean much to us, we only later on realise just what this time or space or contact has meant to us. For example, someone I know drove her son to school every morning for five years. It was the only time they had alone together during the day and it was an important contact for them both, without much being consciously made of it. When he moved to another school, they were excited and pleased, but this needed to be balanced by allowing the loss of the close contact which they both missed. This kind of subtle experience can undermine our lives unless we consciously allow for the sadness of the loss.

MEANINGFUL LOSS

These forty days
The discovery of pain
The twisting still of knife in flesh
Lord, grant they never come again.

My days of speculative theory
I long have lived unknowing
But truly walk the desert once
You'll eat the sand that's blowing.

Forgive too-human blasphemy
And give me grace to bear it
This Lent that you have offered me
Oh God must I accept it?

My individual Easter comes,
O Lord, don't let me lie there
Bound round with shroud's bewildered doubt,
Whip up your Spirit rare!

April 1981

Bereavement

We never know how we are going to react or feel when someone close to us dies, even though we may be prepared for the death in the sense that we know the person has an incurable illness. The shock of losing someone you love and have felt close to, or a person who you may not love but who has had an important place in your life, can never be anticipated. Our experience of loss is individual and the impact on us is personal.

After the death of his wife from cancer C. S. Lewis wrote in *A Grief Observed:*

> No one ever told me grief felt so like fear. I am not afraid, but the sensation is like being afraid. The same fluttering of the stomach, the same restlessness, the yawning. I keep on swallowing.
>
> At other times it feels like being mildly drunk, or concussed. There is some sort of invisible blanket between the world and me. I find it hard to take in what anyone says. Or perhaps, hard to want to take it in. It is so uninteresting. Yet I want the others to be about me. I dread the moments when the house is empty. If only they would talk to one another and not me.

And later on:

> An odd by-product of my loss is that I'm aware of being an embarrassment to everyone I meet. At work, in the street, I see people, as they approach me, trying to make up their minds whether they'll say 'something about it' or not. Some funk it altogether. I like best the well brought up young men, almost boys, who walk up to me as if I were a dentist, turn very red, get it over, and then edge away to the bar as quickly as they decently can. Perhaps the bereaved ought to be in special settlements like lepers.

People remember the smallest detail involved in death. It will be written up in neon lights inside them. 'She was wearing this'; 'He said "I'm just going into the garden"'; 'I was peeling carrots, I remember'; 'We got this phone call and I had just got out of the bath'. People remember the ordinary everyday details of bereavement and all the things they did and wish they'd done, all the things they didn't do and wish they'd done. 'I couldn't face looking into the coffin, but now I wish I had' or 'We never spoke to the children about it, but I think it would have been better, they wouldn't have been so worried.'

People who are bereaved need time and space to talk about these details and about the feelings attached to them, for some time after the death. Death is not something that can be mourned for a week or two and 'got over', but so often that is what people feel is expected of them. In cultures which have strong religious rituals for the dead there are organised settings and spaces in which the dead person can be remembered. Some of the feelings associated with them, some of the unfinished business, can be shared and expressed with others. In the Jewish faith people close to the dead person stay in mourning for a whole year. In the Catholic religion there is the custom of the wake which may go on for days, and we are all familiar with the Spanish, French and Italian widows in their seemingly permanent black clothes. Some may go on mourning for years, like Queen Victoria, but the effect of the 'rite of passage' of mourning gives people permission to be sad, unhappy, not do too much, not have to socialise, and from time to time just scream and wail. I remember reading an account of the families of Aberfan, after the disaster there, written by someone who had no ritualistic belief, but who warmly described the obvious comfort of the ritualistic, chanting embrace of the churches' prayers and music which drew people together at a time of great need. People often feel very angry with God after a bereavement and denounce their faith, but the church offers a place for people to go and be gathered together in a way that no other organisation has yet produced.

The way of death

The way of death affects us in different ways. 'He had a good death' I heard someone say once, referring to a colleague with cancer who was nursed at home by the lovely Macmillan nurses. He had his wife and family around, his books and whisky, his favourite paintings and he saw the heron pass his window every day. When he knew he was dying he did as many of the things he'd always wanted to do as he could. He showed his wife something of the world she hadn't seen. They had time to talk about what they'd meant to each other, what they wanted after death. They had time to explore their different beliefs. These conversations are now very important to the friends and colleagues who miss him. This process made death and dying somehow a dignified and less frightening event.

However, afterwards there is a reckoning, and it is during this time that we come face to face with many parts of ourselves we may not have encountered before. For example, our resentment and anger, our fury and incomprehension, our feelings of being abandoned, left alone to cope. There may be cynicism that there is nothing good in the world; or rage about having to carry on under impossible odds when all we want to do is curl up and have the mass of conflicting feelings go away. Often there is terrible isolation when the look in people's eyes implies: 'Haven't you got over it yet?' Bereavement is something so individual to the person, like the process of breakdown itself.

Types of bereavement

Different types of loss create different problems. Each has its own difficulties which we may not appreciate unless we or someone close to us goes through the experience.

Death of a parent

If one of our parents dies, we are brought closer to our own mortality. In the words of one young man, 'I am now right out there in the front line: I'm next.' If the person has acted as a powerful tyrant in our lives, we may be relieved at first. Later there may be something of a void, and an uncertainty. We may wonder 'what will happen to all my aggressive feelings when X isn't there to bring them out and contain them?' If the parent who has died was a wise counsellor and friend we will have lost something precious which can never be replaced.

Death of a partner

Married couples who have been known to actively hate each other act as if doubly bereaved when one of them dies: as if hate is a stronger force than love. Of course when someone dies with whom one has a difficult, negative relationship there is often a tremendous feeling of guilt and remorse over 'what might have been': the longing to put it all back and have another go and do better is strong.

126

But when someone has been much loved by another their presence leaves a huge hole that cannot be filled by anything else.

Sudden death

A person who dies suddenly 'in the prime of life' challenges us in all sorts of ways. One woman said to me 'Why did it have to be him ... why him? He was so much a better person than me. I am expendable. Why couldn't it have been me?' And she meant it. With sudden death there is no chance to make amends and there is often unfinished business: 'I never told her how much I loved her'. Sudden death can make us feel very uncertain about life, afraid to trust anything. We may feel as if the person we knew was spirited away. Sudden death can have a particularly traumatic effect on young children.

Mysterious death

If it is uncertain how or why someone died or even if they have done so, the situation is extremely painful and difficult, and it leaves people with many unanswered questions. Soldiers lost in a war, sailors lost at sea or young people disappearing while on the trail to India, for example, leave people in a state of constant search.

Women who have miscarriages, or whose babies die at birth or are born dead for no apparent reason can leave the individual not only with their grief and loss but also a sense of personal failure. 'What did I do or didn't do, what could I have done?' The cot death syndrome provokes the same questions. If no one is really sure why the baby died, as is often the case, the situation really is hard to get hold of.

The death of a child

This sort of bereavement is a particularly heavy burden. To have to bury your own child is a great suffering, so often it is hard to make any sense of.

The impact of loss for young children and 'magical' guilt

Bereavement which occurs early in life has a major impact on us. When we are small we cannot quite understand what death is. Families may try to protect their children from the pain of death by obscuring the truth: 'Grandma's gone to Heaven' or 'Your brother is safely away on a long holiday'. These are open-ended concepts which encourage a child to believe that the dead person will some day be returning. Any grieving they need to do will be postponed until the painful realisation hits that the person will not be coming back. When that happens the child may not have words for what he or she feels but may begin to panic, to have distorting dreams, to suffer physical pain or act out in some way. These symptoms will occur out of context, perhaps some years after the death, when other people have grieved and moved on.

Fragments of overheard conversation at the time of the death may ignite a child's imagination. He or she may hear: 'put her head in the oven', 'lost her temper with him she did and then he went and died' or 'I'll never trust hospitals again'. These fragments and the images they create play upon a young imagination, creating the possibility of phobia and anxiety later on. It may also be that the young child didn't like Dad very much or perhaps that the afternoon Mum took her overdose or suffered a stroke she had been very cross at something the child had done. It is easy to see how a child can blame himself or herself for the death, either because of 'bad' thoughts or because he or she witnessed or was part of a row. Later on this can grow into something we call 'magical' guilt, or taking magical (because it's not logical) responsibility for what happened. In some cases this unconscious paradox is so disabling that people are unable to claim their own lives freely. They jeopardise their chances, can be placatory to destructive lengths and actually do not allow themselves to have anything good. We saw an example of this in Kathleen's story, where her eldest brother was found hung when she was only three, and how she later on became an extremely responsible woman but allowed herself little free life of her own.

All kinds of complications may occur when a death in the family is not talked about. Pat's father died at work when she was six. Her mother sent her to an aunt and she did not know until one month later that her father had died. Her mother suffered a breakdown and Pat was sent to boarding school. Father's name was not allowed to be mentioned. Pat was not allowed to mourn for her father. Years after when she came into counselling because of her difficulty in sustaining relationships with men the whole issue of her ungrieved-for father arose. It was, for her, as if she could not allow herself another man until she had properly said goodbye to her father. I think it would be true to say that uncompleted mourning from an earlier time in a person's life is present in over half the people who present in later life with emotional or 'nervous' difficulties.

The four stages of mourning

William Warden describes the four stages of mourning:

To accept the reality of loss

The first task, which can take a very long time, is to come full face with the reality that the person is dead, has gone and will not return. A natural protection against loss is denial: we cannot take in or cope with what has happened or we find ways of explaining, 'it doesn't matter', 'I was expecting it', 'we weren't close anyway'. Another way of denying the loss is to feel somehow that the person will come back in some form: we keep seeing them in the street, have their things ready for their return or we project all the feelings on to another person so that they take the place of the deceased. All these reactions are natural to a certain degree, but when they go on for an extended period or seriously disrupt our life or become bizarre, then the person is unable to move away from this stage of mourning.

The pain of grief

The second part of the mourning process is to really experience the pain of grief. Because it hurts so much, and sometimes physically manifests itself all over the body, we tend to push it away and find something to do, quickly. And because we find that others don't want to talk about the loss or the person but avoid any mention of what has happened, this part of mourning can go underground, only to surface at some other time in the form of a severe depression or a breakdown.

Adjustment

The third task of mourning is the adjustment necessary after someone close is no longer there. Whatever the relationship there may be a loss of financial security, or emotional backup and support. There may be the loss of all kinds of role: playmate and sexual partner, cook, handyman, gardener, mender and fixer, childminder, dog walker, window washer, companion and soul mate. Adjustment means taking on some of these roles ourselves or adjusting to their loss. Often we are not aware of how much the person has done for us until after they are gone. Just knowing that another human being is in the building makes a difference to our sense of aloneness and isolation; there is someone to interact with, even if negatively. Many women have never handled money matters and have to learn to; many men have never learned to take care of the house and food preparation. If people withdraw from taking on board these skills, necessary for their continued life, they are not letting go of the person nor are they fully engaged in separation from the person.

Final stage of mourning

The last stage of mourning is when we withdraw emotionally from the person who died so that we are able to make other close relationships. Sometimes people feel that to love another person is to betray the one who has died, as if there were only a limited amount of love within oneself and as if this had to be rationed out. This can hold up the final stage of mourning.

Identity crisis after loss

Sometimes there is an 'identity' crisis after the loss of a close loved person. We feel that we cannot cope or accommodate the gap that is left in our lives. Sometimes we may have an image of ourselves before the loss, and feel we somehow cannot get back to this state. There is a strong feeling of 'if it hadn't happened I would be all right'. We may feel that before the loss we were good, alive, happy and successful and that now we are bad, miserable, depressed and a failure. It seems then as if all the good feelings get tied up with the deceased, and he or she becomes idealised within that perception, so that we feel cut adrift from anything good or happy.

There is no doubt that bereavement is the most challenging life event to hit us. It hits us in the ways we've described here and it also hits us in places we may not have been aware of before. This fact, coupled with the possibility that we may, for many reasons, not be able to mourn properly for the one we've lost, means that personal loss from the death of an important person is a major trigger for breakdown.

PHYLLIS

Phyllis began to suffer symptoms of a prolonged kind of breakdown just under two years after her husband died. When we met, she was still struggling to incorporate what had happened to her and to understand some of the reasons behind it. She still suffered from anxiety and found it very difficult to go out of the house, she still had many worries and guilts about the past. Feeling guilty about her feelings for her husband and the 'unfinished business' between them possibly got in the way of her mourning his loss appropriately. What also may have contributed to her breakdown was her exhaustion, as she had nursed her husband after his first stroke for six and a half years at the same time as keeping her job going.

My doctor can't praise me enough for the way I looked after my husband, but I do tend to look back a lot, which is my failure. I try not to but I think I've got a guilt complex about some things. When my doctor said 'you must get out' I arranged to go out every Wednesday with a man friend. I have often thought since, that I was being a little unkind to my husband. I don't think he was a jealous man really, anyway, and I think he was quite pleased I went out. For a patient he was excellent. He had his funny ways. He was very fastidious but at the same time, if he cried (he cried a lot) I used to shut the door and Gerald, who lived next door, he would come in and they would talk man to man. He'd get over it so he wasn't a bad patient, not by a long way. I got impatient sometimes, I used to walk in at lunch time and he used to put his tongue out to show 'I'm thirsty' and instead of saying 'all right dear, I'll make a cup of tea I'd turn round and say 'let me get in, time to take my coat off'. That sort of thing has struck me again and again. The doctor says after six years you must wipe out all guilt.

The burden of guilts and regrets about her marriage began to weigh Phyllis down and prevented her from getting on with her own life.

131

I suppose in lots of ways we weren't all that close. He was the type of man who just lived to come home and sit by his fireside. He handed all the money over to me to do all the business side, the shopping and so on. He wouldn't come with me, we weren't compatible that way and maybe that's what all this is about. When I see my friends with their husbands and they go out together ... the things I've done that were wrong – I've brought home wall-paper and it's not been very good. We had to tear it all down because I got the wrong kind of paper. It was terrible for him to put it up, instead of coming with me. I know I'm going back a long way. Some people have companionship, don't they? I think companionship in marriage is far better than, I suppose, love really.

   None of this came up until after I had my breakdown. I do feel I've made a mess of my life.

Another contributing factor was that while she was nursing her husband Phyllis had a definite role to play, and possibly this activity prevented her from expressing some of the more negative and painful feelings about the real relationship.

After he died I had nothing. I woke up to find I had nobody to nurse. My daughter had moved away to Devon so I think that was the beginning (of my breakdown). At least I was very tired. I began to feel – not all the time, but periodically – that I would practically collapse. Collapse physically, not knowing what it was.

One of the ways Phyllis tried to cope with her new situation was to move to London, to be nearer her sister, but it didn't work out, and after fifteen months she returned to the town where she'd lived with her husband. This gave her an added sense of failure and guilt. She lost money on houses and began to feel much worse about herself. Her physical symptoms continued.

I still kept getting this sort of not collapsing, but feeling very ill and not knowing what it was. I kept going to the doctor and saying 'I've got this pain here.' I think I've been to the general hospital three times with them investigating different pain areas. I had one of the pains in my back and one down below. There was nothing the matter, it was all invention. The pains were worse at times and at others not too bad. The doctor, I don't think he knew what to do with me in the end. It was kind of invention ... I invented all these things, you see. Physically I was a hundred per cent but I didn't think I was. He would say 'there's nothing the matter with you physically' but then I got a pain in my chest and had an ECG. That was the time I went to the hairdresser's and my hair was very wet. I just looked in the glass and passed out. They sent for an ambulance and sent me up to the Cardiac. I had an X-ray, my heart was all right. They kept me in hospital for two weeks and then I came home. I went to stay with a friend, sat in a chair and passed out again; and again went to hospital. I was put in the Cardiac Department again. They said it was angina. I didn't feel right. I didn't know what was the matter with me.

When I was in hospital the third time they thought I was a hypochondriac. I was right near where the nurses report. One of the nurses said 'Mrs. P's back. What's she got this time, heart failure?' That was painful. I kept on saying I had a pain here, a pain there and they kept checking but finding nothing. It was awful and I felt so ill. No one told me anything there about how pain links with anxiety. Eventually I did see a psychiatrist. He said 'I wish you had come sooner'. But how could I? I didn't know what was wrong with me. So many people, maybe my own doctor, don't like the word psychiatrist. I've got a friend that doesn't. I won't dare to speak to her about it.

I was ashamed about seeing him. But after I came back from my daughter's and was at rock bottom I said 'I want help'. I can't describe how I felt. I've had major operations and it wasn't like that. It was worse than that: after major surgery I was walking about the next day. This was something I just couldn't understand. And still doctors weren't saying what the matter was and, in fact, they were quite cross. One said 'Look,' and showed me my X-ray, 'it's quite clear, there's nothing the matter with you; go home.'

As well as her conflicting feelings which she was unable to acknowledge and, therefore, to share with anyone, Phyllis felt bereft of a definite pattern in her daily life and was unable to bring about any change. She retreated, with her fears, inside herself.

The first year after my husband died I was very limited. I got into a pattern. I was at work for a year and I used to say to my colleague

'I must go to the bank today' but I never got there. I just went straight home and it would get to Friday and I wouldn't go.

I had to come home and it's been like that ever since. I found being inside was a security to me. When I had the breakdown I couldn't drive because of the tablets. I didn't feel confident enough to drive and haven't done so since. I was here on my own and had to rely on friends to look after me – shopping and everything. I would ring up the doctor if I was in a panic. I didn't see the psychiatrist again for about six months and this surprised me. I would get a taxi to go and see my doctor: he doesn't have much time, just fifteen minutes, they can't do a lot for you. I did ask the psychiatrist about counselling and he said we didn't have anything like that here, and then I found out this volunteer place, then I was put on different tablets and they were marvellous and I started to feel better. They did a lot for me and then the psychiatrist started to take an interest in me. I was going every month but they still hadn't got to the bottom of the problem. I went into a clinic and that was the worst place. I went there and he put me on tranquillisers and anti-depressants but what frightened me were all the other people. I was petrified of the place.

The front door was locked and they wouldn't let me go home to turn my heating off which I'd forgotten, and I didn't live far away. Then this manic depressive followed me around for days, calling out. Another one emptied my drawer out at 6 am with all my underwear. Whatever they put me on, for three nights (I can laugh about it now) I was roller-skating around the town and my heart got so fast it woke me up and I called the nurse. They put me on a tablet which didn't agree with me and which had terrible side effects. It was a terrible place: for the manic depressives and schizophrenics it was fine, but when you sat there and someone threw a metal stool across the room at you and it just missed you, it was terrible.

All this has taken nearly four years. My doctor says 'You've got to help yourself'. Well I do: I don't sit about any more than I can help. I try to go out. I go for a walk. I go to the voluntary place and the counselling I've had there has been wonderful. When my daughter comes I still have the anxiety, but there is a lot to take it off me. I like to help and look after people, it's always given me a lot of pleasure. When I drove my car I'd go shopping and get prescriptions for people. My daughter had high blood pressure when she was here and I looked after her. When she went I had no pain at all for one day. It can happen, but how to make it happen when she's not here?

I saw Phyllis again six months after this interview and she looked a different person. She was smiling, had colour in her face and a much less frightened look in her eye. She was feeling very much better, had benefited from counselling and relaxation classes, and she was calmer and more confident, able to enjoy friendships and to contribute to life in ways she had enjoyed before her breakdown.

MARGARET

Margaret had a breakdown 28 years ago, soon after her fiancé died.

I was in my twenties and working in the field of music. I enjoyed that and worked with people I liked very much. What triggered the whole experience was that I had one particular man in my life who was everything to me. He was a lot older, a marvellous companion. When he suddenly got cancer and died, it was as if literally the bottom dropped out of everything. I can see now and could see then probably, that I had remained too dependent on him, too emotionally dependent. I grew up with the myth that in some way I wasn't quite right, wasn't the right shape. I somehow was a bit of a misfit. I was the visionary dreamer but could never tell anybody the dreams, because I knew nobody would have understood. I think he was the first person to whom I could really express myself. We had an extraordinary rapport – he was very intuitive about me and the way I worked and the way I conformed. He would guess all sorts of things. It was a tremendous relief to have found somebody who understood me, to feel that perhaps I wasn't a misfit.

Margaret feels that her fiancé's death was the trigger for her breakdown, but that the cause lay in her over-adaptation to her family structure.

I was the weak link, or the sensitive member, and I took the brunt of not only my own disorder, but also the family imbalance. My father had died when I was twelve and my mother was a busy working woman. The family were all extrovert types and I was the exact opposite. Although I was living independently when I broke down, I was still trapped and enclosed in the family structure.

I still hadn't given myself permission to free my own decision making, based on my own ideas. I think this was beginning to happen, and if that man had lived perhaps I would have been different, and I wouldn't have needed the breakdown. Definitely I did need (the breakdown) to shake me out of the problems that I had left over, assumptions that I was carrying around from childhood.

It was a very severe and harsh experience. It felt – and other people have said this too – it felt unfair. Whatever the word means. Here I was, doing my best, trying to earn my living, doing all the things more or less required of me and suddenly everything dissolved into chaos. I now see clearly enough that all initiations involve treachery, betrayal, and without that one isn't going to be able to make one's peace with the past. I think there is always that element that wants to take us back to the world of childhood where something is always fair or not fair, and that's where we live, we either share out toffee apples or we don't, and it's on that kind of basis.

What I felt had let me down was in me rather than outside. It was as though I had found suddenly some kind of enemy within myself. Some attacking kind of energy which I experienced as a voice at times, which was all hostile and mocking and which was stripping down all the ideas I had about myself. This stripping process seemed to take them right down to the bare bones and the bare bones of me felt extremely inadequate, extremely small, extremely defenceless and vulnerable.

The idea of betrayal was so strong, such a feeling of 'Why should it happen to me? What have I done to deserve this?' The attacking voices actually incapacitated me. I had to give up work and I went to hospital. I went to a very good and caring psychiatrist. He saw me for a little while while I was working but he could see I'm sure that my condition was deteriorating. I needed hospitalisation. I think I got caught in the food problem too. I stopped eating. I'm not sure how central it was but I do remember not eating very much, and that probably alarmed him. I had medication and, once a week, a meeting with a young psychiatrist. It wasn't at all intensive psychotherapy which I now wish I'd had. I believe my progress would have been better and the whole situation improved if I'd had psychotherapy as well. What I had was caring containment and the staff were carefully chosen but that doesn't mean that there wasn't horror within it; the horror was inside the patients. And a lot of the healing came about from talking with other patients, accepting other patients. Sharing our experiences was very important to some of us.

One part of me was like a tidal wave, a disaster, and I knew it couldn't hold out. Another part of me, or a voice somewhere within me, would occasionally come up with a clear message, and it was expressed in words 'suffering is privilege'. I could see that the words made sense but then something in me said 'this is nonsense' and the tidal wave would come back. It was as though there was a seed of light, or hope or strength, trying to form itself; and associated with that, I expect, came the impulse to go and read the book of Job, which came out of the blue as well.

I can now see how wise that was. It's the blueprint for this breakdown journey. It did keep on coming back, this sense of light. There were occasions when I could almost see it, as though there was a being standing there at the foot of my bed, emitting confidence and hope. Then, suddenly, it wouldn't be there any more. It was just like a light coming through the mist and going away again, and expressing itself in these ways. There may have been other incidents that I've forgotten – it all felt like a total disaster – but there were these threads of connectedness and a new order of reason within it.

After this time of hospitalisation I went back to work. I suddenly felt that I hadn't dealt with the issues and my symptoms returned very quickly. I think I'd always had a suicidal tendency – I probably still have, I think some people do – but I actually made a serious attempt, ended up in hospital, but very briefly. It was as though that was the squeezing out of the worst of the poison, or something like that.

This very intense second breakdown brought about an experience from which my interest in healing stemmed. In the hospital, where I was taken as an emergency, there was a very good chaplain and he came to see me. He listened to my story and made a suggestion that to me was a completely novel one: he asked if I would like to go to confession. I had never thought of such a thing, but said 'yes'. He prepared for the occasion and found a room available (I was in an open ward). That night I had a very strange experience which I can hardly describe now, it was hard to find words then. I never saw anything – it was not a vision, not a visual experience at all – but it was one of the most powerful experiences of my life and I can only describe it as being aware of the presence of throngs, millions, innumerable consciousnesses. It was as though the ward was full of points of consciousness, all of them beaming good will, and I just lay there, aware that some words came to me.

I found myself repeating these words, they came to me out of the gloom. They were quite simple words, repetitive, and I repeated them inwardly and each time I did I became more free and well. In the morning I just felt totally transformed and quickly I was back at work. I feel I have to add that bit of experience although I cannot account for it. I can only honour it because it was so real and effective.

There's a phrase that's used within the Anglican Liturgy 'the communion of the saints', a mysterious phrase. One might use that phrase, the communion of the saints, to describe the experience that night of just being aware of all these consciousnesses without seeing them. I know that I could never evoke that experience, could never repeat it, it was a gift of grace you could say, out of the blue.

After her breakdown Margaret had to work with the whole issue of depression. Her dreams helped her, and later on she went into analysis and became a psychotherapist herself.

I regard my breakdown as a very important part of my training, in effect. My work sprang, I think, out of some of the insights, of the knowledge I gained through that experience, hard as it was. I could never wish it again. I could never wish it on anybody else. But having found myself flung into it, it really was a total kind of fracture. At the time it didn't seem like anything but a disaster, it was only afterwards that I could see the necessity for it.

Necessity is the word I'd use in hearing other people's stories because you can see that perhaps other things could have happened earlier but didn't, and it came to a point where this was the needful thing because life was being, in some way, thwarted.

I still look upon my fiancé's death as an irreversible ending of a particular stage of my life. One of the things that arose from that experience (and it's part of the breakdown itself) was the need to gain a new understanding of death, the need to integrate death in some way. In this very forced fashion I think I was able to do this, and now I draw on its strength and occasionally people recognise this in me, because I believe death has no longer any power to frighten me. It never has since that experience.

It was as though part of me was taken over into the experience of death by his dying. Something of my ability to make sense of my life went with him when he died, and I felt near to death too, and I had to be brought back to find it for myself. He had a very special hold on me, almost magical. So a lot of me was perhaps held by him and perhaps I never could have grown up if he hadn't died.

The death of Margaret's fiancé provoked her to find her own depths and powers, her own magic, which as she says, was to a great extent carried by him in the relationship.

I'm perfectly sure that still nothing is finished, as far as I'm concerned there's a lot more to come. But the point is, one goes round and round these weak areas in oneself and gets a better idea of how to handle them.

I sometimes use the phrase 'choosing what I have darkly chosen': it's taking responsibility for something that happens to you that you couldn't possibly have chosen and yet it chose you. I often think of this idea: the unconscious chooses things, then we have the power to choose for ourselves what has already chosen us and I think something very important happens.

RELATIONSHIPS ENDING

When a relationship that has been important to us ends it can be a hard blow. It may have been a relationship with a friend, teacher or lover; or it may have been a long-standing marriage. Whatever the nature of the relationship, its severance from our life means adjustment and change. Some of these changes are welcome and we may be ready for them because they are part of our passage through life. It is when we are not ready, or when the changes are sudden, or when the loss of someone or something hits us in places that we hadn't recognised before, that our world gets taken over with new emotions that can be frightening. And with the loss of a relationship can go a whole pattern or way of life. Our routine is upset, our expectations are suddenly changed, our future together with that person is gone. We are not always aware of how much of us is wrapped up in another person until the relationship ends.

Separation

Our very first separation is usually from our mothers, either when she goes away to have another baby, goes away with father or to work, or when we leave the home environment to go to school. The way in which this very first separation is experienced does set the tone for other separations we come across later in life. The initial separation may have been sudden, a rude shock, unprepared for, unwanted. We may have felt abandoned. We may presume from this event that we are worthless, unlovable, rejectable, no good. What we make of this first separation lives on unconsciously, informing the way we protect ourselves and proceed in life. The strength of the original feeling may surface again when a major relationship ends. As well as all the current emotional turmoil and changes, we sometimes feel as if we were five years old again, and the feelings associated are just as powerful as they were then. The main difference is that we do have the choice of the adult world in order to make it different. We can seek help and comfort from those who know us.

Sometimes we form relationships which help to protect us from parts of ourselves we find frightening. For example, Alex married Jim because he was strong and safe and she needn't feel frightened about being on her own any more. She was frightened about feeling lonely because it reminded her of the time when her mother and father went away and she thought they were never coming back. She had always felt terrified about being on her own as she believed that she couldn't cope because of her panicky feelings. She was happy and content until Jim's mother died and he became very upset and withdrawn. Alex became frightened again because the man she had seen as strong and dependable needed her and her support, and she just couldn't give it. The relationship broke up because they were unable to bridge the gap. Alex couldn't let Jim be other than big and strong and Jim's needs were too great to carry both Alex's emotional needs and his own. So Alex was left feeling more alone than ever: she had layers of feeling vulnerable which had never been worked out.

Every time we look to a relationship to live out parts of ourselves we don't like or feel we can't handle we are in fact making our situation worse. Sooner or later life calls upon us to work out of our 'no go' area. For example, men who have unconsciously expected their wives to carry all the emotions may suddenly be forced into confronting their feelings. Or a person who feels he or she can only operate by being in control may have an 'out of control' experience, that person then has to take on board his or her own vulnerability, help it, make it stronger and make it grow.

Divorce

A divorce is always painful and deeply sad. It signifies the death of a relationship and often the death of the hopes and aspirations, ideas and future plans, sharings and confidences that were part of the relationship. It can be a wrench, a scar, a wound from which it is difficult to recover. Even if there are benefits – for some relationships are destructive – there is always the feeling of failure and of personal loss. The very concept of divorce is a painful one for those people with strong moral and religious beliefs about the sanctity or commitment of marriage. Divorce is often complicated by the pressure of dividing property and finances, and especially by what happens to the children of a broken marriage.

Sadly some people are so furious about the break-up of their marriage that they forget to attend properly to the world of the children. This can be particularly distressing when the children are used as bargaining devices or messengers or are asked to take sides. Divorce is rarely amicable or completed with each partner feeling equally and fairly treated. Divorce proceedings sometimes make people very self-centred and obsessed with what they can salvage for themselves, and the battles which raged during the marriage are often accentuated by the break-up when recrimination and blame, misinterpretation and dishonesty reign. One woman said to me:

> It's all so terrible. Here is the man with whom I've shared the last 12 years: births, miscarriages, houses, redundancies, the death of his mother, his weight problem, his secretary's problem. There's all the sharing, being young, having hopes, building a life, going together, telling each other everything, believing we'd be together through it all

141

into old age, in just the same way we'd weathered everything so far. And all the things we've both tolerated that we didn't really like in each other: his jokes, my untidiness. Suddenly everything's being seen through a different lens. Things are being made reasons for unreasonable conduct, cruelty, unfaithfulness. Things I said to the children in the heat of the moment are being dragged up to prove a point, to make me look worse. What was once tolerated is now being made into some 'ism', some awfulness that broke up the marriage and it wasn't *like that*. All the intimacy ... when you think of all that ... it feels such a waste. It makes me bitter and I begin to hate him. Some days I can't think of anything else and I know I take it out on the kids.

Many people find it difficult to get through the times in a marriage when one or both partners are sorely tested out, especially when the 'in-loveness' wears off. There is a passage of time when something deeper has a chance to grow but has to be worked for. Marriage is difficult: it requires maturity, generosity, tolerance and a lot of humour, but unless it is seriously impairing a person's development it seems worth trying to work the difficult patches through. The National Marriage Guidance Council is inundated with calls for help, an indication of the number of couples in trouble who want to do something about it. The number of people seeking therapy as couples is also increasing.

We marry for such peculiar reasons, often with expectations that bear very little relation to what we find when we are married. 'I married her for her family', 'I married him for his laugh', 'I married him because I didn't think anyone else would ask', 'I needed a wife and she was perfect', 'I wanted to get away from home', 'I thought she would stop me roving', 'I thought he would stop my spending' or 'I wanted it to be just like my Mum and Dad: never a cross word in 28 years'. If we set up expectations like these, they are doomed to let us down. If we can get over this we're on the way to developing a full and richer relationship. But it takes two, and when this doesn't happen divorce is often sought after.

Divorce and children

Children caught up in a divorce crisis can break down two or three years later. There is now a Family Conciliation Service which solicitors encourage couples seeking divorce to consult before deciding determinedly on this course. This can be of great help to the children, as they can have a forum in which to have their say, and a space in which some of their feelings may surface. With a trained counsellor as third person, children can often speak up without fear of punishment from a parent; but it is always a difficult area and fear of recrimination later on is strong.

John Eldred, head of London Samaritans, says:

> We see young people perhaps having a crisis at 18: they've failed exams, lost their job, something is wrong in their life and they take an overdose ... and you find their parents divorced when they were 13 or 14 and they've no stability to fall back on when their own lives suffer. The trauma of divorce on children is not enough recognised by schools and doctors. Children in their teens are still very tied up with their parents, and the divorce may have left them brokenhearted, but with no place to express themselves, no one to talk to. They can't talk to Mum because she's upset and Dad has gone off. It's hard for them, they need more help because of their parents divorce. They need time to mourn the loss of the family and they need sometimes to be freed of guilt – that it was their fault, etc. This causes tremendous problems later on. We should all value the significance of divorce or partnership ending, on the children around ... and there is a link between the parents' marriage break-up and the crises of young people a few years later on.

The impact of separation and divorce on young people whose parents are separating is discussed more fully in the section in Chapter 4 on adolescent crisis.

Adult breakdown after divorce

For adults who are divorcing there are so many questions that leap up out of the turmoil. 'How will I cope? Will I ever get over the shock and be able to get on with my life in a way that's satisfactory? How will I tell the children, Mum and Dad, Gran, the people at work, the vicar? What will become of me? Will I be too old, too unattractive to find anyone else? Can I think about meeting anyone else or going out with anyone else after all these years? Marriage was all I wanted and now it's ended, I feel as if I've got nothing, I feel there's no point. Who am I if I'm not married, if I'm not married to Jeff or Rita? He or she was the star of the relationship ... will I sink into the shadows now? Will the children stick by me? What will happen to my sex life: will I ever have sex again? Divorce is a stigma: how will I ever tell anyone? How will I cope for money? I'll have to support wife and kids and I'll never be able to start again for myself ... I've lost my home, my family, my routine, my reason for living.'

Divorce is like a bereavement, with the added complication that the person we've lost or said goodbye to is still around. News of them may be very uncomfortable or painful. We may find ourselves feeling competitive, jealous and hateful. We may want the other person to fail, to have a bad time, to wish they were back with us, so that we don't feel so awful about being rejected. Coming to terms with rejection, restoring our self esteem, repairing the wounds inflicted by a destructive and painful relationship and by the ending of a relationship, all take time. Sometimes the unfaithfulness of a partner and impending divorce can act as a trigger, unleashing uncertainties about ourselves that lie dormant as long as marriage is going well.

TOM

Tom had a breakdown very soon after his wife told him she was having an affair with another man.

> I remember feeling the bottom had dropped out of my world. I wanted to go to a monastery or something like that. I wanted to escape. I couldn't cope with what was going on. The stupid thing was that I didn't make a stand. I felt, I can't have anything to do with all this, so I just walked out. I think I decided that I was ill – I had this idea I could hide away in a mental hospital – or a monastery. The GP gave me tranquillisers. A few weeks went by. I left my wife and went to stay with a friend in the country. I had a bottle of pills and immediately took the whole lot. I told my friend. I remember telling the GP I wanted to go into a mental hospital and he said 'Oh you've got to do something really desperate to do that: jump in the river or something', he actually said that, 'or take an overdose'. So I did ...

It sort of blacked out my mind. I didn't want to kill myself, just to go somewhere safe. I did go to hospital but discharged myself after one or two weeks. I had a lot of pills: anti-depressants, tranquillisers, and I decided to throw them all down the loo. I had a bad reaction to coming off them, a strong feeling of dread and terror. I was readmitted to hospital, I think I was there for about six weeks. I can't remember because I was so full of drugs.

I remember odd things like going out of the hospital without permission and having my clothes taken away. I kept being naughty, doing things wrong, upsetting staff. Largactil was injected into my backside as I was held down in a room with things on the window. I had to behave myself to get my privileges back. I had this religious thing. All to do with the life and death of Jesus. Friday was the day I would be crucified. Days leading up to Friday were the worst ... how would I deal with Friday? The religious image was to do with my children. And then I had a dream in which my children were killed in the back of a car. It really upset me. If I didn't relinquish them they'd be killed. If I did relinquish them they'd not be killed.

Tom had previously suffered a breakdown during his first year at university. He feels it was triggered off by a relationship with a girl ending without him knowing why it ended.

I felt a great loss of self esteem and confidence. I couldn't ask her what was going on. I remember reading the Sunday papers and bursting into tears when I saw the headlines of things going wrong in the world, big disasters, people being killed. I felt really ill, uncertain, couldn't cope. I'd ring my parents in the middle of the night and talk for three-quarters of an hour. The college sent me to a psychiatrist and I took tranquillisers. During the summer holidays they wrote to me to say that I should have a year off as my academic standards were not satisfactory. I was upset, no one had said.

During his year off Tom met Peta who became pregnant and they got married. He got a job and settled down and thought that everything had turned out well. He felt safe when he was in a close relationship and his life free from difficult emotional demands. Soon

145

after his second child was born he returned to college to train as a teacher. He did very well but got caught up in his earlier anxieties when he had to take a difficult class during his third year.

> There were discipline problems with this class and I thought it was ridiculous for me to continue if I felt so anxious. I had only one term to qualify but I decided to leave. Everyone was very upset, but I felt there was no point going on.

Tom's sense of insecurity about himself as an independent, grown adult seems to have expressed itself in his need to keep things safe and unchallenged, both inside himself and outside. Each time he ventured out to take his place as a bright, clever young man with a lot to offer, he felt overpowered by feelings which sent him searching for a safe 'womb'. He says this about his early life:

> I was ten before my brother was born. Until I went to school I thought life was heaven, just one long blissful experience. When I first went to school I was stunned by it: it was absolutely awful, I was terrified of the teachers. They were all emaciated spinsters. I thought this teacher was a witch. She told me I just had to sit still where I was, until the end of the day. My best friend remembers I was given bricks to play with. I was in tears all the time. I wasn't prepared for school at all. It was a terrible shock. My image of home was that it was full of love, reassurance, my parents encouraging, supportive. They were always pleased to know what I had done and would praise me. I felt buoyed up, confident.

Tom coped and got by because he was extremely bright, but when life challenged him on an emotional level he found he had few resources with which to cope. It was as if his childhood had been too magical, too overprotected, with little or no help over the difficult rite of passage from nursery to outside. In his family there were few rules or sanctions, so he had very little experience of dealing with basic raw human emotions, only too present in adult relationships and in teaching classes. When his first girlfriend 'went cold' on him he felt he couldn't challenge her. When his wife was having an affair he did feel jealous and angry but he didn't know what to do, he couldn't articulate how he felt.

In some ways I see my life as a series of times when I'm climbing up and becoming really confident, exuberant, full of creative energy and then times when something really disastrous out of the blue knocks me flying and I have to pick myself up and start all over again.

His breakdown put him back in touch with that world of childhood – the desire to be 'naughty' and the need to be looked after. His nightmares perhaps contain an image of the 'lost children' he feared were being sacrificed, something about himself that he was dragging about helplessly in the back seat of his personality and which was vulnerable to accident because it had not been allowed to develop without fear. During teaching practice, going back to the school where there was the same smell of stale milk as in his own primary school, he says he was 'Filled with the same awful feelings.'

Tom feels he is still vulnerable to breakdown.

Nowadays I have a sort of sense that because it's happened (the breakdown) it could happen again. Although there's no indication of it at all. I think it's all related to security and insecurity. Providing that I feel secure these things don't happen. It happens if I go too far or climb too high … like hubris, over-weening pride. I am careful not to overexpose myself because it's that that is likely to precipitate it. I don't think I have the inner resources to cope with anything that might come my way. If I get into a situation where I'm overstretched then I find that very frightening and that's potentially dangerous. Like most people, as soon as I feel strong enough, I always want to overextend myself. What I would like is not to have any kind of working life where I have to appear in public, run workshops or train to teach. I always feel quite uptight before anything like that. I've been trying to write, and I would like to be a writer very much, I think that would suit me … more introverted but satisfying.

Several years later Tom provides the following update:

I now work as the manager of a mental health charity, with responsibilities for a staff team of fifty and an annual turnover of more than a million pounds. I have to address large public gatherings, run workshops, in fact all the kinds of thing which I'm quoted in the book as saying I should avoid. I still feel a sense of vulnerability: it happened once, it could happen again. I also feel that I have never regained quite the sparkle and *joie de vivre* that I knew before all this happened but perhaps life is inevitably less exciting, less full of expectation as one grows older?

I still vividly recall the images of sacrifice which I associated with my children. In the book this is interpreted symbolically and this may have been a kind of truth but it also had a literal truth – I felt I was going to lose them. I am glad that I have managed to keep in contact with my sons and I feel very close to them. It was hard because they always represented and reminded me of the failure of my marriage and the deep pain associated with that failure. Time has healed that pain, the scar tissue is still there and like some old wound can suddenly, out of the blue, start hurting. What I now realise is that like many other men, I tried to shut the door on painful experiences and that this is a foolish strategy. In the end one has to face, confront these deep hurts.

Through my work with people who have been caught up in the psychiatric system, I realise I was lucky to have escaped. Many people become inextricably enmeshed in the system and become life-time service users. I believe that I owe my escape, partly to a realisation that I was falling into a trap but more to the fact that I met the woman who became my second wife. This relationship has helped to re-establish my self confidence and self esteem. I came into this relationship deeply wounded and it could have easily failed, but my wife 'hung-on-in' through thick and thin.

MOVING HOUSE

Moving house is fairly high on the Rahe scale of stress. It involves a great deal of organisation and reorganisation and much adjustment. At the same time as uprooting ourselves from things that are comfortable and familiar we are having to settle into a new area and atmosphere, learn new ways of operating and develop different habits. Moving also usually incorporates some change in status socially, but this factor may be hidden among decisions about carpets and curtains and whether things have got lost. Most challenging of all is what moving house can represent to us about ourselves. Moving may be a way of showing the world our success; or it may be a difficult but necessary evil because of our work in which case we may be very ambivalent about it. Moving is complicated when there is more than one person involved, for rarely does a move suit everyone in a family equally. Most of us have to make huge and unexpected adjustments after a move.

A new house or area may also represent an idealised 'new start' after which we feel we will be different in a positive way. We may feel that by moving we can shut out past unhappiness. When this does not work we come face to face with ourselves and the way we have perceived our life and our options. The move may offer the opportunity for a breakdown to come to the surface.

PEGGY

When Peggy's marriage broke up she decided she wanted to cut out the whole of her past life. Then in her early forties with an 11 year old daughter, she moved to a new area of the country where she knew no one.

> At the time my marriage went I felt I was walking out on the whole of my past, absolutely the whole of my past. It was not just that I didn't like my husband but everything was wrong. I wanted to cut off and forget ... just shut myself away. I wanted to do that when I came here, but I had a child and I had to settle her into school, help her establish friendships and reassure her that everything was going to be all right. I clung on to my level-headedness until I just couldn't do it any more.

Peggy had felt unhappy about herself for a long time, and she had thought these feelings meant that she was mad or mentally ill, that there was something seriously wrong with her. She coped by burying these ideas and getting on with her life in an efficient, level-headed, organised way. Her move represented a way of getting away from all these fears, but it in fact brought her face to face with them. The fear of madness and of being driven mad began during adolescence.

> I felt as if I were being brainwashed by people who were totally wrong for me. I was sent to a boarding school run by nuns: they were

149

strict, there was no freedom to go out. I am a great outdoors person, I need to be free. I would go out there on my bike every minute if I could ... I just cannot be fettered.

I had made a friend. I was a bit of a loner in a way, unusual I suppose, not particularly social; some people thought me odd. But I remember the day I met Angela: I went right up to her and said 'I like you' and we became friends. We protected each other. We were both children of parents a long way off, often abroad. We were both very unhappy at school. One day we couldn't bear it any longer. Angela was twelve and I was ten. We had nowhere to go. Occasionally we would have money for books and I remember we had a shilling between us. We ran off to the station where we thought we would buy a ticket. I don't know where we thought we would go to, but of course the Station Master recognised our uniforms and he called the local police station ... perfectly reasonable one can understand now, but ...

She falters, tears pouring down her face:

We were beaten publicly. They made one Sister we actually liked do the beating ... Sister Mary. She was actually a rather goodhearted woman, we trusted her and she would not have wanted to do this. I have a picture of her I carry with me all the time in my mind: a rather strong, muscular woman, beating down on my little friend wriggling and squirming on the bed and all the girls ranged round to watch this, every senior girl watching so that no girl would ever run away again.

I did write to my mother explaining, but my letter was intercepted – all our letters were read before being sent – and I was told 'You cannot write this kind of thing to your mother'. So I never did write again and my mother never got any kind of explanation. She just thought I was a naughty, disobedient girl, not appreciating my good fortune in being sent to a special school you had to pay for. She didn't want to know, to hear my side of things. Nobody wanted to know ...

I think I gave up then. I felt bullied in my spirit. I think I stopped growing then. I became physically bigger, got more intelligent, entered my twenties, fell in love, married, had a child and all that ... but I wasn't grown up in my own personal, individual way. I was still a frightened, dispirited child underneath.

150

And the worst thing was losing my friend Angela. You see, we were sent to Coventry and all that, and then I was taken away from the school by my mother. Angela wrote to me but my mother took the letter and I never knew. She thought I should be separated from this friend whom she thought a bad influence, so we lost contact.

The first two years after my marriage broke up were pure tension. I also realised that my own daughter was exactly the same age as I was when things started to go wrong for me. I was torn between being a proper mother to her and my own desperate needs to be listened to properly and looked after. I kept getting into a terrible panic. I just couldn't handle anything or manage my everyday life any more. I had this image of myself: I could feel myself sinking in a pool of water, with my hands pulling on my lapels to raise my body but, although I was determined to pull myself out, the weight of the water was dragging my body down and I could feel myself deep in the water and ripples all around. I had to stop work, I just couldn't cope. So while my daughter was at school I was totally free and I took lots of walks; but I was able to wash my face, dry my eyes and be at home, be sensible, by the time she got home and we would have a chat about her day. It was important that I was able to do it although I wasn't very communicative at other times. I was so tired and I needed to sleep a lot. I used to write a lot to help my feelings. I was very isolated.

After nine months, Peggy began seeing a therapist at the local hospital once a fortnight. She met another woman who had had a breakdown and her friend Angela came back into her life.

We arranged to meet at the station. I was terrified I wouldn't know what she looked like with all the people on the platform ... and then there was this little face, just the same. It was wonderful. During the whole period of my breakdown, four years, she was very generous. I couldn't afford long telephone conversations but she would ring up and my talks with her were very valuable. I started having long bicycle rides during the day, exploring the whole countryside, and at the same time I was having all this grief and trying to mother my child. I was very withdrawn from life. I met very few people, spent a lot of time on my own. I was afraid of people, I didn't know what sort of person I was. I didn't know how to deal with people socially.

I did feel as if I had moved on somehow, that what I was struggling with was much more important than 'How many children have you? Are you married?' and so on. It became very important to me to get it right. Nobody was going to stop me. Maybe I'd never get another chance because I was middle aged and there were so many questions. I was born into this world, what was there for me? To go right back to the beginning, what am I? There are these people, there's this river, these fields. How am I going to live in it? Do I fit in? Am I going to stay? I often thought of killing myself, but I felt I would have to take my child with me, I couldn't leave her on her own. I imagined ways I'd do it and no one would ever have bothered, no one would really know, but I felt how awful it would be if I died and she didn't and woke up ... that was too terrible.

Peggy had coped through her level-headedness with an enormous amount of brutality, with abuse, loss and sadness. The rejection of her natural seed self by her parents, school, husband and herself stretched her survival self to the limits and exacerbated her fear of letting go, which she equated with going mad. Although her move was an attempt to escape from this fear, it led her to meet it within herself on a most profound level. She dared to meet this terrifying place – of loneliness, isolation and vulnerability. From within this she reconnected with her 'seed' self – including her love of nature and the spirit – and she found a sense of meaning. Through this reconnection, she started rebuilding: she became stronger, experienced herself as more confident and developed real friendships.

I am glad my breakdown happened because now I'm me, but I regret it had to be that way. I need time to think about all the experiences I've been through, I need to learn, I need to be detached from it. To trust people, I need to break with the myth my mother carried that women were not able to stay with men and with her mistrust of men and her bitterness. I need to grow now. I am back at work and have built up a good relationship with my employer. I find I have considerable strengths and can be very useful to him. The friends I have made are real friends: they understand when I need to be on my own. I feel a great sense of achievement and deep relief about my daughter. She has a sense of responsibility, she's a good judge of character, she's starting her career and has a stable relationship with her father. I never talked to her about my breakdown but recently she said she realised what had happened. I have stopped being a mother now and am embarking on a new life.

For the second edition of this book Peggy writes:

It is good to learn that this book is being widely read; it means that my outstretched hand is being taken by others into theirs. Since the time I first talked with Elizabeth McCormick an important new chapter has begun. I have a grandchild to whom I will have, in due course, a lot to tell and for whom I am already a part of her history. I have a new and highly rewarding career. I look back sometimes to the disorganised and uncertain person I was and to my weakness when faced with trying or tempting situations and am relieved to have changed so radically. When thinking of political change, which occurs so rapidly, it seems to me, nowadays, rather than merely feeling frightened and incapable I don't doubt that I can face any consequences indomitably. I'm not glad now that the breakdown occurred because it did take up a lot of valuable time and resources but of course I am glad to have come out of it and to be the stronger, abler person I am today. I *am* glad, too, that I am not insensitive either to my own feelings and needs or to those of others. I look forward to a busy future and to realising more ambitions.

HAVING A BABY

Having a baby is often the first serious commitment we make to another human being. Love and marriage have their special commitments but of a flexible kind. You can get cross with your spouse and not speak for a few hours, then make it up; husbands and wives can spend time away from each other and keep their bond; within a relationship there is freedom to walk around, sleep, eat, play, ask questions when you want. In the early years after having a baby one's life is dominated by the timetable of the child or children. This is often the first time we are in a situation where we cannot see an end, the end of term, the end of the week, the end of one's shift or winter stint; a baby cannot be handed back to anyone, put back, no one else is his or her mother. Together with all the thrill and wonder of having a baby, this is a sobering thought.

Baby 'blues'

Women are very vulnerable after giving birth both physically and emotionally. They are usually extremely fatigued from the last months of pregnancy when sleeping is difficult. This is hard to make up for after the birth because of the baby's feed schedule. As many as 20 per cent of women are thought to be anaemic up to four days after giving birth because of blood loss and the reduction of blood volume in the body (up to 30 per cent is taken by the baby). Multiple hormone changes occur in the adrenal and thyroid secretions and most significantly there is a sudden decrease in the amount of oestrogen in the blood chemistry. These factors make mood changes inevitable during the post-natal period. Most women experience what is called 'baby blues', which pass after a few days. One of the family doctors I spoke to said: 'When I walk into a post-natal ward on the second or third day there will be two or three women crying, especially new mothers. I tell them and the husbands they will feel awkward for a while ... it's such a biological change and with the first baby I say "You're not a girl now, you're a woman" and they know it; they know they're committed for life, you can never go back and not be a mother, and they are overwhelmed sometimes. Post-natal depression is a separate illness from this. It's a separate, hormonal biological entity, all on its own, not endogenous depression or reactive depression. It's a hard thing to teach young doctors to notice. People with post-natal depression need a lot of support. Health Visitors and District Community Nurses are very useful, and family can be helpful by taking children off parents' hands, giving the mother a break and so on.'

Post-natal depression

A woman can suffer from post-natal depression very soon after her baby is born and it can last for some time. It is best to seek help from a doctor straight away and get the help and support you need rather than struggle on alone and exacerbate the symptoms. There may be different reasons for depressed feelings, a mixture of physiological, emotional and psychological upsets which can be helped by proper hormone balancing, medication and counselling. A baby challenges a woman's whole way of life. If the birth has been traumatic, help will be needed to relieve the shock and trauma of the event. A woman may feel ambivalent towards her baby and feel bad about this, and not want to admit how she feels. Some of the difficulties she may come across may plunge her into despair, such as not being able to breastfeed, not being able to bear her baby crying or just not feeling 'maternal'. There are also expectations from immediate family and the outside world that a baby will make one wonderfully happy, that one will be busy and bustling, overjoyed and proud. One may not feel like this but want to be quiet for a while. Now the attention is shifted from the pregnant woman to the baby and a woman can feel left out. Husbands often feel left out too, at birth and afterwards, and some men feel very cut off and so cannot support a wife who is suffering her own depression.

Occasionally women can suffer from what is called post-partum psychosis, or delusional ideas about themselves or the baby, or about where they are. They can act out in bizarre ways which may include harming the baby. This state may develop gradually over the first year and does require medical attention.

Giving birth challenges what has gone before

Whether or not a woman becomes 'blue' or depressed after the birth of her child, giving birth is a major life event. It challenges a woman's sense of identity, role, place in society and in the family. Many issues are brought to the surface – the need for time and space, an awareness of vulnerability, and helplessness; it challenges our concept of control. Having a baby is not just a job, it is an event that contains many, many opportunities. We may be thrilled, overjoyed, delighted to have a baby and in a state of wonder about the miracle of birth, especially if we've waited for a long time. At the same time we are provoked into strong feelings, brought about by the persistent demands of the helpless bundle – we feel angry, trapped, at times furious and we feel guilty for our Impanence.

We often become more aware of our own neediness and helplessness. For some of us the meeting of the actual infant and the one we feel inside us is overwhelming. Women who have been mother to their own mother, if she was dependent, and who have never been allowed to be needy and dependent themselves, are very afraid of dependency, and tend to need a good measure of control in their lives in order to cope with this. When a child comes along many of these fears come alive again. When we hear of a woman being near to battering a child it is often because she has no reserves with which to cope with the screams of the child outside and the screams of the child inside.

Women who have high expectations of the difference that a child will make in their life are often disappointed and then get depressed. The experience is not what they imagined or hoped for. People who are idealistic may feel a failure if they don't have a natural birth or can't breastfeed, if they have a boy when they wanted a girl, if the baby is not as pretty as they hoped or if the child was intended to mend their marriage but cannot do so. A woman who has a painful, traumatic birth and who is sore, stitched and angry afterwards may not know how to handle these feelings, especially if she has no one to help her.

Some years ago a young mother came to see me who was alarmed at the terrifying fantasies she'd been having about knives and her infant, then one year old. She was an articulate, intelligent woman, who had an excellent bonding with her child, and a good relationship with the father. Over the two months before she had been becoming increasingly afraid of handling knives and of harming the child's neck. She was very distressed at these thoughts and afraid of what she might do, although consciously she loved her child and would never think of harming her.

In talking about her child's birth she told how unpleasant an experience it was and how little she was prepared for it. She had hoped for a natural birth at which her husband was present and she had been to natural childbirth classes and learnt breathing techniques. She had a long and painful labour, was given medication against her will and her child was born with the use of forceps. She had a large episiotomy scar which had taken a long time to heal. Her anger against the doctors was evident. When we did some active imagination work on how she felt when knives were present, and she imagined having a knife in her hand and using it, her imagination took her immediately back to the cut inflicted on her own body, on her own most vulnerable flesh at her most vulnerable time. Powerless at the time of giving birth to exert her rights of choice, and overpowered by the medical profession, she could only take her anger into herself. Now it was surfacing in the form of fantasies about knives, projected on to her little child's neck – her most vulnerable exposed place. We needed to go through her traumatic experience of birth several times before the horror of it was exorcised and she was free of her fantasies.

NADIA

Nadia, an artist and mother, began to break down immediately after her daughter was born. For four years, she was on the edge of breakdown, during which time she had another child, a son, and looked after her husband during a severe illness.

Her story tells us a great deal. The seeds of her being were potentially strong, active, passionate, physical and imaginative, and her feelings were powerful and expressive. There was no ground for them to be safely planted when she was young, for her family were unable to listen or respond, and so this part of herself became split off and shut away, but held unconsciously by powerful images which could be recalled and made conscious through dreams and through her painting.

Some of the energies were turned in upon herself. For example, she coped with her anger with her family for their coldness and inability to communicate by making a secret resolution, very early on in her childhood, that if things got really bad she would take her own life. She struggled to fit in with what was expected of her: to get on, not feel very much, cope with everything and not make a fuss; but this survival device was a fragile covering for the self she was underneath, which was vulnerable and frightened and which did not feel very grown up. Her art helped to keep her natural instincts alive, and she married a man who was right for her on a feeling, instinctual level. Their relationship worked well as long as she saw him as 'strong' and herself as 'weaker', and as long as this was unconscious between them. This hidden concept of herself did not come to the surface until her daughter was born and her own unmet needy childlike part became more exposed because she had to be a mother.

> I had always wanted to have children. I used to think that life wouldn't be worth living if I couldn't have children. I don't think I thought of having a teenager or a person, just a baby. Maybe, I thought, something, someone would love me. I thought it lucky I'd married a man who also liked children. I became pregnant after four

years of being married, had a very happy pregnancy and then the birth was completely messed up by an unneccesary induction.

Nadia had been attending natural childbirth classes and felt in control of her labour, but she was given pain killing drugs against her will and her husband was sent out of the room. From then on she found that everything went against her, she was treated harshly and not taken seriously. Later on, when her daughter, who was born prematurely, was in intensive care, she was forbidden to feed her more frequently than four-hourly. Her frustration and anger at being overcontrolled nearly pushed her to the edge and she feels it contributed to her inability to bond properly with her first child.

When she returned home from hospital she found more problems. Her daughter cried a great deal and suffered from colic. Nadia found her exhausting.

I knew I was getting depressed and unhappy. I didn't realise I was getting near a breakdown. I carried on, running a playgroup; my friends thought I was very efficient. But some days I would spend just rocking in front of the fire, crying all the time. The worst of it was that I was a very bad mother. I'd always assumed I would be Mother Earth herself. I'd always been very good with other people's children. It never occurred to me that I wouldn't enjoy my own, and I didn't.

Part of the trouble was that my husband and I were pulling in different directions. He was such a natural mother, so loving, so easy going; he never had any difficulties about getting up in the night, or with any demands. He made me feel, without meaning to, totally inadequate. I think if we'd realised this it would have made a difference. I couldn't tell him. I wanted to be like him. I desperately tried and I couldn't. I couldn't have had a nicer, kinder, gentler man to support me. I knew that he loved me very much but was desperately worried about the way I was as a mother, and it upset me. At one time he would have swapped roles, and I probably should have. But because I'd been brought up all my life to feel that I wanted to be a mother and to expect fulfilment from this I couldn't actually bring myself to do that. I felt I couldn't take the responsibility apart from anything else.

The shock of the birth and the guilt I felt ... the tension between me and my daughter was so terrible. I remember we got a kitten for her when she was about one, but I was so tense about everything that I hated this kitten. One day I threw it out of the house ... this tiny creature, just because it had made a mess ... slamming the door on it and breaking its tail. Then I felt very guilty when it came home with a broken tail and was very frightened of me.

I went on like this, doing my best, and then my husband got ill. He was very ill for three years but it was undiagnosed. His personality changed. Instead of the gentle loving man I'd known he was uncooperative and irritable. He insisted on going to work everyday and would collapse at the weekend. I relied on him to help me and he wasn't around. After three years I couldn't cope with this. I resented him for being ill. I'd started to feel so badly depressed about my daughter I'd had another child, a son, who was born easily and with no problems with bonding ... but the relationship with my daughter was still terrible.

I got to the point where I could not bear to be alone. I arranged to stay with my parents when my husband had to go away. It was all right until the last day when I couldn't reach my husband on the telephone. I got panic stricken. My parents wanted me to go out to lunch but I couldn't face it. They were very cross. They didn't seem to sense anything was wrong, they thought I was being very selfish. They took my daughter and my son stayed with me ... he was about two. I felt so awful, so desperate. I felt I just couldn't go on. In the end I phoned the Samaritans and they kept me talking for about two hours. I feel terrible about it now because my son was sitting on my knee all the time – I think it's going to come out in his life. I don't think I was talking coherently, but I remember telling them I couldn't cope and wanted to kill myself. When my parents came back my father stormed into the kitchen and said 'You've been here all day and haven't even washed up'. I went into my room and swallowed a bottle of pills.

I was so desperate, but I remembered I had two children. I went and told my parents what I had done. They seemed not to react. My father said 'How do we know she's telling the truth?' Then I started screaming at the top of my voice. I remember screaming and screaming. They took me to hospital. I felt more trapped than ever, alien from them, desperate.

Perhaps Nadia hoped to find the love and acceptance she had never felt as a child when she went to her parents' house at this point in her breakdown. Many of us do feel a longing for a real and loving link with parents from whom we have become alienated and find ourselves journeying back home with the hope that this time all will be well. Unfortunately it is often the inner image of the ideal or archetypal parent with whom we are longing to meet – the parents we would have so liked to have had – rather than the mortals who were our physical parents.

It was a tremendous help for me to say at last 'I've had a breakdown'. I realised my parents couldn't help me, but my husband's family rallied round and got me painting again.

Nadia started to feel better, as if she had a 'net' under her for when things got really difficult with her daughter. But the shadow of suicide hung over her. She began working out ways of killing herself and taking her children with her in order to protect them from their grief at losing her. She says: 'only recently have I fully realised how totally mad it was'. She was able to tell her psychiatrist what she was thinking of, and was admitted into hospital, relieved at being able to let go.

I loved being in hospital. There was nothing I wanted more than to go away and be safe. People think you are mad, so mad, when you actually like being in a psychiatric ward. I was very relieved to be away from my family, not to see the distress I was causing other people, not to hold back. I was allowed to have my paints, and I painted really strange paintings – most of them depict sheer terror.

I believe my breakdown was a metamorphosis ... a way for me to find the real me, to reach into what really matters and to truly find myself spiritually. In the ward there was a great deal of love with no expectations and no reservations, no judgements. I found that extraordinary. The people there meant more to me at that time than my husband, and that's amazing for I've never loved anyone as much as him. But I really loved some of them: some were so pathetic and so much more ill than I was and with so much courage. The closeness might have been because we didn't get much from the authorities. We were like children in so many ways, we all had something in common and there was a tremendous amount of support even from the most violent, aggressive people. I found it quite comforting seeing people who were behaving quite wildly helping others when they were upset.

Nadia stayed in hospital for six weeks. Returning home she felt very vulnerable and was afraid of being with people, even those she knew. Her husband's family helped her to resume her painting by helping with the children. After two years of 'thawing out' she began to like herself for the first time. She began to feel energised by her work and to return gladly to her family responsibilities. She became successful with her work, exhibiting her paintings, which sold well.

I think this is where my energies went from negative to positive. Before I was using energy wrongly, I had no outlet for all the difficult things that were going on inside me, and it turned against me. I think this is one of the reasons for the breakdown. I thought when I became a mother I had to give myself one hundred per cent to the children. This is idealistic. I also feel that I wasn't growing up: my development had been blocked, and I had to break, it was the only way of getting out of the block. As a child I was very unhappy ... I was sent to boarding school at eight. I was miserable, but my parents never listened. Both my sisters have had breakdowns, and all of us have had to exorcise the coldness of our childhoods. So many things led up to my breakdown, but it was triggered off by having my daughter. Once you have a child everything is different: you can't be something you're not. Everything you are comes out. All the things I'd hidden, suddenly they were there, either coming out because of the way I was as a mother, or in my daughter ... little me ... that I hated. I hated myself and there I was.

Nadia saw in her daughter all the things she had put away in her own childhood: her vulnerability and her need. As her daughter was high-spirited and active like herself, she saw this as a threat and as hostility, and her daughter became the part of her that she had put away long ago and which she had to reclaim and learn to love. Nadia wishes she had had more help during the four years leading up to her breakdown. She visited her GP but was told she was 'just another neurotic woman'. She also felt ashamed of what she was feeling and judged it as her own inadequacy and so felt she needed to keep it hidden.

If someone had come along and said, 'You're unwell', I would have been very relieved. Also, If someone had helped me make sense of it, had pointed out that it was to do with the child on all levels, it would have been helpful. All my dreams and images during this time, and my paintings, were of foetuses being ripped out, an abortion taking place, children falling out of buildings, children being swallowed up. If you don't experience great pain nothing much happens to change you does it? I had always been so self-centred, closed up. I have gained an understanding and can reach out to people so much more. I am much more self-sufficient not so dependent. I feel I can cope with life, and myself. The real thing is that I no longer see the journey I've been on as negative.

Several years on Nadia reports:

In an effort to build myself up psychologically and to come off antidepressants after my breakdown I first joined a dream group. Through analysing my dreams I discovered the central key to my breakdown – a series of events which, as a child I was unable to cope with and upon which I had completely closed the door.

At the age of seven I was sent to live with my grandmother in another country as there was no school where my parents lived. After a year grandmother died and I was sent to boarding school. It was like losing my my whole family. I never went to the funeral or had any momento, and my grandmother was never mentioned to me again. It was as if I was too young to have feelings. I was not considered at all.

I moved from the dream group into weekly psychotherapy which I have continued for over three years. I have had to re-experience that childhood pain in order to come to terms with it. I discovered that my mother had had a breakdown in similar circumstances to my own but she had closed the door on it. Her inability to cope with my feelings as a child was very much to do with her inability to cope with her own feelings.

I can see a chain passing through the generations – both my sisters have had breakdowns even though they had very different childhoods to my own. I may have passed on the chain to my own daughter because of the way I behaved towards her after her birth.

It's as if I had to experience my mother's breakdown because she could not and the chain can only be broken by tracing the root causes and having the courage to go through that pain with the help of a therapist. It is such a relief! My sisters have been in therapy too, and maybe at long last we are putting to rest the ghost of my mother's unhappy childhood.

I am now cutting down on antidepressants, so far with no side effects. I feel stronger than at any time before. My marriage is richer and my work as an artist has benefited from the therapy – I have learned how to channel my most intense feelings straight into my work. My relationship with my daughter has changed beyond recognition and I hope that I may have undone at least some of the damage I inflicted upon her as a small child. Having re-experienced my own inner child I have managed to move into a (fairly!) responsible adulthood, a goal my mother never attained.

4
Vulnerable times

We have seen that breakdown occurs when the individual is in a situation in which all his or her known resources are challenged. There may be months or years of gathering symptoms before there is an obvious crisis. There are some times when we are more vulnerable than others. We gradually learn what are our personal most vulnerable times. This chapter is devoted to some of the traditional times when we are prone to breakdown ... times when external change demands an internal adjustment, that maybe cannot be met.

BREAKDOWN IN YOUNG CHILDREN (0–12)

Linda was born after her parents had been married for 12 years. Her mother had suffered three miscarriages and had one baby who died two days after the birth because of encephalitis. Soon after Linda was born her mother lost her own mother upon whom she had grown very dependent. Linda was the light of her life, the longed-for precious child, doubly precious to her mother now that she had lost her own mother.

Sometimes when we finally receive something we've always longed for we get overwhelmed with feelings, and not all of them are happy ones. Linda's mother felt very guilty about the other babies she had lost and guilty about her own mother. Could she have done more? Was she too wrapped up in taking care of her pregnancy, in her own baby? Soon after Linda was born her mother became depressed. In her depression she clung to her child, taking her everywhere, never letting her out of her sight. Linda was a naturally bright, high-spirited child who liked to crawl as far as she could as soon as she could crawl, who liked to find out how things worked – the taps, the plugs, the television. Her father was a kind, outgoing man who enjoyed making things, and because he was lonely during his wife's depression took the little girl into his workroom and showed her how to make things out of wood. Linda's mother was terrified that something would happen, and even though patiently soothed by Linda's father, would take the child away and sit her on the best armchair whilst she listened to the radio.

Linda became very torn. She needed her mother but she needed her mother to be happy and above all quiet – she didn't like it when her mother screamed and shouted at what she was doing. She also needed to find her own way of doing things, but it became too risky: she learnt that if she did anything other than what was acceptable to her mother all kinds of bad things happened. Later, when she could understand what was being said, she felt that she was putting her mother's health in jeopardy if she did certain things. This became an anxiety: if she was herself it was at her mother's expense, so she must sacrifice what she wanted for the sake of her mother and her mother's needs.

At school she discovered a whole new, free, bright world, with other children, books and ideas. Linda was naturally bright but all her achievements were tinged with guilt. There was the constant image of her mother sitting at home alone – who knew what she might be doing without Linda there to keep her going? The anxiety and the dilemma posed by this situation proved to be too much for Linda. At the age of six, she began refusing to go to school, she started sucking her thumb, lying on her bed a lot, withdrawing into herself. She began wetting her bed at night.

It is easy to see how, if only seen superficially, this situation could be misjudged. People with a strong sense of 'oughts' and 'shoulds' might see Linda's behaviour as wilful and naughty, deliberately causing trouble, and 'only wanting attention'. I know many children whose behaviour was interpreted like this and who were punished 'to make them better'. Fortunately in Linda's case, because her mother was so depressed and because she had a kind and thoughtful father, her plight came to the attention of the practitioners involved in the school welfare. After some family counselling sessions, and some

ANIMI – VULNERABLE TIMES

Who is it that walks around my skull?
a troop of red-coats
made of tin.

What battle do they wage there?
first ask who is their
enemy?

I shall be their conqueror
and jump upon their fragile limbs
in a rage.

individual sessions for Linda's mother plus some medication over a short term, the family could grieve for their losses and take up their lives again. Her mother allowed Linda more space and freedom to be herself, and allowed herself the joy of having a child who was high-spirited and outgoing, trusting that she would stay healthy. This was a breakdown with a good outcome. Too often breakdowns in children go unnoticed as such, but get termed 'bad' behaviour.

What can children do when they feel they have no significance, no power, no autonomy? They have to make a protest of some kind. They have to express what they feel, and because they have few words or sophisticated strategies, it tends to be through action: through bed-wetting or soiling, through refusal to eat, get dressed, go to school or be nice to grown-ups. It is the only behaviour open to them. We owe it to them to try to understand what they are hoping to communicate.

Having to be special in order to feel 'someone'

Many eldest or only children, who have been very special to their parents, believe that unless they are special they are insignificant or 'nothing'; they feel under tremendous pressure to go on producing behaviour that is special. This can later on lead to an obsession with achievement (the 'workaholic') or to placatory behaviour ('If I don't keep supplying people with what they want I won't exist'.)

Dr. Lillian Beattie, Senior Clinical Medical Officer in Aylesbury, who specialises in working with children describes an example of this.

> Maya was an eldest child, the eldest of four. Her mother was pregnant with the fourth when Maya was six and first came to me. She was a typical eldest child who wanted to be mother's super special daughter. As each child came along the mother had been more stretched and under tremendous pressure to care for the younger ones. This little one was sort of pushed aside, there was not time for her to be super special and she retreated into encopresis (soiling) and into aggressive behaviour. She was in bunk beds and would lift up the mattress and soil on the child underneath, and of course she was super special to her mother in an unacceptable way. When spoken to, it was put to her that she wanted to be super special to her mother and she agreed, but she didn't know how to do it any more: she was

only six, after all. At the end of the session she was asked what she would like to say to her mother: she burst into tears and said she wanted to tell her mother how much she loved her and rushed off to do just that.

Later on, at a school medical, her mother was worried about her because she wouldn't eat. She had stopped soiling but she wasn't growing any more. Once again she was the focus of her mother's attention. She was referred by her doctor to a paediatrician who had her in hospital for tests and investigation because of her failure to thrive. Significantly since she's been in hospital and the centre of attention her growth has gone up.

As Maya's story illustrates, if we cannot carry on living up to the position expected of us, our only other option is to withdraw. When we become discouraged because too much is expected of us, we may suffer from exam phobia, work block or fear of failure so that we stop trying. We face a terrible impasse where it becomes too frightenlng to move forward.

Parents can guide a child into feeling useful and significant by allowing him or her to make a useful contribution to family life. They can relieve a child from the burden of being especially wonderful or especially difficult. Maya's parents were young and inexperienced and their resources were so stretched that they hadn't the time to lead Maya into a competent way of behaving. Lillian Beattie says:

> It isn't just the specialness one needs to reinforce. Maya actually needs to learn by example to work with others in order to deal with the situation, but unfortunately because the other children are so young and the mother young in experience there's no guidance to bring Maya into cooperating within the family. Now that she's being allowed to make a useful contribution to the caring for the youngest child she's achieving a place within the family without having to be special.

ADOLESCENCE (12–22)

Any early trauma from infancy and childhood that is not resolved carries on into adolescence. By this stage the problem has become

168

overlapped by a few more years of repression and a whole lot more strategies for coping or avoiding whatever is painful.

Adolescence is in any case a most painful time: a time when we change from boy to man, girl to woman ... the biggest change we ever make. Physical changes often happen long before we can understand or accept them. Many of us don't want to grow up in the way that our bodies are demanding or our parents are instructing. We don't see much in it, unless it is of the glamorous, dare-devil kind, unless it smacks a good deal of freedom, the freedom not to be a child. Many adolescents are very split: they develop quickly in terms of street wisdom and subculture, joining forces with their own kind to dress, parade and promise special things for themselves; but there is a part of them that is still a child, young, afraid, weak and longing for safety and comfort. It is the most enormous challenge for any adult to communicate with both these parts appropriately.

Parents and their teenagers

From about the age of 12 onwards most parents no longer know as much about their children as they previously did. The physical, emotional and mental welfare of the child which was once their responsibility, is becoming the responsibility of the child. We do not know our own children's inner worlds after this time, for they do not usually share with parents what they are thinking, dreaming or longing for. Their dreams are private and this represents their first right to adult choice for privacy. They desperately need that privacy, trust and respect; and at the same time we owe them the distanced kind of vigilance that allows us to notice when things are going wrong and make helpful suggestions. If we are rejected we need not to take it personally but to see it as a sign that our child is striving for independence, and if something is wrong, we need to stand firm and find out what it is.

Crises during adolescence actually give us an opportunity as parents to do the things we were unable to do in our children's infancy. We may be further on ourselves and able to understand more, we are certainly older and perhaps wiser and these crises do offer the opportunity to put some things right or to contribute more than we were able to do earlier. Many adolescent crises plunge the individual back into an earlier stage, in the same way as many breakdowns have

169

a period of regression. The adolescent may be petulant, cross, foot-stamping, fist-bashing or may rush out of the room, just like the toddler who threw himself on the floor in an uncontrollable rage, refused to eat or spat at Grandma. It is testing, trying and stretching for the parent and should be seen as such.

The added complication is that now the 'child that was' is probably six foot tall, weighs eleven stone and is physically very strong. Problems during this time tend to be acute and serious. An angry impulse which earlier would end in tears and rage can now bring about a suicide attempt. Protest over food can become anorexia nervosa. Hitting out can lead to serious damage. Acting out in protest, rage, a bid for independence or to resolve some imagined or real family conflict can lead to drug-taking, stealing, unwanted pregnancy or imprisonment.

Swings of mood

Adolescence is an important formative period and a time when polarities both within and without are at their most extreme. The emergence from *dependency* to being *independent is* a lengthy, fraught, zig-zag course and rests upon the structure and flexibility of the family and how the family receives and encourages those steps to independence. People need to have been allowed to be comfortable with dependence and have these needs satisfied before they can become properly independent. Only then, when they have a firm core inside them, can they happily and freely fly off and start a new world for themselves, occasionally coming back for rest, reassurance, comfort, welcome and a reminder of good nourishment.

Swings from *depression to euphoria* are another common feature of adolescence. In extreme cases, these swings can verge on psychosis, paranoia or delusion. It is important to see this in the context of the adolescent's growth period, a journey most make and come through with much inner experience and adventure, to go on to live comfortable lives. People around need to be as strong as possible, so that the young person can crash around like a wild sea against a rock that is steadfast. It is a somewhat wild, difficult and challenging time for everyone. Sometimes the disturbed feelings need expert medical attention.

Adolescents also often swing from feeling *powerful to powerless*. Because adolescence is a time when young people's idealism and ambitions are heightened they feel the weight of their powerlessness and they struggle to have some say in things. Too much power and adolescents can go berserk without any boundaries or the grace of maturity. Too little and they feel the rage of impotence.

Love or hate are felt strongly by teenagers. Passionate love and intense relationships, with an individual or a cause, are part of adolescence. Extreme hate for what is seen as needing to be changed can charge up the feelings of young people, often unconsciously so that they act without thought or feeling, straight out of this place of hate.

Adolescence is also about physical change: what can you do with the full grown body of a man or woman when inside you still feel like a child? How can you include facial hair, breasts, a deeper voice or sexual desire into a scenario that is already full of so many questions?

And against this background, we demand that our young people be taking on such things as highly competitive exams with increasingly high standards, and that they make major decisions about their lives and futures.

Understanding the extreme swings of mood that occur during adolescence helps everyone involved to allow tactful space for them and a caring eye. This group can be extremely good at helping each other if allowed and trusted, and a strong peer group who have different individual swings at different times forms strong bonds which can be extremely supportive.

What young people say

I have been able to talk to young people informally, some in confidence and alone, and some in group discussion. Here are some of the things that have come out of this about adolescent breakdown.

There are no words. It's impossible to put it into words ... what you feel. You know you are doing daft things and you feel like shit but you can't say anything. You just feel awful, and daft, and cut off all the time. You have a drink and you blot it out for a bit, some of us do hash. You always know the ones that are going to do the hard stuff ... they're just out to lose out, they're weird.

When I started going up the wall in this bedsit where I was studying for my degree, I checked into this hotel in Brighton. I thought it was a good idea, it would help me to get myself sorted out. It was awful, except that there were things to do, like going for meals and things. I wandered around for about a month ... I just wanted to disappear but I didn't know how to. I didn't talk to anyone. It never occurred to me.

Everyone goes on at me about my eating. Eat this, eat that, it will be good for you. I don't want any of it. I just wanted to be left alone. People watch you all the time. And now there's all this talk about it (anorexia) it's worse. You become a 'case' or a 'problem' child. You're never just a you wondering what's it all about. I don't know why I do it really (not eat).

CHARLES

Charles ran away from school at the beginning of the second year of his A levels. He couldn't stand it any more. For a while he had a job in a café but he felt trapped and scared, so he left and lived at home on social security. He turned his world upside down in ordinary terms. He slept all day and was up all night, pacing and smoking and writing. He wrote a story about a 14 year old boy who murders his father and mother, stabbing them with a large carving knife violently and with the blood dripping over every page. In the story the act is blotted out from the boy's memory because a burglar, who just happened to be making his robbery attempt at the same time as the murder, is accused of the murder and the boy, now an orphan, is sent to a foster home. Later on, a face in a pub crowd jogs the boy's memory and he remembers what he has done and tells it to a kind friend.

Charles was bringing to consciousness much of the rage he felt against his parents who divorced when he was six. Two years earlier his grandparents had divorced noisily and unhappily and his grandmother had told him how wicked and cruel his grandfather was and how he had left her alone and helpless. A very feeling and sensitive boy, Charles was very disturbed about this but had kept it to himself. He felt let down by his mother who had promised him that what happened with his grandparents would not happen to him. He was in a fury about the hopelessness and instability of adults whom he was torn between pleasing and hating because they messed up his life. When he was in the transition period from childhood to adulthood he felt that growing up was one big let down, an entry into a world of evil, untrustworthiness, meaninglessness, petty squabbling, money lusting and the misuse of power. He saw becoming a 'man' as having to become evil, wicked, abandoning and overpowering and this idea had been exacerbated by his boarding school and its masculine ethic of anti-woman, anti-feminine. He wanted no part of it.

He fell deeply into the drug culture, and wandered through different cities in Europe trying to escape organised life. What he was looking for was some kind of role model or way of life with which he could identify and express himself. He could not identify with the harsh, masculine images in his family and school. But his breakdown allowed him the space to process his feelings, and break through to a greater sense of seed self. He moved on to a different, more appropriate path.

Many young people feel they have no 'map' of future life. Fred, another young man now in his early twenties, says

> It's like all your life you are programmed to grow up and move on and it's all supposed to be very exciting and it's what you do and it's all planned and supposed to be easy and then when you get there it's awful. Going for interviews where they grill you time after time and you don't get the job anyway. Then you sign on. And you smell the smell of the underside, of poverty. You smell the defeat. You live in the poorest part that no one cares about and even the shops have awful food. There's no choice. You can't really live anyway on what you have and when you've given up trying to get more by working at whatever's going you can feel yourself slipping down into just not caring. You go numb sort of. Drugs are important. You get them where you can. They make something better for a bit. It's easy to be a pusher. It's so easy. I haven't got that far yet because basically I'm against it. And I have got parents who care I think about me and they wouldn't like it. It's the last drop. But you look around and it's all just not what you've been expecting. There's all this evil, it's awful.

CYNTHIA

Cynthia took an overdose one evening when she couldn't bear the strain she was living under any more. Three years on she finds it very difficult to put into words what was happening to her, at that time.

173

When I was a child I could never really express some things, I could never really talk about it. My mother always encouraged us to but I just, for some reason, I couldn't. Perhaps because of that, not consciously, I didn't have much self-confidence. I have this fright about people being fed up and bored with my problems. I was worried about my A levels and I had split up with my boyfriend. I felt I was facing it all at once. I hadn't done enough work for my A levels and I was going to fail, and I had failed at my relationship with my boyfriend and there was the failure of my parents' marriage. I don't think I felt responsible for that, but it was just there were so many changes happening, and I couldn't cope with them all at once like that. It was just like a really big, maybe heavy weight or something, and every time I woke up early in the morning it was there, it was the first thing I thought about and I couldn't get away from it, I couldn't enjoy anything else. I couldn't sort of notice anything else because it was there the whole time, like the centre of my world the whole time.

People would say 'Things will get better' and it's the sort of thing I would say to someone, but I just couldn't believe it. I just didn't think it was going to happen because it wasn't getting better, every day was the same for what seemed such a long time. I'd go to school, sometimes I'd talk to someone and then feel embarrassed and the next day I'd think they were talking about me behind me, I just didn't want anybody to see me – to see certain things that were happening to me. I escaped as much as I could, just went out walking. I didn't sleep much and I had nightmares. I'd just do what I had to. Very remote. And then I took this overdose. I'd thought about it for a while. I thought ... I just can't go on for another day. I didn't really want to die, I know I didn't want to die, I just wanted it to end there, I just wanted it to stop. As soon as I'd done it I felt ashamed and guilty. Everyone rushed around but I didn't want to know. I just didn't want to know.

In the hospital I saw a psychiatrist who was very nice but she had an assistant and I just wanted to talk to the psychiatrist not in front of anyone else. I didn't know what the assistant was doing, how she was listening. So I couldn't talk. The nurses were very nice, very kind, it helped a lot. My father was terribly upset and my sister and I felt awful about it. It was very stupid and dangerous but I just couldn't do anything else. I think it helped me in the end. It became easier to

174

talk to my family and not to keep things inside, but I still can't get over what I did and what might have happened. And my sister bore it all, she's the one who's taken so much from everyone, she kept the house going when my mother left, all the cooking and looking after my little brother, and then I did this. She was wonderful to me.

After that I had more time. I didn't take my A levels until the next year so that pressure was let off and it gave me time to look at things. I was very upset. I'd thought to go to University, and then I realised I didn't want to, that I would do nursing instead. And I spent some time with my mother and got to understand more and talk to her. You see no one told me what was happening. I came back from a weekend away and my little sister told me she'd gone, that my parents had split up and I was so shocked. It was a real shock to me, I had no idea that things were so bad. And it was like you couldn't rely on anything any more, the decision wasn't yours about what happened in your life. I think I'd got to be dependent or something. I was dependent on my boyfriend and he had let me down. I was dependent on my parents and they had gone. So I couldn't trust anyone.

What I would have liked was to be able to trust someone to see me through all this, but I couldn't. I'd never have rung the Samaritans. It wasn't that there weren't people it was just that I couldn't speak about it. I felt silly and all trapped. I went to college to do my A levels in the end. I wanted to prove myself and prove I wasn't a child.

I got through it myself really. I've learned a lot about myself and don't feel quite so bad now. If I saw someone like I was I would try and do something, give them some sort of satisfaction, an hour or something, but people can stop themselves breaking through, they won't allow it. I did get very bottled up and couldn't let it out. I know now not to get like that.

Who can offer appropriate help?

Breakdown during adolescence is a special area of its own and has been the subject of major studies over the last 20 years. There are places for young people to go who feel they need help and these are listed under Useful Addresses at the back of the book. Some conflicts may be so tied up with the family that contact with the family is

175

important for all concerned. If young people are afraid to go back to their families or confront their parents some organisations do help to ease this pressure and offer support, sometimes going back to the family with the person concerned or arranging for proper consultation with a professional who can act as a kind of 'referee'.

Drug induced breakdowns need to be carefully controlled under medical supervision. During adolescence we may experience 'peaks' which may appear drug-induced but are not. It is important for these peak experiences to be contained and processed by being recorded or drawn or shared with another.

MID-LIFE CRISIS

> Wholly unprepared, we embark upon the second half of life. Or are there perhaps colleges for 40 year olds which prepare them for their coming life and its demands as the ordinary colleges introduce our young people to a knowledge of the world? No, thoroughly unprepared, we take the step into the afternoon of life, worse still, we take this step with the false assumption that our truths and ideals will serve as hitherto. But we cannot live the afternoon of life according to the programme of life's morning; for what was great in the morning will be little at evening, and what in the morning was true, will at evening have become a lie.

> C.G. Jung, *Structure and Dynamics of the Psyche*

Just as everything in nature matures and dies, so do humans. During the first half of life most of us are concerned with the development of ego consciousness and the adaptation to outer reality. We are involved with our place in the world, what we are going to do, who we will take on as partners; we acquire skills, make money, build homes, gather possessions, we explore and gain experiences. Jung referred to this phase as the 'natural' phase. He writes: 'Man has two aims. The first is the natural aim, the begetting of children and the business of protecting the brood; to this belong the acquisition of money and social position. When this aim has been reached a new phase begins, the cultural aim.' The second half of life is our time for reflection, for being rather than doing. Schopenhauer writes:

Life may be compared to a piece of embroidery, of which, during the first half of his time, man gets a sight of the right side, and during the second half, of the wrong. The wrong side is not as pretty as the right, but it is more instructive; it shows the way in which the threads have been worked together.

If we were all programmed like the computers we have invented we would pass through the stages of our life according to some well laid out plan. But for most of us this is not so. As we have seen, much of the first half of life is governed by our survival self and by what we have come to believe is required of us by others. Mid life is a natural point for taking stock of what we have done during our first 'half'; it is also a time when we may be literally forced, by the unconscious, into a new phase that at the beginning we really do not understand.

This may take the form of some kind of mid life crisis during which we are forced to stop. Women may reach a crisis in the last few years when childbearing is possible and the dilemma is to have a child or adjust to not having a child; women may also begin their passage to menopause at this time and suffer loss and disorientation. Mid life is often a time when we begin to lose parents, relatives and friends from sudden death, accidents or illness; it is a time when a heart attack may lay us flat on our backs, wondering what has happened and why. At this time statistics tell us we are more vulnerable to using alcohol, to inappropriate love affairs, moves or changes of job, and to the onset of depression, phobia and anxiety.

We are challenged to find meaning: what has my life been about so far? what do I want to let go of? what do I want to keep? The crises we find ourselves in do not immediately let us know this is what our struggle is about. In her book *Passages,* Gail Sheehey writes 'Without warning, in the middle of my thirties I had a breakdown of nerve. It never occurred to me that whilst winging along in my most happiest and productive stage, all of a sudden simply staying afloat would require such a massive exertion of will. Some intruder shook me by the psyche and shouted "take stock! Half of your life has been spent. You have been a performer, not a full participant."'

The intensity with which we receive mid life experiences forces us to pay attention, and we will be moved by the new experiences if we are able to glimpse their meaning and to incorporate them. If we resist any kind of change and throw all our energies into our conscious

177

world we risk becoming rigid, and the dragons of the past do not lie down but take the form of events or people around us.

JEFFREY

Jeffrey's breakdown, two days after he was 35 years old, took him into therapy where he began to put two very different sides of himself together: the idealistic boy in him who loved to go flying and feel romantic about women, and his more serious side with which he felt more uneasy.

> I just woke up one morning feeling very strange. I'd been very ill in my life, living and working in India, and I've had all kinds of near death experiences like during cholera ... but this was something completely different. My stomach felt just like a cavern. I was heavily sensitised I could feel my whole body, from inside as it were, literally. I'd always felt an extremely confident middle class boy ... I was still quite a boy I think. I've done a lot of things and rarely felt scared: heights, flying, being alone never got to me, although I had avoided physical violence at close quarters – that scared me. But this feeling was such a new experience that it took me a time to think about it. I did feel very nervous but I had no idea why. The only thing I could think about was that I'd been poisoned by some stuff I'd been working with on a building I was doing – pretty nasty chemicals and they can get into your nervous system. I think in some ways I wanted it to be that. I wanted it to be a physical manifestation and I could get something for it and it would go away.

Jeffrey went on feeling 'strange' like this for several days before going to his GP who said 'work hard and play hard'. Later on Jeffrey consulted a homeopathic doctor who prescribed remedies, which Jeffrey calls his 'crisis pills'.

> The real thing I was worried about was the heebie jeebies late at night and I was petrified it would stop me sleeping. That was one fear that took over ... of not being able to sleep. The worst thing that happened when I couldn't sleep were horrific faces appearing – large, mushrooming, unpleasant faces – just like a horror movie. I was

worried that if I didn't sleep I would get exhausted and wouldn't be able to work: I work for myself as a builder. When the faces appearing went away there were sweatings, and I was afraid I was going mad. That one became progressively more pronounced. The real fear about going mad was not the fear that I would not be able to return to sanity one way or another, perhaps with the help of drugs, but that I would be deserted, dumped on a place somewhere and that people would lose interest in me; after all if you're mad, people lose sympathy for you after a while.

The other thing that was happening to me, which wasn't very nice, was that I was having vaguely violent thoughts towards women. It was really scary and made me feel for a long while a real traitor to the cause of feminism, which I've been supporting, albeit a man, for a number of years.

I had this thing about knives: if I picked up a knife in the kitchen I would think 'What would happen if I stuck it into somebody?' Then it would pass, but there was always a kind of chill crept over me when I thought that. It wasn't forcing or stabbing, just like testing a jacket potato or something, a very innocent kind of prod.

It was the shame of it that really upset me, just wanting to touch women, not actually being violent. I became worried that I might actually touch them ... somebody in the street. I might touch them on their backsides or something, you know. I could understand it in a way. People do this and get away with it and people who know that men do this wouldn't say they have any mental illness: they're just unpleasant people, or whatever you think about it. It's touching somebody up – there's almost a way in which it is encouraged and accepted by our society. I have always thought it horrible. This is an area in which I've had a whole lot of thinking to do.

At the time I thought of all these things as excessive sexual feelings or a behaviour that I had because I'm oversexed. I thought I wasn't getting enough sex, and that this was a kind of leaking out of desires. It may have been that the leak was under real pressure, a blow out rather than a leak. When I talk to my menfriends they feel the same.

I always felt bad about my sex drive. For a long while feminists have made me feel that it's wrong, that men shouldn't want sex too much. It's only in the last few months that I have begun to be happy about having a strong sex drive.

179

Jeffrey began having this confusion of thoughts at a time when he had decided to settle in England with his Indian girlfriend who was expecting their first child. Up until this point he had been a wanderer, throughout the world, carefree, but taking part in projects which suited his idealistic nature, supporting causes.

> I liked what I experienced when I was first in India: an amazing purity. I felt very pure, I had no meanness and I had virtually no avarice. I was a very nice person. I had a five pound note in the bottom of a box, a passport and half a ticket to get home.

A few months before his breakdown Jeffrey had returned to India and felt very disillusioned.

> My later trip was a big disappointment in terms of the area I lived because it is still a real shit hole, 15 years on from when I first went there. The same filthy streets, filthy scavengers, higher incidence of TB, leprosy, hookworm fever … it just crushed me. So when I broke down all these things became somehow fixed in my mind. I realise that I have a lot to sort out about what I really want to do. Political convictions carried a lot of decisions for me and were sufficient reasons for staying out of the real world … don't take responsibilities because if you do you'll be screwing somebody. I haven't found a comfortable way to work where I can balance my political beliefs and feel OK.

Therapy has helped Jeffrey to explore how he feels on the issues that confronted him through breakdown: his attitude to women and what is feminine, and his attitude to power, focus and what is masculine. He has also been helped to strengthen the part of himself that was very nervous about the more pragmatic responsibilities of a house, wife and family and of being a breadwinner. As long as he was in his 'hippy' days he could feel free and idealistic, but when he came down to earth, he met with uncomfortable feelings to do with commitment, especially to women. His support of the feminist cause, which made him feel bad about his sexual needs as a man, could also be seen as his way of coping with ambivalent feelings about women which he inherited from his family.

I suppose I didn't actually think women were up to much for a long while, although until recently I would have denied that; but through therapy I've done a lot of collecting together. The great mystery is about my mother: where was she? I don't like this thing of pinpointing things that have upset me to the family, but the one idea I have come round to accepting is that the dynamic that was going on in my family while I was growing up was one which very much excluded my mother. I have this very persistent memory of being in the back garden with my brother who was sports-mad: we would be playing cricket or football, rain or snow, we would be there playing something in the garden half an hour before tea. My Dad would come home (from the army), take off his uniform and come out into the garden and play because he was very into sports as well. The three of us would get on fabulously. I've very strong memories of this half an hour, and my mother was the person who spoiled all this by saying 'Tea's ready'. We would say 'Hang on, just one more goal', and she would always be put in a bad position. Now I know what it's like to cook and put your heart in it, even if it's not something special, and people don't come. It's not enough to say 'well if it's cold it's your fault': she wanted a social occasion, she wanted to feed her family, and they just weren't around. I think also one of the hardest things for me is to see my father put my mother down, intellectually ... they're both working class. I think unfortunately I got used to her being discounted. When I got to university in my twenties, I was on the river with a girl, and she took a turn rowing, and I said, 'You're really capable, aren't you, rowing really well' and she said 'Thank you very much' (why shouldn't I kind of thing). I was quite offended she didn't take the compliment, but I do see I didn't think of women as being as good as men. In sexual terms I've always found potent women a bit of a challenge: are you going to be in control here or am I?

I think in that sense my breakdown was about a mid life crisis, and it was something to do with incorporating what was masculine and what was feminine for me. I've discovered through therapy that I've got a very strong feminine side ... but that I'm very much a man. I'm very sensitive to other people's needs, so much so that I want to care for them quite a lot, but the way of caring is taken over by the man's side so it becomes fixing, sorting out arrangements for them, or arguing on their behalf with authority. When the opportunity offers itself I'm quite capable of physical comfort. You can see what I mean: the impulse is what I consider to be very feminine but the mode of carrying it out is where the man steps in. I would like to be more open, more listening than doing, less active in my care.

If any of my friends now had a breakdown I'd be able to talk to them without being formal. I would suggest they try psychotherapy, especially before trying anything esoteric and I would definitely advise people to stay away from drugs. It seems to me you can so easily get off on the wrong track: and in my case, all that was wrong was a crisis of identity and responsibility inside, and I hadn't sorted a lot of things out. I was kind of stuck, still living as if I should be an idealistic kid flying about. Therapy has helped me to put many things together.

RETIREMENT

The word 'retirement' is misleading when applied to the phase of life when active, full time, paid work ceases. Retirement suggests withdrawal, seclusion, removal from something, and to describe a person as 'retired' gives the impression that they are not in the real world any more. In fact this period can be extremely active, fulfilling and happy: it is often the first time people are without obligations to others and can have time for themselves. I have known many people to blossom and flourish at this time, finding out all sorts of things they are able to do that they hadn't tried before because of commitments. People who have not enjoyed their jobs feel released from duty and the daily treadmill. However when much of our identity has been shaped by the nature and status of the work we do, leaving that work can be sorely challenging and frightening.

Mark said 'I see the men come back after they've retired, and they sit and have a coffee and want to talk. So often we haven't time for them, things have moved on: someone is in their office doing their job and we're all so busy. You can see in their eyes that they miss the place, however much they hated it when they were here all the time. They miss having a place somewhere that's got their name on it. Suddenly they're not important any more, there's no community for them, no group, no crowd to go out with in the evenings. Many do try to keep up after they've left but it's not the same. I don't want that for myself, I don't want some bloke patronising me, having to be nice to me, pass the time of day, feel obliged. I don't want to be washed up like that. I'll try not to retire ... if I'm forced to I'll go abroad.

Harry said 'When you go through that door marked 65 you go to death. That's all I can see beyond work. There's nothing else I want to do with my time. I don't want to be poor. I don't want to have to be careful with my resources. I don't want to be thought an old fart.'

Retirement from full time work forces us to face ourselves in a truly profound way. The issues brought to the surface at this time may have surfaced at other times but we found ways of dealing with them, postponing the deeper realisations of what we are afraid of. At this time of our life we can no longer put off what we fear most. If we have a collection of things we have avoided it is possible that during this time they will have to be reckoned with. For many men, their crisis comes through the loss of work and its accompanying identity and peer group; this is doubly hard if there has been no time to develop other interests or groups of friends. For many women, their crisis comes through a relationship or lack of a relationship. This is a time which many women face alone, or they face being in a marriage that has little warmth or companionship.

Powerful issues at this time include work and identity, meaning and joy in life, purpose and gathering in all that life has been about so far, unfinished business from the past – regrets and old wounds – loss, and going forward into the unknown, to death. Many people make sudden decisions at this time of life: to move to another part of the country, to split up after 30 years or more, to go off abroad. Sometimes these decisions work out and are part of some longed-for plan, but if they are a way of coping with some inner fear or turmoil they will not solve the problem but exacerbate it. We often hear remarks such as 'After his retirement he was never the same again', 'Two years after her retirement she had a stroke' or 'They moved away after retirement and always regretted it, they couldn't settle, make friends, find things to do.' If there are unresolved conflicts around the time of retirement from work, they may surface in the 18 months or two year period following, as illness, accident, depression or uncharacteristic behaviour.

ANTHEA

Anthea became extremely depressed after she retired from her full time job as receptionist in a busy dental practice. The depression was gradually increasing each week until her feelings of despair built up to the point where she had strong suicidal feelings and decided to consult her doctor. She said

> I couldn't see the point in living, in going on, I was right down in the depths where everything was black. Everything I did seemed pointless, I became aimless, and I was also extremely anxious, I didn't like being on my own in the house ... it seemed to hold all the terrors for me. And I'd always been afraid of storms and this fear increased. I had to make sure that someone was with me if there was going to be a storm. It all got to the point where I didn't see how I could continue. There was no one I could go to for help, no one I could talk to.

Anthea was referred by her GP to a psychiatrist who saw her and prescribed anti-depressants, but also asked to meet her husband and son and daughter. The family had stopped being close during the children's teenage years. Anthea's son had drifted abroad and gone his own way and her daughter had married a man with whom Anthea and her husband could not share much feeling because of his strong political views. And the relationship between Anthea and her husband had been 'on automatic', without much feeling, with little conversation, no sharing, just living their own separate lives. This was barely tolerable while Anthea was working but became quite intolerable when she no longer had the support and the acceptance of a work structure.

Anthea saw herself as a very sensitive, easily hurt person who disliked and avoided arguments and getting cross. She realised very quickly how she expected other people to be as sensitive to her feelings as she was and to anticipate them. She saw that she tended to interpret things not being done as being against her when in fact it might be because of other people's lack of knowledge, understanding or awareness. She quickly saw the need for being more assertive with her family and with other people about what she felt, what she wanted and needed. This helped her to feel slightly more in control and less depressed, but she

184

still felt extremely sad about the lack of warmth and affection between herself and her husband and with her daughter. She said she felt she had to learn 'to be immune' from her family, and she expressed her bitterness about her family's attitude – the lack of spontaneity and thoughtfulness. It felt as if all the disappointments and disillusionments of the last 20 years had piled up while she got on with the order of her life, and suddenly caught up with her when she no longer had the structure of work, and the position of being a needed, useful and valued member of a team. It is a very hard thing to come to terms with a disappointing marriage. The possibility of leaving and starting life on one's own becomes impractical and inappropriate, but the decision to stay with the difficulty, coldness and intransigence is a painful one.

Anthea used her counselling sessions to express her feelings about her situation which could not be expressed anywhere else. In doing so, she let go of some of their burden and in the process was able to release some energy for new meetings with people. She was also able to gain more acceptance for how things were: that they were difficult and not as she would ideally like, but they were the stuff of her life, of what she had.

She began to trust her feelings more and to express them, to risk 'explosions' and she found that at times this was effective. She and her husband resumed their sexual life, after a gap of several years, and as he drew near to his own retirement she found that she had a great deal to offer him, even though he was not able to acknowledge the value of this. She did get much closer to her daughter, who came to live reasonably near by, and was thrilled at the birth of her first grandchild: she could take part in this event and be of help, now that she was no longer so depressed. She continued her interests and found herself being asked to talk to other women in her village who were also suffering from depression. She was wary of being 'sucked in' but surprised herself when she found she had a lot to offer other people.

Retirement challenges us all – men, women and families – and needs to be thought about and discussed long before its time draws near. If we are able to view our lives as a whole and see that each age or phase is part of a necessary journey and has something to show us at each turning, we will be less rigid in our approach. Seeing the cycles of life as a natural, ever-unfolding process, in the same way that a good farmer rotates his crops, will help us to value and reap the harvest of each of the cycles of our own life.

5
Suicide and parasuicide

All of us who have been sorely tested by life and provoked by strong inner feelings will have thought about our own death, and about the possibility of bringing it about ourselves. In the whole animal kingdom, human beings are alone in their capacity for consciously bringing their own death. There are few societies where suicide is unknown, although at one time the aborigines of Australia had never known suicide, until their invasion by other cultures. Suicide poses a great dilemma for all of us. It challenges our beliefs and convictions to do with religion, morality, society, meaning in life and soul.

DIFFERENT KINDS OF SUICIDE

Impulsive and immediate suicide

The most devastating is the impulsive leap in front of a train or seizing of a butcher's knife while standing in a shop queue waiting to be served. The thoughts of not wanting to live and deal with unbearable pain are already there but there is no apparent process of thinking out what to do. We don't know what happened with the person because he or she is dead, but it appears that suddenly he or she saw the means of suicide and at the same time experienced an impulse strong enough to be acted upon without hesitation. The accepted wisdom is that the person really wanted to kill him or herself, really meant it. But the phenomenon is that it is *only in that instant*. Who knows what

186

thoughts a person has in the split second while in the air after leaping from a building or in the movement of the arm to grasp the knife. Their action makes for no second thoughts. It is from actions like this that we learn about the power we all have all the time, every minute of the day, to release the 'suicide' inside us if it has been activated in some way. It makes us recognise a sobering sense of responsibility.

Premeditated suicide

Some suicides are premeditated: overdose, driving into a wood with a hosepipe to attach to the exhaust, putting Sellotape over the windows and one's head in the oven. There is always the chance that someone will come. Sometimes people feel they must tell someone else what they have done so that the matter becomes shared, the cry for help moved into community spaces.

Parasuicide

When someone gambles with their life, perhaps frequently, this is known as parasuicide. The person may injure or poison him or herself in different ways. The thinking is 'If someone comes I'll have another go at life; if not, well it doesn't matter'. The aim is to change what is happening within the person's life, and the purpose is to evoke a response from someone specific or from society in general. Parasuicide is a desperate attempt to change something when no other way has been found; in contrast, someone who hopes for suicide has no expectation of change.

WHAT IS SUICIDE ABOUT?

Perhaps because in our culture we don't like to talk about death, it has become something of a taboo. People who are brave enough to share their longing for death or their thoughts about death being welcome tend to frighten others. Historically suicide has long been associated with evil and blasphemy: John Wesley in the 1700s ordered that female suicides should be dragged naked through the streets and hacked about by anyone who cared, to make an example and deter other women from the act. If everything is centred on life, death goes

187

SUICIDE

God knows I'm weird and incomprehensible –
    confusing to others, confusing to me.
Have I a soul?
Is there an axis for all my emotions,
    is there a centre of gravity?
How can I tell?
These divergent feelings, mercurial moods
    and awkward sensations they change constantly
And puzzle me much.
I wish I was shallow, responseless and heartless,
    quite unaffected by people around me
And quite out of reach.
But I didn't create me or cause my existence,
    so I can't explain my impossible self
And can't understand,
But just have to endure my strange self as it is
    and accept the perplexities of my muddled mind.

about in a dark cupboard, and we meet it secretly inside ourselves in our fears and imagination or in the awesome figures from the collective. In *On Death and Dying*, Elizabeth Kubler Ross writes that we are not able to embrace life until we have confronted death. This means confronting our own desire for death and our ideas about what death is like, what it means.

Most suicides are not seeking death, they are seeking a solution to their unbearable suffering. We have seen some of the ways in which people suffer and which bring them into a state of breaking down. Nothing is more pertinent to a person breaking down than the question of suicide, which could be termed for some the ultimate breakdown. For it is a breakdown of life when death is seen as a better alternative because it symbolises the cessation of symptoms of pain. Successful suicide is a decision made out of an altered state of consciousness brought about during breakdown by the current dilemma and the current journey. It is not the best time to make such a major decision about one's life or one's death. Such a huge irredeemable act needs to be made after a great deal of conversation with one's personal belief, whoever or whatever is God for us. The impulse to suicide which is part of a breakdown is not to do with dying in the real, physical or existential sense.

Suicidal and parasuicidal impulse

We have seen from earlier chapters that during the path into breakdown suicide appears to offer a way out or solution to the unbearable pain from which the person is suffering. Nadia spoke of the logic which went with the idea of killing herself: that it became the only thing to do and that this seemed at the time to be so obvious.

> Before I took the overdose the thought had been coming more and more frequently that I had to do away with myself. It seemed very logical. I did all sorts of things rationalising about it, planning. We had a great friend and I decided she would be my children's step-mother. In my mind I tried to match her with David ... if I could get them together everything would be all right. Nobody will miss me. I'll be out of the way.
>
> Although I didn't have the courage to go ahead with it I did intend to kill myself, really. I had been thinking about it seriously, what I

should do. After the first attempt, to my astonishment, I realised David actually minded. It hadn't occurred to me that anybody would mind because I hated myself so much. I realised how I'd hurt David – he was devastated – how much I'd hurt the children and how much they loved me. So when I cracked up again, realising all this, I thought to myself 'I can't. I can't carry it out – I've got to take them too'. I was very frightened because I knew how one tiny thing can knock you over the edge and make you do what you're thinking about. I got to the point of knowing how I was going to do it.

I'd been seeing a psychiatrist for some time and I told her all this very haltingly, thinking she wouldn't believe me; it was the most tremendous relief. The first thing she said was 'You must tell your husband'. That was the most painful thing to have to tell him: 'I'm thinking of killing our children'. That's the last thing, the last layer, I said earlier that things come off in layers. It's only since talking about it this year (I hadn't talked about it for several years until my friend had a breakdown) that it all flooded back. I can actually see now what I was doing in terms of murder and see that as a sane person would see it. I still know how I felt about it but I can really see how totally mad it was. Until recently the logic was still there. I could still understand how I felt. Whereas now I can see how I felt but I can't understand it. It was logic turned on its head. I had to protect the children – not killing them, the whole idea of murdering them didn't come into it – I was going to protect them from what I had to do. I think I could actually have done it. I don't think I could bring myself to tell you how I was going to do it (I've never told anyone). It was absolutely painless and they'd never have known.

My husband was absolutely wonderful. I had to tell him and he had to know about it. He managed, he coped in his usual way. He didn't hold it against me because he was so used to his mother and her dotty ways, she was manic depressive. When the psychiatrist made me say it all in front of him ... it was still the worst thing, awful to do that to him. Then she said 'I think you need some time in hospital' and of course my husband agreed and I think both of us were heartily thankful.

Charlotte (p. 47) spoke of the thought she had while watching a bus, that the thought was without passion of any kind. Cynthia (p. 174) told us of her own suicidal thoughts, how they began and then seemed to take over, so that this in the end seemed to offer the only answer. At the extreme of suffering suicide seems the next logical step. Suicidal impulses can be seen as the ultimate anger turned inwards. Instead of being able to recognise and allow the murderous rage against someone or something in the life of the person, it is turned inwards, against the self.

In order to understand the impulse to suicide we need to know what has been going on in the individual's thinking and feeling, and we need to know what it is the suicide intends to solve, bring to a head or delete. Suicide is often misunderstood: it tends to make other people feel extremely angry and upset, frightened and impotent. Although the drive behind a suicide attempt is about forging better communication, so often the result is the opposite. Suicide impulses usually bring the person to medical attention and, as the vow of medicine is to prolong and protect life, suicide is often seen as something self-indulgent, self-induced and not to be tolerated. It is often considered attention-seeking and provokes great fury.

Common factors in suicide

Edwin Schneidman has made extensive studies of suicide and suicidal behaviour, and in his book *Definition of Suicide* he indicates ten commonalities of suicide and suggestions for appropriate response. The following two sections are taken from his work and research.

1   The common purpose of suicide is to seek a solution

Suicide is not a random act: it is never done pointlessly. It is a way out of a problem, dilemma, bind, challenge or difficulty, crisis or an unbearable situation. It has its own logic. To understand what the suicide was about we must know the problems it intends to solve.

2   The common goal is cessation of consciousness

The person wants to stop hurting, stop the intolerable pain.

3   The common stimulus is unendurable psychological pain

No one commits suicide out of joy: the pain felt is impossible to

191

imagine unless you have been there. If the level of suffering is reduced the person may be able to choose life.

4   The common stressor is frustrated psychological needs

This is what creates the pain.

5   The common emotion is helplessness-hopelessness

The feeling is one of 'there is nothing I can do, there is no one who can help me'. Different emotions may underlie this: shame, guilt, frustrated dependency, hostility.

6   The common internal attitude towards suicide is ambivalence

We call for help and try to end our life at the same time. We feel we have to go ahead with it and yet we yearn for rescue and intervention.

7   Our thinking state is severely constricted

Our range of thinking is limited to two views: we think that there must either be a magical and complete solution or nothing at all. Nothing else is on our horizon at this time: family, friends, abilities, are not so much disregarded as simply out of range. This is not psychosis or character disorder, this is total constriction of the person's thinking. This must be seen to first and attempts made to widen the constricted view and suggest more than the two fixed options.

8   The common action in suicide is escape

Suicide is the ultimate escape: a radical and permanent change of scene.

9 The common interpersonal act in suicide is communication of intention

There are always clues that someone is thinking of attempting suicide. People signal their distress in a number of ways: talking about death and suicide, inquiring about suicides, and showing interest in methods; the watching of the river or standing by the railway, counting the number of pills. People often tidy up their affairs, make a will, speak to people they haven't for a long time, get over unfinished business, behave as if saying goodbye.

10 The common consistency in suicide is with life coping patterns

There are always links with ways in which the person has behaved before.

Helping yourself or others

1 Try to understand what the suicide is about, what problem it is intended to solve. This may be very complicated, for it is not readily accessible to the person or he or she would be forming their ideas in another way.

2 Try to help reduce the level of suffering: a) by understanding and reaching out; b) by being available without judgement or constraint; c) by allowing a safe space for the person to open up.

3 Try to help remove the frustrated needs; in the case of Nadia (p. 157), she was offered asylum and safety and she took it with relief.

4 Openness, such that the person feels that he or she is being cared for and that his or her point of view is respected can help to reduce the level of lethal perturbation that accompanies the fixation on suicide. Head-on collision, over-interpretation or moral persuasion do not help: they only antagonise more and increase the arousal levels.

5 Time, lots of time, is needed to allow the person to explore other scenarios than his fixed, either/or polarity. Giving time and space can allow for the ambivalence to be amplified into a state of comfort.

6 We may need to be practical and remove means of suicide thus blocking physically the way out and allowing the person time to look at other options.

If you realise you have been thinking of committing suicide

1 Find someone to talk to in confidence about what you are thinking and feeling.

2 Try to put into words or pictures what it is you want ended in your life, what it is you want to go away. Be still with yourself and ask your unconscious for an image of what you are struggling with.

3 Go toward the person you most trust and ask for asylum and sanctuary so that you have the space, privacy and encouragement to explore the dismal landscape in which you find yourself.

193

4 Before you make up your mind, give yourself 'borrowed' time from which to examine your options.

If you realise someone close to you is thinking of committing suicide

Read through this chapter carefully to see if you can get any clues to what it is the person is up against. Make a list of just three major priorities for this time in order of importance. This is a crisis and not a time for deep meaningful dialogues, arguments or persuasions. The main objective is to keep the person alive so that they have time to be released from the intolerable pressure inside them, to widen their thinking and choices and to begin to build in a new way. Sometimes when a person realises the seriousness of the situation, and realises that their secretly held view of suicide as the answer has been taken seriously, they are able to begin to respond. That someone has noticed can be a relief in itself. Someone is saying 'I have seen how bad things are for you'. If you are unable to do this and you recognise that someone is heading this way, you can ring the Samaritans for help. If the person you are concerned about is a young person they now take third party calls – calls on behalf of someone who does not want to or cannot ring. They have an enormous wealth of experience in dealing with suicides of all kinds. They will help you to approach the person you are concerned about and they will talk to you about your own distress about the person.

WHO COMMITS SUICIDE?

There are over 20,000 attempted suicides in Britain of which 4,000 do succeed in killing themselves. This makes suicide one of the top ten causes of death. Suicide is the second most common cause of death in young people under the age of 25. The number of suicides among young people has increased threefold over the last ten years, all over Europe and especially in the United States. The figures were approximately 600 ten years ago and today are between 7,000 and 8,000. The groups most likely to attempt suicide are again the vulnerable groups mentioned by Dr. Roland Littlewood: adolescents, women and old people.

Vulnerable minority groups

Adolescents, women and old people share a number of things in their vulnerability.

1 They are all in transition, wondering where they are going and how to get there.
2 They are all wondering what their life is about and what it means to them.
3 They all have to fight very hard for genuine acceptance, rights and power.
4 They are all vulnerable to disillusionment.

Adolescent suicide

Adolescence is a time of powerful mood swings and suicide may be attempted because of a passionate need to find answers to a dilemma, or during a fit of fury at something going wrong that cannot be dealt with. There may be such a strong demand upon adolescents as a group to get themselves sorted out, find jobs, take up careers, leave home and grow up, that no one listens properly to what they are saying. And this is a time when young people aren't sure what words they would choose, so they cannot communicate their needs or feelings except by action. This time, so highly charged for the teenager, is often a time when parents have started going their own way, divorcing, separating, taking lovers or starting their own careers. They may be so preoccupied that they do not attend to the behaviour of their offspring. They may be stuck in the traditional 'Me parent, you child' role without realising that their teenager is bursting with life, wanting to move on and needing to be able to communicate fully and to be valued as a separate human being.

6

What can I do to help myself through the stages of breakdown?

This chapter contains some ideas which may help us to look in a different way at the problems we have which, if left unexplored, could lead to the impasse or chasm experiences of breakdown; or, which we may find we still have after the experience of breaking down. Having identified our problems in this way we might then seek professional help in order to process our experience. The following sections are for people who feel that they need to be reframing their symptoms; or for people who can recognise they are 'on the edge'; or for people who feel they are at the 'rebuilding' stage of breakdown.

TIMES TO GO FOR HELP

We all have our own individual times when we are ready to recognise that we need help. Sometimes it takes a serious crisis before we will ask for something for ourselves.

It would seem that the process of breakdown tends to get more entrenched because we don't find the answers we need in the initial stages. From what I have seen in my own life and work there are times when we are ready to 'hear', and times when, whatever is said to us and however wise, words fall on deaf ears. This may be because of a terror of being seen as fragile or 'needing' something and having to succumb to the understanding of another, or it may simply be that on the journey of life there is some kind of pattern to our development process which means that we take in or confront issues only when we are ready to deal with them psychologically. And it must be said that some people do seem determined to carry on treading a self destructive path despite what is being offered them.

Whatever the reception we receive from someone suffering in whatever way, whether we are friends, family or professionals, we should not underestimate our contribution. People have often surprised me by saying, 'Oh, after you said that I started thinking ... and then about six months later I heard this radio programme ... and then my sister went into therapy' and so on. Sometimes what is being said registers and is being stored away. A collection of ideas starts gathering along the same theme and the person concerned can hear the common note being played and start listening. People need to come to things in their own time but the length of the time should not make others waver or give up.

Some people have said in this book that they felt they wouldn't have been able to change without having something extreme happen to them like a breakdown. They would have liked another way because the breakdown was so painful, but they recognise the intransigence of the over-dominant part of themselves that had to be challenged, by force if necessary.

No approach to helping people should ever aim to 'cure', remove, or 'save', because people aren't machines that need to run to order. We need to accept that breakdowns are part of life, they happen for a reason. If they are seen as a weakness or illness they will be seen as something to get over or avoid, like measles. These latter two go together. If we seek to cure breakdowns because of an idealised image of how we should behave then we will make these crises necessarily more frequent. If we see them as a necessary course for some people in certain situations and work with what the breakdown is about we will allow people to move on, rather than leaving them stuck in a myth of illness.

How to recognise we're 'on the edge'

1 Knowing something is very wrong but not knowing what it is.
2 Feeling bad about the way we feel.
3 Feeling that it's all our 'own fault': 'I brought it all upon myself' and should 'snap out of it' or 'pull myself together'.

4 Feeling trapped by the way we feel so that there really are no words for it.
5 Thinking often of suicide as the only way out, the only solution.
6 Being frightened of our own feelings or frightened at the loss of our feelings.

Going off at a tangent

It is during the initial phase – the onset of symptoms or the realisation that something is missing – that we may unfortunately go off at a tangent from what we really need. We may recognise in ourselves a pattern of ill health, depression, phobic anxiety, or desperate coping strategies such as avoidance, alcohol or drug abuse, that actually seem to make our problems or symptoms feel more absolute. This may be dominating our lives and making us feel angrily resigned and bad about ourselves. We may doubt our capacity, and be angry about what we see as our limitations. We may have become convinced that the problem is something outside ourselves: a virus, or the way our bodies work; or difficulties in our backgrounds or education; or tragic life events in our past, and that it is these which are limiting our lives or what we see as our chances.

If we have been convinced that it is our body or our 'weakness' that lies behind our problems, and we are continually trying to overcome these factors, we are limiting our perception to only one area and our difficulties are actually exacerbated. If, for example, the only way we can allow ourselves to be vulnerable and helpless is within the framework or 'permission' of illness, we might get repeatedly ill, have countless unnecessary operations or invasive tests which all have their own reactions, giving us another set of problems, while our real underlying problem may be to do with asserting ourselves, asking for help when we need it or acknowledging what we feel. This real problem has not been addressed and we are getting further away from any solution to this with the added burden of unnecessary surgery. The same goes for alcohol or drug dependence. Instead of reaching the spot where help is needed, alcohol and drugs give us another set of physical and emotional symptoms.

If we can get the help we need during the first phase of a breakdown then we don't necessarily have to move on to the later stages: our symptoms are understood and the necessary changes are accomplished. But even when we find the help we need we may still need to go through a period of trap, impasse, thawing out and rebuilding as we face the parts of ourselves that we know least and perhaps fear most. This process of breakdown is then contained during therapy or alongside some new understanding we have of ourselves.

Some people feel that consulting someone who is not a doctor but someone who works with the 'mind' is shameful and frightening, or that they have to be mentally ill in order to see such a person. Other people feel that trying to seek help with what they are feeling is somehow 'copping out', that they should be able to sort things out for themselves. Pride, fear and lack of information can lead people to put off looking for appropriate help until their condition becomes severe. This need not be so. All of us can claim the right to seek and assess information about what might be beneficial for us or our families. This is taking control, not giving up, and it is using resources wisely.

REFRAMING OUR SIGNALS

Many people spend a lot of time and money looking for solutions to their problems within a system that is offering cure for what is presented, when what is being presented is only the signal.

Symptoms are signals from our seed self informing us that our survival self is no longer appropriate. Our survival self may have all kinds of mistaken ideas about the sort of person we are, about how we should make relationships with others and how others see us, and what we believe we have to do in order to be effective, loved, happy, successful. When we get symptoms we don't want or life doesn't seem to be working out for us in the way we hope and this causes us problems, it is worth examining what kind of beliefs we have.

Exercise: preparation for reframing

1 First thing in the morning, before you get out of bed or, if you share a bed, before you have spoken to anyone (creep out somewhere private the bathroom if necessary) take a notebook or large blank sheet of paper, and write down anything that comes into your mind. Any words, colours, shapes, thoughts, phrases, anything ... without making an order or judgement. Do this for a week.

2 Then, when you feel up to it, choose your best time of day and read through what you have written, picking out all the words and phrases you use most. Pick out any feelings or sensings you get. Pick out two things that seem to dominate the week's creation: this could be a black mood, or 'I'm no good', or angry sounds

3 Then for a week, keep a journal of all the times when you feel or think like this. Write down the time and place, what is happening when these thoughts or ideas or feelings come to you. Just simple notes, such as: 'grey and miserable, shop assistant rude, forgot toothpaste, saw reflection in shop window, not enough change for milkman, new neighbour bought six rose trees or six Mars bars.'

4 After one week, again when you feel like it, sit down with this week's creation and see if there is any pattern in it. For example, you may find that Tuesday was a good day and Friday a bad day and your notes will tell you something of what ingredients made up that day so that you begin to separate out what makes you feel good and what makes you feel awful.

5 The next process is to evaluate how these processes are governing your life in terms of how you see yourself and present yourself to the world. Often our moods and symptoms are a response to an imagined situation rather than to a real one. By writing down when our symptoms or mood changes occur we help ourselves get a distance from them. By recognising them and what triggers them we have more control over them. If, for example, we recognise the compulsive need to clean an already over-clean bathroom as a response to feeling bad about something, we can take an active part in changing this habit.

TRAPS, DILEMMAS AND SNAGS

At Guy's and St. Thomas's Hospitals, Dr. Anthony Ryle has designed a successful method of working therapeutically in a focused way which helps people to reformulate their problems and difficulties. Therapists working with this method known as C.A.T. (Cognitive Analytic Therapy) share a helpful paper called 'psychotherapy file' which divides the way we perceive being and doing into traps, dilemmas and snags.

Read through this next section and see if you recognise any of your own patterns. Make a note to yourself when something you read rings a bell, and allow this recognition to inform you about yourself. Noticing our patterns of thinking about ourselves, and the choices these patterns often limit us to, is the beginning of our taking control of our behaviour. As we understand better and see more clearly how we can get muddled up in procedures that end badly for us, we are able to challenge old ways and learn better ways of dealing with things.

Traps

These are what we cannot escape from: certain kinds of thinking and acting are self-perpetuating and can be called traps. In 'trap' behaviour a negative belief makes us act in a way which inevitably becomes a self-fulfilling prophecy, reinforcing the negative belief and the feeling that there is no escape. Here are some examples:

Fear of hurting others trap

Feeling fearful of hurting others* we keep our feelings inside, or put our own needs aside. This tends to allow other people to ignore or abuse us in various ways, which then leads to our feeling, or being, childishly angry. When we see ourselves behaving like this, it confirms our belief that we shouldn't be aggressive and reinforces our avoidance of standing up for our rights.

Avoidance trap

We become anxious in certain situations, such as closed spaces or crowded streets, because of our underlying insecurity about ourselves ('I won't manage, it will be awful ... people will laugh'). Going back into these situations becomes fearful and we develop a fear of the fear itself, so we avoid these situations, but at the cost of personal restrictions and deeper insecurity ('I can't ... I'll never').

---

*People often get trapped in this way because they mix up aggression and assertion. Mostly, being assertive – asking for our rights – is perfectly acceptable. People who do not respect our rights as human beings must either be stood up to or avoided.

Depressed thinking trap

When we feel depressed we imagine that we will do things badly. We think 'they won't like me', 'I'll never be able to be as good as him'. Often if we are depressed we don't feel like doing things and we don't feel up to managing things as we might or are used to. We may actually do things less efficiently than usual, and anyway we tend to remember only the negative. We don't remember the positive value of actually having a go at something. This further deepens our depressed view of ourselves. Keeping a diary of times when we cope and times when we have pleasure, on a scale of 1 to 10, for each hour of the day, can help to give us a more objective view of our depression and the hold it appears to have on us.

Social isolation trap

We feel under-confident and have a poor view of ourselves and we think that people will find us boring and stupid, so we avoid being with people or looking at them or responding to friendly moves. We are suspicious of anyone who seems likely to like us. As a result we seem unfriendly and then in fact do become isolated, from which we conclude that we are boring and stupid. Our isolation deepens and our feeling that we are stupid and boring is apparently confirmed.

Low self-esteem trap

Feeling worthless, we feel that we cannot get what we want because a) we will be punished, b) others will reject or abandon us, or c) we feel that if we receive anything good it is bound to go away or turn sour. Sometimes it feels as if we must punish ourselves for being weak. From this we feel that everything is hopeless so we give up trying to do anything which confirms and increases our sense of worthlessness.

Placation trap

We feel uncertain about our worth and we feel guilty and anxious about our right to be assertive or to ask for what we want. So we try to please others by doing what they want or seem to want. We can end up being taken advantage of which makes us angry, guilty or depressed. Hence our sense of uncertainty and lack of self-worth is maintained or increased. Or we may feel suffocated and taken over by others and deal with this by withdrawing emotionally, standing people up, not answering phones or letters. So people get irritated with us, we feel guilty, and we end up still more uncertain about our self-worth.

Self-effacement tends to invite abuse from others and this makes us cross. The very nature of becoming a 'pleaser' or doormat to others means that we have probably never been able to develop anger or assertion appropriately and we feel it to be forbidden. So, when we get rightly cross in these trapped situations the anger may come out as a childlike tantrum or we may withdraw into passive and manipulative kinds of anger. This, too, can invite ridicule and more abuse and so our trap goes on, often accompanied by bad moods and physical symptoms. Assertion based on mutual respect is an appropriate and essential skill for mature adult life and one which can be learned. In most situations assertion is acceptable and one then receives the behaviour one earns in this way. The people who do not allow us appropriate assertions and are aggressive to us need to be fought aggressively or avoided. Birds sing, usually, to define their territory, warning off other birds of the same variety. Most of the time, rivals respect this, and fighting only occurs if the line is crossed. People often need to be instructed in the art of 'singing on the boundary'.

Dilemmas

We very often carry on doing certain things, even when we don't much enjoy them, because we believe that any alternative will be as bad or worse. Yet there are in reality other ways we could do things, it's just that our particular history has offered us a narrow view of possibilities or strategies. Dilemmas force us into the splits and polarities which we have been talking about throughout this book: they put us in an 'either/or' position, for example, 'I'm either in firm control of my feelings or in chaotic confusion'. They also put us in an if/then position: for example, 'If I'm feminine then it will mean submitting to others'. We are not usually aware of how narrowly we view the options or possibilities open to us. But if we sit down and look at the patterns we make in our life we may see that we act as if we did indeed see things in this extreme way, like Melanie who saw herself as if not 'saintly' then horrifying (p. 108), or Charlotte, who believed 'If I'm not working I will be nothing' (p. 45). As long as we see things through only two-dimensional spectacles we will apparently find only confirmation of our simple view and will not learn other ways, and stretch the muscles that are waiting in the wings. Some dilemmas restrict the ways in which we believe it possible to relate to other people. Others are to do with how we control and look after ourselves. Do any of the following dilemmas restrict the ways in which you go about your life? Knowing this is the first step to being able to find alternatives.

Dilemmas about attitudes to ourselves:

In relation to ourselves, do we act as if any of the following false choices rule our lives? Recognition is the first step to change.

1   Either I keep feelings bottled up or I risk being rejected, hurting others, or making a mess.
2   Either I feel I spoil myself and am greedy or I deny myself things and punish myself and feel miserable.
3   If I try to be perfect, I feel depressed and angry; If I don't try to be perfect, I feel guilty, angry and dissatisfied.
4   If I must then I won't; it is as if when faced with a task, I must either gloomily submit or passively resist (other people's wishes, or even my own feel too demanding, so I put things off, avoid them).
5   If I must not then I will; it is as if the only proof of my existence is my resistance (other people's rules, or even my own, feel too restricting, so I break rules and do things which are harmful to me).
6   If other people aren't expecting me to do things, look after them etc., then I feel anxious, lonely and out of control.
7   If I get what I want I feel childish and guilty; if I don't get what I want, I feel frustrated, angry and depressed.
8   Either I keep things (feelings, plans) in perfect order, or I fear a terrible mess.

Dilemmas about relationships with others:

1 Either I'm involved with someone and likely to get hurt or I don't get involved and stay in charge, but remain lonely.
2 Either I stick up for myself and nobody likes me, or I give in and get put on by others and feel cross and hurt.
3 Either I'm a brute or a martyr (secretly blaming the other).
4a With others either I'm safely wrapped up in bliss or in combat.
  b If in combat then I'm either a bully or a victim.
5 Either I look down on other people, or I feel they look down on me.
6a Either I'm sustained by the admiration of others whom I admire or I feel exposed.
  b If exposed then I feel either contemptuous of others or I feel contemptible.
7 Either I'm involved with others and feel engulfed, taken over or smothered, or I stay safe and uninvolved but feel lonely and isolated.
8 When I'm involved with someone whom I care about then either I have to give in or they have to give in.
9 When I'm involved with someone whom I depend on then either I have to give in or they have to give in.
10 As a woman either I have to do what others want or I stand up for my rights and get rejected.
11 As a man either I can't have any feelings or I am an emotional mess.

Snags and self sabotage

Some of us play down, deny or actually dismantle the achievements, pleasures, gains and assertions we make. If we find we are doing this, that there is a 'yes ... but' about what we do, and we find that we do want to change but cannot take on board any gains we make, we are being caught by an underlying process we call a snag. 'I want to ... but.' These prohibitions may have external origins: parents, spouses, friends and lovers can be quite resistant to our changing and may appear not to be able to cope with the changes in us. Their reaction may take the form of indirect obstacles, like their becoming ill or depressed if we show signs of becoming more assertive or successful.

The prohibition however is often within one's own being, and it stems from our need to avoid guilt. For example, if we feel that our being well and on top of things will result in someone else's feeling bad or that they won't like it and therefore us, we will avoid doing well or getting better, in order to keep the status quo to that we know, safe.

Does any of this ring bells? Do you feel you have a tendency to avoid, deny or dismantle your own achievements and gifts? Do you feel you have to restrict your pleasures and interests or to 'pay' for them by self-punishment or symptoms? Spend some time on this one and try to get a sense of where this personal restriction is coming from in your present or past life.

What to do about snags imposed by others

If you are up against snags imposed by other people make a list for yourself of all the changes you would like to make in yourself and imagine the reaction such changes might provoke in those people close to you. It is probable that in principle these people want you to feel better, to change, but this message may not always be clear. Sometimes there are powerful conditions attached to relationships. Many of these conditional relationships with specific rules work for a long time. But when they are not working any more and one person is getting serious symptoms, it is time to reevaluate, rethink, to become flexible and to allow the relationship to change and move. Nothing stays still in relationships. If it does stay still for too long the relationship becomes 'fixed', and symptoms are signals to say something's wrong, let's take a look. As we said at the beginning one person exhibiting symptoms drawing them to breakdown may not be expressing only individual symptoms but symptoms for the family or for the marriage or relationship.

There may be other conditions upon which we base our image of ourselves. The family or spouse may say 'You're the one who can go anywhere, do anything, you've always been so strong', making it hard for us to be otherwise. There may be powerful family rules: 'In our family we never wash our dirty linen in public', meaning that we never talk about what's really important and to do with our emotional life to anyone outside the family. And with this there is a strong implied instruction to cope alone, to get on with it without showing any feelings. Now these reactions may not be very obvious: they are part of our lives, taken in with our early milk, and they become as if part of us. Only when we feel bad and aren't coping do we have to look again at ourselves: Is this true? Is this me, and if not, what is me? Learned views about ourselves, and the positions we've taken on board for survival and adaptation, can be restrictive and they do not allow us to see our other parts.

When we realise we want to change and we can, some people will be pleased for us and help us. We may get surprised. Sometimes we are confronted with a major opposition, people close to us feel they just cannot accommodate what we need to do at these times, and we have to make a choice between our desire to change and the continuation of the relationship.

Snags imposed on ourselves

Snags that we impose on ourselves are more difficult to locate because they are sensed as being part of our nature and are usually based upon unacknowledged or irrational guilt. If you can trace a pattern in your life that shows you have avoided using your gifts, or feel that you have to pay for your success or for your actual existence, or if you habitually sell yourself short, hurt or deprive yourself, then you should suspect that you are 'snagged'.

The guilt underlying a snag is often unconscious; common sources are the illnesses, deaths or disasters of parents or other family members during childhood or adolescence, for which one has assumed 'magical' responsibility. This can lead us to feel that our life and in particular any evidence of a full, happy, successful life, is at this person's expense. We saw an element of this in the way Kathleen felt about her dead brother (p. 69), for example. This is an intensely powerful undermining feeling, one which paralyses some people, and cannot be strongly enough stated. I have met many women who are negating their own lives and potential because of magical guilt for their mother's limitations, for her neediness, her helpless 'inner' child, for her jealousy, for her sense of threat at her own child growing up. They are living believing, 'If I'm beautiful mother won't like it; if I'm clever mother will be threatened; if I'm powerful or successful mother will be annihilated.' And because mother, or whoever is mother for us, is central to our early safety and protection we bend our natural shoots of seed development to adapt to mother's needs for fear of having nothing. Any mother, however neglectful, angry, punishing, hurtful, cruel or negating is better than none at this early stage.

What can also lead us to jeopardise our own life and gifts is envy, particularly from the same sex parent or sibling. Active envy is sometimes acted out in repeated comments like someone telling us that we are bad or that we will never come to anything; or it may be that our every action is penalised: 'What did you have to do that for?' or 'trust you to make the most complicated dish for supper'.

If you recognise any of this pattern at work in your life, undermining your efforts and your progress through life, you will begin to see that your self-sabotage is a learned mechanism to cope with difficult circumstances and totally undeserved. There is another issue here, and that of family myth. These myths are very powerful indeed and we tend to take them in on an unconscious level. In this way we carry something of our mother's or father's unconscious. We absorb more of our mother's (or whoever was mother for us) unconscious life because it is usually her with whom we are intimately imbedded. We may pick up many unspoken messages that she was unaware of. Your family map will help you look at the myths of women or men in your family and see how much you have been caught up in this in your own life.

For example Sylvia realised in the second year of her therapy that most women in her family were either alone, had been left by men or were martyrs to men. They were unhappy, unfulfilled women coping with a saintly resignation for what they deemed their fate. Early messages had permeated: 'Men are very difficult and usually unkind but you need to get one'; 'Don't expect to be happy with a man' and 'Any man will do as long as you get one'. Sylvia herself was a bright, progressive thinking, alert and ambitious young woman, furious inside at these restrictions which tended to be played out in her life in the form of unsatisfactory relationships with men. She was caught in two ways: one was magical responsibility for her mother's impoverished emotional life, and the other was the feeling of doom and gloom that settling for cold, unloving, unresponsive men produced.

Her anger and desire to get on top of this situation, to find and win her own way of being in the world with work and men is beginning to pay off, although the constraint and power of this message has caused her a great deal of pain and frustration. For a long time, in her twenties, she made no relationships at all with men, but established herself in a career and didn't actively seek relationships. In her early thirties she started meeting men and going out and found herself to be plagued with these difficulties. She felt a teenager, a 16 year old with no skills or understanding of men, of whom she was both afraid and resentful. She has had to start afresh and learn to experience herself in a new way with men so that she is not dashed upon the rocks by their coolness and cruelty. What drew her into these difficulties was both the experience of a cold father and the collusion from her mother that this was what one has to put up with. When she could see this, and how it lived on, she could begin to change and rebuild her experience and to free herself of past magnetic pulls.

Recognition of patterns is the beginning of change

Having recognised and recorded any of your own traps, dilemmas or snags, you might like to ponder on them together with a close friend or counsellor. It is always helpful to share any self reflective process with another trusted person. A trained counsellor or therapist can help take the process further in terms of being present as you give up redundant, unwanted patterns and dare to let the true or the seed self out. Although very liberating and fulfilling in the end, this process is sometimes scary. Like the hermit crab who has grown out of one shell, we must emerge in a somewhat vulnerable stage before finding a more appropriate shell. Encouragement to go on and let the seed self become stronger is very important to the process of this strengthening change.

If you recognise any of these traps, dilemmas and snags in your life, keep a diary of the times and occasions when they operate. Don't be alarmed if the list seems a long one. Recognition is the first step to being able to let go of the tendrils of these obstacles to your seed growth. You are allowed to be free of them.

THE IMPASSE ... THE CHASM ... THE DEEPEST, DARKEST PIT

This is the experience described by people when their breakdown state becomes an acute crisis. They just cannot manage any longer alone. They have tried all they know, struggled to make things different and they have worked hard to bring about a change, but it has made no difference. What happens then is that we feel totally out of control. This affects our thinking – we might feel as if our mind is 'blown'; our feelings – we feel terrified and anxious to the point of paralysis; our sensations – we might feel wobbly, shivery, stiff and immobile, or sick, or we may cry as if we'll never stop; and our awareness – which becomes acute and at a distance. We can actually be aware of the most bizarre things: the moustache on the doctor, the smell of the person's breath may hit us like a huge force, but we will feel apart from it, detached. This crisis state puts us into an area that is totally new and unknown. Nothing that has gone before feels useful. We feel separate from the rest of the world, from people, from anything familiar. What has been a build-up of our symptoms seems worse, and our problems seem to spread into other areas. What has been one particular problem becomes 'I can't manage any longer' and a general issue 'How can I go on ?'.

The impasse stage of breakdown is often when people suffering do need to be taken care of, they need to be able to ask others for help. When we are in this place it is very difficult for us to be objective about what is right for us, we depend on others, and we can only hope and pray that this type of care will be as appropriate as possible for our needs. Some people do get through this time on their own, and some with very little help. In Chapter 7 we look at some of the options open for families and friends to help those near to them suffering at this point.

Other experiences of the impasse are of the despairing, desperate, depressing, tearful, lost, abandoned flavour, where the person feels a failure, a no-hoper, alone and lost. People talk about feeling 'in pieces', broken and shattered, as if they need to be put back together again, mended. Jane wrote to me:

> With the night terrors came a paralysis, not daring to move or take
> a breath in case something heard me, or I aggravated something
> alien. I feel I am being persecuted, something is waiting out there in
> the dark to trap me should I make a wrong move. A wrong move is
> just being there, in the wrong place and at the wrong time, like the
> victim of a rape, burglary or other people's unconstrained violence.
> It would be something in me that would remind them of something
> they didn't like. It could be so innocent – the colour of hair, eyes, the
> shape of a mouth, an expression, smell, shape of body, clothing. I can

see a man in black coming up the stairs. I can sense him waiting out there in the dark. I think about violence, how it is something in the person that has to be projected out ... it cannot be borne. Like my eating: when I eat to push away the raw and hungry feelings that I'm so ashamed of, that plug away all the time inside, that have no voice other than a craving for food. Eating to numbness and oblivion. But no physical food ever meets the spot, just as it is with violence. A violent act may dull the pain, increase the feelings of powerfulness, but the waking is with an increased heaviness and feeling so bad, so very bad. I just don't want to be any more.

The sadness and melancholy of the depressed place in the impasse needs time to reveal some of the underlying issues that have been camouflaged by the depression. It can be a time of the utmost emptiness, where just existing is a struggle. Some people feel very stuck in this place for a long time.

Peak experience or transformation

It is in the midst of this sense of 'nothingness' that people report their experiences of meeting with a figure or presence with religious or some special qualities. They report a feeling of oneness with a force never before experienced but which transcended what had been previously known, which linked up with the individual's spiritual past, where they found their spiritual self and from which they could begin to become whole. Someone whose full story is not reported here said that at the worst of her chasm experience she met a figure of a strong man who took her into his arms and held her, awakening in her a belief in the 'goodness of life'. From then on she had a sense of strength, something strong, good and living in her, beaming help and strength, upon whom she could call when necessary. Another person wrote to me about her experience of walking alone in the woods one day after her discharge from hospital and at a time when her family had deserted her. She had no home, family, she had lost her job and income, she was 'stripped bare'.

I sat down underneath one of the oak trees and pondered on all that had happened to me. I couldn't go any lower. I had lost everything. I had given up everything that had felt important to me, or it had

211

given me up. I felt as though there was nothing for me to live for, no point in my struggling on to get better, whatever that meant, to learn something else, to struggle back into normal life, whatever that was. I just couldn't imagine how things could go on. And suddenly I had an awareness of something else, some other force that was much greater than me, and that it didn't really matter, that I could be anyone, that I was part of something else, bigger, more of a sort of gathering of things, a throng; I spontaneously started to pray. I'd never really done this before – only when I had to at school – but I felt so thankful, so joyous, so grateful for this other Being which was a something I cannot describe but I knew it was there. It made all the difference.

To try to analyse or define such a deeply meaningful experience would be wrong. The fact that such experiences were reported by over half the people I spoke to and had such a profound effect on their healing does suggest that here we have a collective phenomenon which is often referred to as a peak experience or manifestation of the transpersonal. The experience helped each person to go beyond the limits of the definition of the person by their illness, disease, disorder. It lifted them out of the patient status and gave them something deeply personal. It is my belief that every one has such a place, which is transpersonal, that can heal and transcend even the greatest adversities.

THAWING OUT

Perhaps the hardest phase of breakdown is the thawing out period. The crisis has happened, the impasse has been entered and lived through. We are beginning to look up again, look around … like someone coming round from an anaesthetic who feels a sense of relief because they are alive but who feels the pain of the wound, stitching and medication. These early days are like learning to walk again, trying to resume bodily functions which may or may not work, getting to know the body – is it still really there? The similarities are manifold, and we wonder whether we can make it, whether we have the strength for the biggest struggle yet.

What can I do to help myself through the stages of breakdown?

As more energy and clarity come back, concentration improves, and we have a number of choices. How do we use our energy now that we are feeling better? If we have made it this far we have got a lot going for us. We may have fought off all kinds of demons and destructive impulses and thoughts, we may have met many different creatures, figures, people from our past during the journey we have just made. What we have now is a jumble, a collection of miscellaneous experiences and feelings and the most important thing is for us to process them. We need someone to help us. What we don't want is to go on to automatic again only to start feeling the same familiar dreads in a few months time.

This is a very wobbly time, when we are more vulnerable to suicide attempts and successes because we have a bit more strength and energy. We are looking around and we might not like what we see or think it worthwhile to battle on. If you are the family friend or helper of someone coming out of a breakdown this is the time when they need as much support as possible. And if it is your breakdown know that you are vulnerable to swings of mood, and to the cynical grab of 'Is it worth it?'. Now is not the time to take major decisions. You cannot know yet what you are going to get out of your experience. What is needed at this time, before you are ready to do some active rebuilding is to treat yourself as if you had just come home from a war.

1   You will be suffering from shock. You will feel wobbly, uncoordinated, weak and weepy a lot of the time; perhaps you have become accustomed to the institutional routine of the hospital and are missing it. Shock care means warmth, slowness, routine, support, care and nothing new or challenging.
2   You will be shocked by where you have just been, by your experience and perhaps by some of the thoughts you had. You may be tempted to punish yourself for feeling as you have or thinking as you did. Be reassured that whatever has happened to you has been for some reason and that there are people around who are trained to help you understand what has happened to you. Be understanding and kind to yourself. Later on, when rebuilding, you will be able to discard all that needs discarding because it is now redundant and to build upon the things that have not yet had a chance. This is not a time for recriminations

although this is tempting. Try not to fall into the trap of self
abuse.

3   You will need surroundings that are familiar and comforting:
your own home or the home of a friend that you know and trust.
You will need caring people around: one popping in every day can
be enough.

4   Keep a notebook for everyday thoughts and dreams. It will help
when rebuilding.

5   Keep activities to a minimum. Try to get exercise outside.

6   If you have found yourself drawn to some particular place or
object, to a position or to music, or a shape or colour during your
experience, take this very seriously. Anything that helped you
through your journey is an important part of you: a manifestation
of unconscious parts of yourself that have been attempting to keep
you safe. All of us are naturally mythmaking, image-making
creatures. Believe in this part of you, take it seriously, keep it to
yourself if there is any risk that it will be ridiculed or laughed at.
It is precious: guard and treasure it as the most important thing
in your life. Go every day, as many times as you need, to whatever
thing it is that has helped to keep you safe and be with it.

7   Select and be with the people who give you something, who are
nourishing, caring, supporting and understanding. You take up
the choice. Make a list if you need to. Be aware of the people who
drain you of energy, who make you question your right to be on
earth, who make you feel bad or guilty.

8   Make a ritual for yourself for every day. Organise some limits,
some kind of timetable which is loosely defined and which is
composed of what you know. It may be making tea in the
mornings using a properly laid out tea-tray; it may be the same
walk you make morning and evening; it may be making the effort
to talk to at least one person each day. But make a pattern for
yourself in the same way that a routine is made during
convalescence. Have a rest every afternoon: get into bed and stay
there for at least an hour. Look in the paper and choose a radio
or television programme to listen to rather than randomly putting
it on. Some people find the radio very comforting and like to have
it on all night so that there is noise when they go to sleep and wake
up. This is a separate need from the need to consciously choose
the things that are good for you.

9   Begin to make a list of the things that are important to you. A list of the things you like about yourself; a list of the things you want to do.
10 You may have a lot of questions. Keep a record in your notebook of these questions so that when you are with someone whose judgment or whose words you value, you can call upon what it is you want to ask. In this period you may feel concentration to be poor and tiredness uppermost, so making lists helps you to recall important issues when you need to.

Nurturing our bodies

The body plays an important part in healing, and in breakdown this is often underestimated. Through our bodies we can allow a special containment for all our feelings. It is possible for us to begin to feel more in control of our lives by concentrating upon the needs of our bodies. Taking care of and mastering the needs of the body can help us to feel more in charge and can stimulate the healing processes. Disciplines such as yoga, meditation and tai chi can help us to stimulate energies and contain difficult feelings. We do feel everything through our bodies and it tends to be our bodies which carry the chemicals produced by fear and depression or the 'body armouring' produced by our defences. Most of us know about body language: about how much is said non-verbally by the way in which we sit or stand, move or walk, by the gestures we make.

This time of dethawing is for nurturing and kindness rather than self exploration, but if you begin to become aware of what your body is experiencing you will begin to learn how to take care of the body's immediate needs and thus your own inner needs. Similarly, slow, abdominal breathing does help us to take charge and feel better. People have reported to me how much walking helped them to keep moving and release the tension. Later on, during the rebuilding phase you may wish to return in more detail to learning some of the techniques that involve the body to strengthen your everyday life.

Breathing

Sometimes when we've had a shock or have a period of anxiety it affects the way we breathe. We may 'forget' to breathe or breathe shallowly from our upper chests, taking in great gulps of air to compensate every now and then; sometimes people find that they are concentrating too hard on breathing, forcing breath in as if they weren't getting enough. Breathing disturbances are a sign that we are under stress, and if we notice this in ourselves or in other people it is wise to do some breathing exercises three times each day until this time has passed.

Exercise: Breathing

Sit with your hand over your solar plexus (abdomen) and practise pushing the muscles in and out so that you can feel them working. Sit straight up with shoulders relaxed but your upper body straight. Breathe in, allowing your solar plexus to expand thus allowing air deep into the lungs. Imagine a balloon being blown up as you fill your whole lung cavity with air. When you breathe out, let the air out slowly, pushing every bit out until your balloon image is empty and deflated. Sometimes it helps to make a noise as you do this out breath, such as a low grunting from the back of your throat: this can remind you what you are doing, and those familiar with yoga deep breathing exercises or who have friends trained as singers will recognise this sound! Concentrating on breathing properly at least three times each day helps to restore a regular pattern of breathing, so that this healthy breathing becomes more automatic, and it helps us to gain a sense of relaxation and peace.

Exercise: Relaxation

This may be read to you by a friend. Lie flat and close your eyes. Concentrate on your breathing as above and allow yourself to become totally relaxed. Imagine yourself to be in a favourite place, or a place you can imagine you would like to be, or if neither of these comes to you imagine you are in a meadow with the sun overhead. Nearby is some water that is calm and healing. Stay in the meadow and find a spot – just let your mind wander until it finds a spot where you can sit down and be calm and relaxed. In this place feel into your body. First of all, feel your feet: tighten them and then let them relax, feeling the ball of your foot and the ankle release tension. Feel the calves of each leg: tense them as tight as you can and let them go. Do the same with your knees, and your thighs, and your buttocks (often a place where we carry a lot of tension). Go to the small of the back, then the middle of the back, the shoulders and the neck (again a place where we hold a lot of tension) and work to the head and face. Let your jaw drop, and the forehead. Work on your arms, hands clenched and then relaxed. Concentrate upon relaxing each little bit of your body until you are in a state of deep relaxation.

REBUILDING

After a period of thawing out, we can actively work to mend what we feel has been shattered inside us, to heal the wounds of which we have been made conscious. We work to strengthen the part of us that has kept us going through the experience so that we have a stronger centre from which to operate. Rebuilding is best done with another person. People to whom I have spoken about this-stage have been helped by counselling, psychotherapy, co-counselling. Good therapy or counselling does help very much at this stage. This process is aided by our own contribution, notes, dreams, journals and self monitoring. The section on reframing your symptoms may help you with focusing on what area is most difficult for you. Chapter 9 'Where do I go for help?' and the resources at the end of the book will help you look for the help you may need.

The aims of rebuilding

1 To process what has happened. Telling another consolidates the experience. It may also blow away old ghosts. Once a ghost is named it is never as ominous or powerful. There is power in the knowing and the telling of something.
2 Having processed, to learn from the experience. What have you got out of it that you can use and strengthen? What needs to be let go of?
3 Having processed and learnt, to cast off what is redundant. This means recognising the patterns of behaviour that are no longer necessary and consciously letting them go. When we let something go that we know is of no more use, although we like it because it has become a habit, we allow a space for something new to come in. This needs time to be experienced and re-experienced to become consolidated. Take your time but don't give up.
4 Consolidating the new learning means taking in consciously new things that happen. One of these may be the simple fact of having

217

found another human being with whom you can share what you feel who doesn't shout at you, abuse you or walk off. This is a new experience. Through it you learn that you may not be as unlikeable, unapproachable as perhaps you originally feared.

You may be helped during the rebuilding stage by the section earlier on traps, dilemmas and snags, and you may find the behaviours that you recognise are processed and understood by keeping a diary of times you feel you get into bad or unwanted feelings.

I cannot stress enough how important rebuilding is. It is not enough to have suffered a breakdown and to be so relieved that the worst is over that you carry on pretending nothing has happened, put the lid on it all and carry on as if nothing much has happened. Something very major has happened to you and you can draw on it to help yourself go forward. It is not all negative: parts of all breakdowns feel totally negative but it does seem that the experience of going through the dark without hope or light of any kind is a necessary experience for us to be strengthened in an important way. Once you have walked that path you are different, you have been where you feared most. After that you may go to other places and not be so afraid, so you live more fully because you are not avoiding the ghosts which have been holding you apart from life.

Some people feel stuck after a breakdown because they feel terrified that it will happen again and are afraid to put even a toe out of the door. If you can find a way to share your experience, process it, and hold it in the palm of your hand you may find a way to live with your fears, by going into life with the fearful part of you and helping it to be stronger. Avoiding something makes it worse, it feeds our imaginations, and stokes up the fire of our vulnerability. Having a nervous breakdown is not an excuse not to try. You may have a heavier load than other people to carry through life, but it should not restrict you or be the dominant factor in your life.

Exercise: Rebuilding

Go back to the images in the first chapter of this book ... the image of the road of your life. Try now, at this rebuilding stage, to imagine this road: Where are you on it? What does it look like? What is it you have to do right now to go forward, to proceed? Imagine what is immediately ahead of you –

any obstacles or difficulties; help or encouragement. Try to find an image for what these are. Stay with it and let it tell you or give you a feeling for what step you need to take next in your life. If nothing comes, just stay with the idea that you are on a road somewhere, that this is your unique road, yours alone and that finding your own path and the meaning of that path for you can restore or help to build afresh strengths and beliefs that may not have been around much throughout the last few years of your life.

7
Crisis and emergency

HOW CAN WE HELP WHEN SOMEONE IS IN A CRISIS ?

How do other people know what to do for the best when someone
they love is in a crisis? If someone collapses in the street we send for
an ambulance without question. Intervention when someone is in a
crisis where they no longer function in a day to day sense can be more
complicated. Nadia (p. 157) says 'If only someone had told me I was
ill. That I had an illness. It would have been such a relief. I would have
felt better, known it wasn't just me ... that there was something
tangible wrong with me and I could perhaps have some treatment, get
better.' Melanie (p. 108) talks of the relief when she first told someone
about her bulimia, the relief that it was OK to have these symptoms,
that she would not be punished but, hopefully, helped.

Sometimes people resent what they see as interference or don't
recognise help when it is forthcoming. Dr. Nira Kfir, leader in Adlerian
Individual Psychotherapy in Israel and internationally known for her
work in crisis intervention, says 'In crisis work you must expect and
be prepared to be rejected. You need to be rejected at least three times
before people will accept you. If you're not prepared to be rejected
then crisis work is not for you.' If you are with someone at a time of
crisis, whoever they are, and you are the only person there, then you
are the best person to help. There may be others better equipped, more
qualified, but the fact that you are there is the main issue. The person
in crisis needs to have someone in charge. They need permission to be

let off the hook, to let go, to be taken care of. They need authoritative help – not overbearing but decisive and specific.

This is not a time for democracy or for searching for meanings. What needs to be ascertained is information: the person in crisis is in a new situation and there may be other situations going on that are not new. We can look for what is familiar to the person. Sally Berry, who started the Arbours Crisis Centre fifteen years ago, says: 'Sometimes it's very difficult to get access to a person and others may speak for them ... it's both compelling and exhausting for others to speak for the person in crisis but it makes it difficult to get the right picture. I have to see who the person in crisis was and who they may be. Often people who are very disturbed have some kind of knowledge or insight into what actually is the matter. They may have no idea of what to do about it, but I think they know at least part of what it is that started it off. Once you can get hold of that, pick it out, you have communicated and you have some of the information you need.'

Once information has been exchanged about the current crisis, anxiety levels tend to drop. Someone is alongside the person, someone is getting a handle on things. The priority is *what does this person need right now?* A doctor, ambulance, cup of tea, holding hand, listening ear, warm rug, a good sleep? Once this is ascertained and the support is in evidence, then things may be taken further, if appropriate. Many crises are made worse by other people's panic or by their wanting to be rid of the person and their problems.

EMERGENCIES AND WHAT TO DO

Breakdown is unlikely to be life-threatening, except when there is a suicide attempt or when someone is acting out in a violent way, threatening others or him or herself. In this situation, medical attention is needed urgently. Help is needed to get across to the person obsessed in this way, to see what is going on and try to avert a catastrophe. It is a very difficult matter to talk to someone who has a lethal weapon in their hand and is in a space where nothing to do with the 'known' world makes any sense to them. There are psychologists and psychiatrists who specialise in working with people who are taken over by the more destructive, demonic parts of themselves, and who have amassed a wealth of knowledge and experience in talking to the person affected in this way. A person who is actively suicidal needs to be contained in a place of safety until this period has changed or the person has been able to restore other bits of him or herself that do want to live, that can offer some balance in a very threatening landscape.

Medical emergency

Severe depression during which the person becomes mute, withdrawn, cannot eat, drink or speak, can become a medical emergency and need medication or even ECT treatment (see page 272).

The onset of what is called psychosis can also become a medical emergency. In this situation, the contents of the unconscious take the place of what we know as conscious thought and there are no boundaries between consciousness and unconsciousness. In this state non-organic objects can be seen to move or have voices: the chair that speaks, the vibrations in the form of jelly beans that are coming through the walls, the spies that are in the television, the blood that is pouring out of the tap, constant confrontations with the Devil, with evil forces. During one woman's breakdown she saw the sides of the quarry in which she was walking running with blood and felt they were closing in on her. All these occurrences, which can last from a few minutes to hours or days, are very frightening indeed. Many of us experience such things from time to time but are able to restore our link with consciousness immediately. But, for the person in psychosis they are very real, and because they are experienced as part of the life, there is no beginning or end to them.

Certain aspects of paranoia and delusion can also become emergencies. When these aspects get a grip of the person they appear real and logical, and carry with them a fixed, fanatical, rigid and very determined quality. People suffering in this way cannot be reasoned with, cannot call on other aspects of their personality to give a balanced view. In his talk on paranoia at the Oxford Seminar in Archetypal Psychology, James Hillman took four case histories as examples: Anton Boyson (1920–1960); John Percival (born 1803, incarcerated 1831–1834); Daniel Paul Schreber, in clinics from 1893–1902; and Carl Gustav Jung. He showed that when revelation of any matter becomes too literal, fixed, ruthless, the para-noetic (mind always preoccupied) content forms a madness where nothing else can be expressed. This madness has an incorrigible quality, illustrated by the story of a man who believed himself to be dead. When his doctor asked if dead men bleed the man said 'Of course not, everyone knows that.' After jabbing a pin into the patient's finger and drawing blood the man says 'Well I'm damned, Doc., dead men do bleed.' Here this man's perception supported his delusion rather than contradicted it. Receiving such revelations mercurially, with humour, pondering on what is happening, releases us from fixity. Jung obeyed the spirit of humour, 'Don't let them (voices, revelations) provoke your believing response'. Percival learned to doubt the authenticity of his voices. He struggled with meaning (what on earth is all this about?) and saw it as a struggle with the god in the self. Schreber did not learn. He stayed in madness. The god in us speaks poetically ... we should hear literal commands with a poetic ear.

GIVING SUPPORT

We hear Nadia's story (p. 157), of how she saw her own death as the only way out of her misery, and that this became fixed and determined; and that after her first suicide attempt she found to her surprise that people around her were extremely upset, that they loved her and didn't want her to die. Rather than changing her mind, she felt that it would be upsetting everyone too much for her to die so she must take her little ones with her. When her psychiatrist encouraged her to talk about this, to express it out loud, to bring into consciousness the fixed messages of the unconscious response, and to tell her husband what she was thinking of doing, she was being encouraged to challenge her own fixedity. She was pushed to ask, 'Wait a minute, is this right? Is this true? Is this what I really want? Must it be like this?' It was after this, when it was suggested she needed to have a period of time in hospital and be taken care of, that she responded with relief.

The strain of suffering from the fixity of paranoia, dementia and psychosis, which we label madness, is enormous and the toll of daily battling with a frightening and overpowering inner landscape and all the creatures and demons that we meet in that space is a very costly one. People need space and time to be relieved of their suffering, they need time and space to not be interfered with by other people's fixed view of what is happening to them. Places are needed where people can meet these inner demons and questions and challenge them so that a non-believing response is set up and restored, is strengthened, so that in future times these visitations are not so overpowering.

Nadia says now, with a look of horror on her face, 'Of course I realise now ... it would have been murder wouldn't it? How terrible, awful that would have been – it's just not thinkable – but at the time it all seemed to make such sense.' Soon after I met Nadia I heard the story of Ann Reynolds, now serving a life sentence for killing her mother. Perhaps if she had had someone to talk to about what her inner demons were driving her to do, and that person could receive her kindly, honestly, unafraid, knowing that the fixity and ruthlessness of these states makes the person under their spell absolutely set on that particular course, she would not have acted out literally what it was she was seeking to do and she would not have been branded as a criminal.

8
How do families and friends cope?

The attitude of family and friends to someone suffering in any of the five stages of breakdown is of tremendous importance, but family and friends need a great deal of support to help them cope with the strain and the difficulties imposed by a breakdown in the family. Breakdown challenges all of us on many different levels. People I have spoken to about a breakdown within their family or close friendships report feelings of impatience, fury, resentment, rage, intolerance, hatred, despair and absolute exhaustion, most of which they felt guilty about and were unable to express. They also feel confusion about what to do, and how to be with the person; how best to offer help and support, when to intervene, who to recommend, who to listen to for help, who to talk to about how they feel themselves. They often have feelings of desperation that the situation will never end or be relieved. People do get worn out listening to others' troubles and being caught up in others' problems. Sally Berry of the Arbours Association says 'What doesn't often get mentioned is how tiring people's distress is. So often the nitty-gritty is tiring and boring. People don't often write about this – that so much of people's suffering and breakdown is really wearing. Not everything is a journey into vividness.'

All breakdowns are hard for families. Where a breakdown specifically involves the whole family, as in most cases of anorexia or bulimia, most adolescent crises and in some cases of agoraphobia, the family can be supported by family therapy, by general practice, community nurses or social workers. But most families struggle on alone without much help, sometimes reluctant to talk to anyone about what is happening at home. We are all challenged by a breakdown in the family, not only in terms of how we respond and feel, but in terms of how much we are involved and what the person means to us.

CHILDREN OF PARENTS WHO BREAK DOWN

A child shares his or her emotional life with whichever adult is closest, traditionally mother. If this close adult suffers breakdown, it is impossible to explain to a child what is happening in terms they can take in. Children are amazingly adaptable to 'odd' behaviour and can react well to people who are nearer to the unconscious world than the conscious because that is the landscape they can understand – of trees that have names, winds that have voices, fairy tales and dreams and ghosts. And if there are other stable adults around for the child, the withdrawal of the close adult can be less absolute. But when the breakdown state is severe and no one explains, children can get caught up in a destructive way, being targets for aggression, being deprived of love and affection, and their world can be rendered unsafe and unstable.

Enid, now an established psychoanalyst says:

> Mum's breakdown was disguised as physical for some time – she came out in rashes and had to go back to her mother every time. I remember Mum being useless as a mother. My only memory is when I was three, running away from her; that was when my brother arrived ... I wanted to move house and live somewhere else. I'd repeatedly climb the front gate and take the little boy next door for walks and pretend I was his mother. My mother was unliveable with: I never went to her for anything – Once I fell off the gate and was full of fear to go to my mother so I went to the woman next door to get mopped up. The only way to get through to my mother was to get either very passionate or very funny. Once I cried for twenty-four hours and then she responded. I couldn't afford to start getting hopeful when she did have her nice moments. I knew it would nearly drive one mad. My only way to survive was to defend against her: I couldn't afford to get near to her for a moment because then it would all have gone away in the next instant.
>
> I kept myself going because I had an innate ability to know what's

a disaster course. You focus on saving yourself and go for it: it's born of desperation, knowing you have to.

Martha, now in her forties writes:

I didn't fully realise how much my mother wasn't there because of her own prolonged breakdown, until I was in my mid thirties and had a crisis of my own, my marriage broke up and I was devastated, but I had nowhere to go, no one to talk to whom I felt would understand. I had lots of friends but I had filled the role of listener to them. I realised what a barren landscape I was on.

I began to realise how much I had let people empty me out, starting with my mother. It is such a subtle thing. She was never in hospital but she was always 'delicate' and had to lie down a lot. She disapproved of everything I did and I tried so hard to please her. I can see now that she saw me as a threat – my ability to 'cope' and be strong, to get on with my father – and she reacted to my successes in a really mad way, shouting, raging, retreating into a terrible sulk or a wounding reproach. I suppose I hated her then but I didn't know it. I wanted to please her, to make her like me, to be nice to me. Now I can see that I have tried ever since to mend other people's rather mad and psychotic bits. I have believed I had to absorb it all and it was my job and duty to make it better. I married an alcoholic who beat me up: I thought it was my life's work to understand him and make him well.

The first half of my life has been dominated by this drive. Sometimes it is as if my whole life has been a sham. It has all been built upon this primal need. There is a hole in my heart and so often I just don't want to live. I don't know how. I feel as if I really can't make it. I don't know who I am in truth and I can't see a new way. I can't go on living in the old way but it's hard to get out of the habit. Whenever there is the seduction of a need I supply it. The hole is so heavy. Can I develop a sufficiently protective cover so that I don't let these devils in ? The energy all this takes from me – I realise now why I have been tired for the last twenty years or more. I assume other people are right and I am wrong. I do not stand my own ground. I cannot say what I feel. I cannot stand up for myself or assert myself. It all stays inside like a great big hurt.

227

Using parental crises creatively

When we realise consciously that we have been carrying a parent's early breakdown around with us in this strong way – and often a crisis of our own precipitates this realisation – we can get help to separate from this aspect of our mother or father. It may take time, but it is possible to make this progress and to use the antennae and sensitivity we have developed for something of our own choice.

Crisis in our own life brings us an opportunity to use an otherwise negative experience positively. If we have had a breakdown and are concerned with how this will affect the children we can help them. Nadia says of the effect of her own breakdown on her son then aged two, 'I know it will come out later on for him. I feel sad for this but then I simply couldn't do anything else at the time. At least I know how to help him now should he need this, and I am aware and awake to his responses'.

Most people who have come through their breakdown with a greater awareness of all the facets involved are able to help the children who get caught up. Where a parent is unable to do this, the person who experiences their own crisis and brings mother or father's breakdown to the surface can be helped by professionals to express the locked up feelings and to move on.

WHEN A PARTNER BREAKS DOWN

Some people feel sorely challenged by a partner's breakdown. The emotional bonds between a couple are such that any readjustment on the part of the person breaking down must inevitably involve the other partner in readjustment.

ANN AND MARK

Ann's husband Mark had a breakdown in his early forties – a mid life crisis – and for Ann this was a period of intense suffering and isolation because of the strength of her own feelings:

> I feel that I behaved abominably because I simply couldn't understand what was going on. I saw what was for me a big strong

man becoming tremulous and childlike, depressed and withdrawn. I couldn't bear it. I was like an animal backing off. I couldn't face the responsibility. It was as simple as that. I think I'm pure animal in my instincts and not intellectual at all. I couldn't bear the dead look in his eyes ... so depressed. If I'd sat back and thought things out I'd have thought 'You're an absolute cow. That man's going through a terrible state'. But my instinctive reaction was just like a pack of wolves ... get him out .

I couldn't respond – not that I didn't try to – I didn't know how to. It's not that I don't have compassion, I do very much, and I believe I have this for individuals who are weaker than me, say a child, but I expect a husband to be very strong. I'm sure that's something to do with my past. I associate men, wrongly I think, with success, making decisions, all the things he can do very well in fact. I can boss him around and I don't like that. So when he comes to needing me I don't really want it. I found I despised him and yet for no good reason at all. Here was a man in trouble and I didn't feel he should be in this trouble.

She is extremely upset and distraught about her memory of this time.

He's a very positive, striving man with a wonderful sense of humour – very sensitive, vulnerable, very intelligent – all the things I admire enormously. Now I feel full of respect and good feelings towards him, terrific friendship and love in a platonic sort of way, things are really fine.

He started having problems I suppose about 10 years before he broke down. Forgetfulness, loss of memory, confidence; trying to gather things together and worrying he wasn't. I was slow to realise what was happening ... he kept going to doctors and psychiatrists. My tone was pretty dismissive. I believed naively that he wasn't getting job satisfaction. He has a good mind and it wasn't getting stretched properly, and he tends to be cautious and timid. He found it difficult to make changes and I thought it was all in that area that he needed help. I was looking for a practical reason, explanation. I don't think he wanted to face the fact that it was probably something within himself. I know I was very dismissive, especially when he started dredging things up to do with the past: I felt he was just making excuses.

229

> He got very depressed and didn't want to go out. He didn't want
> to see people. He had this withdrawn look. He was very sleepy.
> Then one day he just couldn't get out of bed and I had to get the
> doctor.

She looks very miserable again, very upset.

> I think what he really wanted was warm motherly affection from me
> – for me just to have put my arms round him and comfort him – that
> would have healed everything but I didn't want to give it. I didn't
> want to be near him. He was crying out for help from me and I just
> couldn't give it. I'm sure if I'd put my arms round him and said
> 'You're going through a hell of a time. We'll get it sorted out … us,
> not you' I'm sure it would have been all right. I feel terribly bad about
> it. I would have loved to have been able to give him that support and
> I feel terribly guilty about it. I deserve to rot in Hell when I think of
> all the support he's given me over the years.

I asked her what it was that prevented her. She shakes her head
sadly, uncomprehendingly.

> Because in some way he revolted me. It made me realise that it is very
> difficult for me to give proper whole-hearted affection and yet I
> think I'm an affectionate person to other people. I don't like a lot of
> closeness … I don't really like the married relationship at all. I'm
> much better at being close with someone for two or three hours and
> then getting out of it. I was very threatened by his need. I felt terribly
> vulnerable and wondered if I could stick it all, the children, the
> husband who wasn't well. I wanted to run away from it.

She is very self-deprecating about her efforts to help. I suggest to her
that in times of crisis we do what we can, what we know, with the
resources we have. She thinks for a while.

> I think I should have confided in somebody. I think in some sort of
> way I felt ashamed and couldn't deal with that feeling. I think I felt
> that this was not to be talked about. I didn't trust people enough.
> This question of public image and private person is so true here.
> People have always thought of us as a pretty close-knit unit but once

you see flaws and cracks people will gossip and chat ... I wanted to protect him very, very much. I just feel that private life is very private. I did try to say something to the GP about feeling awful at not being able to give Mark a big hug and he said 'Here's so many Mogadons for each day'. When people ask me about feelings I'm often quite glib because I can't say anything very much. I think I was always afraid of feelings anyway. I've sat on a passionate nature. If you don't understand things you get frightened and you get rid of it so that when you need to draw upon good feelings to give to someone else you can't do it. Strong feelings rise up, yes, but I have terrific control. I never used to be able to cry. I cry now and basically it's a good thing but I don't think I cried properly until two years ago. Most of the time I try to be very rational and do something else and get on with it.

When we found a good psychiatrist he could see every week he felt a lot better and things started to improve. I did feel that so much of his breakdown was my fault in some way, that I wasn't a proper loving wife to him. But it turned out that it was a much more individual thing, to do with his own ambition drive and his own feelings of insecurity. I went to see the psychiatrist and told him what I feared but he didn't seem to think this was involved in the breakdown. I know some friends did – the more old-fashioned ones thought I was too independent. No one ever suggested going to see anyone as a couple. I don't think that would have worked for us.

For the second edition of this book Ann provides the following update:

In the years since we last spoke my husband has sought many different types of help. Hypnotists, clairvoyants, healers, therapists, psychiatrists. Nothing seemed to come out of it. His self preoccupation has frustrated and annoyed me because I have seen it as an excuse for not getting on with the business of life. I am afraid that I continue to be impatient about it all, and we have reached the point where he does not talk to me about it, and I do not enquire. This is not really satisfactory because if we are to have a proper relationship as we get older, it must involve toleration and understanding so that we can lead richer and more honest lives.

My daughter has recently had some severe emotional problems and been extremely stubborn and uncommunicative. She feels extremely hostile towards us and I feel very grieved that she will not let us help her. Since her problems arose I have had to take a serious look at myself and try and understand why I had so little sympathy with my husband and yet could die with misery and pain for my daughter. I have had some therapy myself but I cannot bring myself to tell my husband of this. I definitely associate shame with the need to have therapy which is pathetic. I've learned that the animal hostility I felt to my husband prevented me from showing my compassion and caring, which I had no problem expressing with my daughter. I can be a complete mother, but not wife and lover. Sex for us has always been a constant source of misery and humiliation, and I suppose I am lucky that somehow our tremendous friendship has helped us to stay married for thirty years.

I still hope to break down the emotional barriers between my husband and myself. This means asking him to accept me as I am – disappointed in our marriage and guilty for feeling this way. In doing this and asking for forgiveness I can start to explain why I was so 'bloody' to him. I think we love each other as loving friends with respect and shared interest and I think it is enough to hang in there until the end.

One of the things I have tried to do is think positively. I believe in the power of prayer. I feel a huge need to connect with my spirit, and I do feel that in some way I am out of grace. I get enormous pleasure from nature, art and music, but I feel hugely impotent the older I get. It is as if I was meant to be doing something, and I cannot find out what 'it' is, and there is no peace until I do. I have tried to be the strong one and put a brave face on everything, but the only way I could do this was by not admitting problems, sweeping them under the carpet. Perhaps my daughter has seen through me and rejected all that I stood for, because in the long run it was dishonest. Having said all this I am definitely more sympathetic and understanding about other people's problems and not judgemental. The conventional side of me, narrow minded and prejudiced, seems like a hangover from another age, and I now want to keep my newfound sense of hope and anticipation alive, to build bridges with my husband even as we sink into old age. I generally do feel positive.

JENNIFER AND ALAN

I met Jennifer and Alan 19 years after Jennifer's breakdown. Jennifer says:

> We were both over 40 at the time and had two small children of five and seven. We were building our home and paying a mortgage, both of us had jobs. I began to get obsessed with orderliness. I was very contrary. I must have been a pig to live with (Alan nods).
>
> I felt if I could keep everything in order it would all be OK: it was as if things were slipping away and I was trying to keep control. I think finally the mental thing overtook me – I couldn't repress it anymore. It was the pressure of work as well. If I didn't do in a certain time what I'd planned to do I'd be an absolute pig (Alan smiles now: 'Oh no I just used to clear off' he says). It was contrary really because what I needed was help but I couldn't ask for it. On reflection it would have been nice if Alan could have taken some of the burden of work off me, in the house, but you see we were both at work – he was building furniture in the house.
>
> In the few weeks before I did collapse I would go through the ritual of doing chores. I felt I could concentrate more if I said out loud things that I was going to do next. That helped to keep me sane. I used to say 'When I've finished doing this washing up, I'll go upstairs and do the beds, see the children have tidied their beds, have a look in at the bathroom and see it's tidy, remember to bring my jacket downstairs ...' If anybody had heard me they'd have thought I'd gone round the bend already. I felt that by saying it, I kept my mind on the level. It became increasingly difficult to go through the door. I'd go to it and come away again, and I'd say, 'Don't be an idiot – you've only got to walk through there, walk down Avenue Road and get on the bus.' I never told anyone what was bothering me ... no one.

Alan joins in: 'One morning at five past eight she rang me up at work and said "I can't get out of the house". I thought the door was jammed or something, but then she said "I just can't go out of the house" ...' Jennifer says, 'That was the point of no return, that was the breakdown.' Alan said:

I came home from work and called the doctor, which she doesn't like my doing. He came and he saw you on your own didn't he? (Alan turns to Jennifer) Yes I was on the settee in the lounge. I couldn't even get out of the lounge. He suggested to me that I go in the local street, and I said no, I couldn't leave this room. So he said another doctor would come. He kept asking me what was the matter with my hands because I was wringing them over and over. I wouldn't look at him, I couldn't keep my legs still, they were completely gone. He drew up a chair and sat and talked to me. I think I was very lucky to have him as my GP and he was at the time doing this course, a psychiatry course, and he was also the prison doctor and it all helped him like an extra interest. I think I was lucky, perhaps I was an interesting case to him at the time. Later on that day another doctor, a psychiatrist came. I didn't know what to do because whatever you did she didn't want you to do. She was unapproachable really ... whatever you suggested she just didn't want to know. I felt helpless.

Jennifer nods, then says: 'I slept for most of the first week, either on the sofa or upstairs. I couldn't go out of the house. We didn't talk. Alan had a week off work'. Alan adds:

I knew it was a breakdown, but I didn't know what to do next. The GP was good because he knew us. He said 'All the tablets we're going to give you will only assist you but you've got to get out of this yourself' ... I just said to the children 'Mummy's not well'. Our daughter, who was nine then, was tearful and frightened because she didn't really know what was happening. She knew it was something that she couldn't help with. Our little boy wasn't really aware of what was going on: he was seven.

In the first few weeks after the breakdown we were getting in the car and going up the road a few yards and then coming back ... a little bit further each day. I was in charge of this, I had to make her go out. As soon as she said 'I can't go any further' I'd say right and we'd turn and go back. Eventually we managed to get round to the supermarket, to Woolworths, and we got in and were half way round and she'd had enough. We left the basket with the checkout girl.

Jennifer comes in:

I felt terribly embarrassed. Eventually we managed to get round and do all the shopping, but I had to keep forcing myself, everyday.

It was work that really cured me. The manageress really valued what I did. Once she brought me this really expensive dress to alter. And I think I did get a cup of relief from losing myself in that job. That was within the first three weeks of my breakdown.

There was always part of me that sort of knew what was going on and observed it all; I was annoyed at what happened to me. I think my strength was in my annoyance that this had happened to me and it had no business to. I had a lot in my life: we'd got children, plans. If people could try to instill in themselves an element of temper about what is happening to them ... I think that is nature's medicine. I think Alan had a lot of patience with me.

I went back to work gradually. My boss used to pick me up and by the time I'd got up the stairs at the workroom I could just about control the nerves in my legs. I could only stay an hour at first, and it got gradually longer and longer. Within your mind you are screaming and at the same time so annoyed and ashamed that you are in this condition. I have an extremely independent nature. My father died when I was four, my mother had a great strength and instilled it in us all. If she had been alive then when I had my breakdown she would have said 'Pull yourself together. Do you think you're the only one who's afraid?' She did pull us through a lot of illnesses when I was a child. Even during the war we were not allowed to show fear ... you haven't got time to think about fear. Perhaps all that suppression contributed to the fear and terror I felt during the breakdown. You are a prisoner of fear – 90 per cent of the breakdown is fear – you don't know really what you're frightened about.

I asked her if she could talk to Alan about the fear at the time. 'No,' they both shake their heads. Jennifer says, 'I don't really know why but I suppose it was the shame.' Alan says, 'In those days these things weren't talked about. Neither of us knew anyone who had ever had a breakdown.'

Jennifer adds:

I feel I was extremely lucky with having Alan. He got me out of it, he kept me going. He was wonderful and it was the strength of our relationship and our marriage which carried us through together.

JERRY AND SUE

Jerry's story is not such a happy one. His wife Sue had a prolonged breakdown over about four years. They tried to make things work, by seeking marital therapy, and giving Sue more space for herself from the children, but the strain in the end was too much for the marriage to withstand. I heard their story from both points of view:

Jerry

Every time there was a problem – and my missing the train home and being late was a problem – she would just go wild. She had so much anger in her. It seemed to be mostly directed towards her father and men in general, but it was terribly difficult to cope with at the end of the day. Nothing seemed right for her: she didn't like the house we were living in, it was too small, and we were trying to buy a larger one, but my heart wasn't in it and I guess she knew that. Our children were very small and there was the thought of all those bills for years to come. I was happy with our house. Looking back I guess she just projected everything she hated onto things outside. The kids got a pretty rough ride and my son has had the worst of it ... being male I suppose.

It just went on and on, there was no let up. Nothing I did was right. It gets so tiring to be attacked all the time. I tried to be as understanding as I could, and as tolerant, and perhaps this was a mistake. I didn't really stand up to her. If I got cross when I came home and was tired and there was no food, just her sitting there with the television on, and I told her, or showed it somehow, there would be an explosion. Or she would retire to her bed and curl up in a ball. She did that once and stayed like it for 24 hours. The doctor had to come with an ambulance and take her away.

I felt as if it were all directed at me somehow. When she was with other people she would be fine. She seemed lively and made jokes. She would spend hours on the telephone to her sister. But for me she had no time. She started to feel that I had produced all her troubles: I had given her children she didn't want but yet said were the love of her life to other people; and she of course went right off sex, unless she wanted something, then she could put on the charm. I would think, maybe she's getting better, she used to like sex a lot ... but afterwards there was always trouble. She would blame me for seducing her and how could I knowing how she felt ... it was all twisted and turned.

Then my business had a bad year and I lost money. We had to give up the idea of the house we wanted and this was the final straw for her. She went in to hospital and had ECT. She didn't want to see me, or the children. I didn't know what to do. Part of me knew it was all part of her illness, and the doctors confirmed this, but I couldn't see it ending. I also felt I was caught up in it maliciously in some way. I don't know even now – and it's six years – if it was deliberate on her part, but it certainly felt like it. The therapist made the point about my being something of a victim to strong women – that I never challenged a woman or allowed her to be an equal – I sort of patronised them without realising it. I've never been able to take this one on board. Sue and I divorced two years after her last trip to the hospital and I'm now remarried and I am very happy. I don't feel there is any problem of equality, I just feel I have met a woman who feels herself to be herself and has no hang-ups about men. I believe it was actually my wife's problem, Sue's problem, and she needed to work it out individually in therapy. She never has of course because she took my leaving as a sign that men were really bad and she was the victim, and she's gone on like that to this day. I don't think she's learnt from it at all.

Sue

Jerry was always detached, and at first I liked this. I have never been able to stand anyone watching me, especially to think they might watch me whilst I sleep. But he wasn't much of a husband. He certainly wasn't the kind of husband I thought he would be. Perhaps I was guilty of admiring his father, who was quite famous, and thinking Jerry would be like this. I don't know. It felt to me as if he didn't try. How could he walk out on me like that when I was ill ? Like kicking a dog when it's down. I haven't forgiven him and I don't think I will be able to. The children have suffered because he fought me for them. After a lot of battles I won. I need to have them and I think children should be with their mothers. I don't think he could have looked after them properly anyway, he was always so wrapped up in his work. I don't think many people realise what it's like, to suffer in a nervous way, to be frightened and not know what you're doing. I did feel as if everyone was against me, and I didn't feel the marital therapy was any good although the person was very nice. If Jerry could have been more a man, just stuck with it and got on with it all would have been well. I've had a struggle since he left but I have made a go of things. I think I was very unlucky in my marriage and I am still angry about what happened. I don't think I'll get over it and I don't think I'll try marriage again; there's been no one since Jerry.

HOW FAMILIES, SPOUSES AND FRIENDS CAN HELP THEMSELVES

1   If you can't talk to your spouse or share cooperatively what is happening, try to find a confidant with whom you can talk in trust and safety. Good friends and strong members of the family can be so very useful and can offer just simple hints on how to cope, what might help. Though it may not be anywhere near the ultimate answer, it always is good to share a difficulty and to remove the isolation. Isolation by itself can make people feel very stuck and depressed. Once a problem is shared, the energy in you is changed, and you may well find that new thoughts get opened up.

2   If you can take an active part in what is happening you may find that it is a learning phase for you too, that you grow in a way you couldn't imagine beforehand.

3   Talking to a professional can also help, perhaps the professional involved in helping your friend or family member. Some people feel shy of approaching professionals and, like Ann, feel embarrassment lest they get blamed for the problem. Just being willing to share and think about how you can help is a major contribution, and professionals or people helping will be able to direct your energies in the way appropriate.

4   You may find reading useful: any of the books or leaflets

suggested throughout this book for specific problems may be helpful. Organisations specially set up to help families may also be good points of contact. For example the organisation Al Anon has proved to be invaluable for the families and spouses of people with an alcohol problem, and all the organisations, especially those set up by sufferers and their families, are always sympathetic to callers from within a family.

5   Don't suffer alone. Choose your moment and person and take the plunge.

6   Remember that you may well feel angry, fed up and exasperated by what is happening and that this is to be expected. No one should desire to be saintly, ever-smiling and turning the other cheek, when inside they are smouldering and furious. The fury will always come out in other ways. It is very difficult to be cross with a person who is ill, especially a person suffering in a 'nervous' way with something that's maybe difficult to understand. But people who are ill still have the capacity to make us cross and we sometimes need permission to be ordinary, to be allowed to speak about our ordinary feelings. We may also be frightened: we don't know what's going on. It's not like an operation which has a predictable course and outcome but we need somehow to hang on to a belief that the person will get through the difficult phase and that we will too.

7   Anything that you can do which bolsters your own confidence and belief in life will be vital for you to keep going during this time. Your own 'safe places', your own friends, interests, rituals, time to yourself, these are all extremely important for everyone.

8   Know that you may feel guilty, cross, alienated, stuck, furious and helpless. Know and expect it. Don't expect yourself to be superman or woman. Know that all you can do is your very best, from what you know, and that you can try to find help, understanding and support that is within the scope appropriate for you.

9   Find one or two things that work and stick to them. Try not to get confused by the variety of advice or old wives' tales available.

10 Aim to be sympathetic but confident. If you are seen to take things on confidently so will other people, and so will your spouse or friend. Life isn't one long, smooth path and these times are difficult and strange, but if we go with it like a campaign or a

process we will win through, and we will look back with surprise and added strengths. You may notice how nostalgic people often are about times of crisis they have come through. This is because it is during those times we learn about ourselves, we find places we didn't know we had, we surprise ourselves and we feel good about this afterwards.

9

Where do I go for help?

As we have seen from the stories in this book, the person to whom we go first in our search for answers is very important. Their response can be the beginning of a fruitful journey or it can send us off at a tangent. Who we consult depends a great deal on what is available in our area and on the sort of person we are. Also, we often don't know what it is we need, let alone have the words to ask for it. This section looks at some of the different professionals who come into contact with people breaking down. You may be inspired to seek help in a certain direction for yourself, or for someone close to you.

Most breakdowns are prolonged so there is time to consider the help that you need: don't panic and take the first option. Sometimes making choices about what is best for us is too much of a burden, too difficult, and when we are vulnerable emotionally we are not always able to make decisions for the best. The assistance of a trusted friend or family member to help us look for what we need can be useful. If this is not available, read this next section, not with your head, but with your heart; and use your feelings to inform you what kind of approach to your problems might be the most suitable.

THE GENERAL PRACTITIONER

The importance of visiting your GP first if you are troubled and feel you could be heading for a breakdown is to get yourself checked out physically, and to make a start on finding the help you need. Your journey may stop there, or it may branch out into supportive counselling or therapy, alongside the medical help.

Doctors are trained to look at the body first – what is going on physiologically. This is always useful, because in any search for understanding what is going on with our life as a whole, we need to be able to rule out actual physical disorders, or get them sorted out. One of the difficulties however is that when we are under internal stress we often produce physical symptoms; and, physical illness is sometimes part of our breakdown journey. General practitioners now have to complete a special training to work as a GP and this gives opportunities to take other courses in psychologically related areas such as psychosexual counselling, marital work, family dynamics and psychosomatic disorders. Many GPs are now adding to their work some of the approaches from what is known as 'alternative' medicine, acupuncture, homeopathy, herbal medicine. The advantage of this is that the approach to symptoms is to see them in the context of the individual life of the sufferer rather than from some disease model. Many family doctors who have worked in the same area for many years know their patients and their families, and the circumstances under which they are all living. In this context it is possible for a GP to use his or her wisdom and compassion about what might be happening in their patients' lives. I talked to a number of doctors about their approach to breakdown. One of them, Dr. Norman Paros, is a family doctor in Essex and is also very involved in the St. John Ambulance movement:

> A common presentation in general practice is something we call TATT – tired all the time – it's very, very common: 'I feel ill doctor.' It really is difficult because you have to make sure there is no physical illness, and sometimes there is a more deep-seated and profound anxiety, what we call endogenous depression ... there in the person, often inherited and which comes out in the person all throughout their life, sometimes severely and which has to be managed. The fear of illness ... this is so common these days, we've built up a nation of people who are terrified of illness and rush to the doctor as if they have leukaemia or something.
>
> Everything you see in general practice is stress triggered in one way or another. A young woman came in today. I've known her since she was a child. She said 'I can't stop ... I just can't stop ... all day ...

there's nothing much to do but whatever I do I have to do it over and over again and by the evening I'm absolutely smashed and I go to bed exhausted and so my sex life is all over and I can't get up in the morning and I feel I haven't been to sleep and once I start I can't stop again, doctor.' And that was really her reaction. She's quite a stable person but she has reacted in a big way: they are buying a house, there's a mortgage and her husband is working six days a week to pay it and she's got a two hour job every evening after her husband has got home and can sit with the kids. I asked 'When did you last have a break?' and she said 'We haven't had one for three years, we can't afford it.' So we spent a long, long time talking about this. She was at the beginning of a possible breakdown but she's an intelligent young woman, she knew something was going on and we talked and turned it into laughter and there was no depression in her. Her reaction to life was making her ill.

I spend a lot of time with my trainees teaching them to be aware of clinical depression: the early morning waking, the inability to concentrate or to cope, the retardation of thought, loss of personality, loss of appetite, variations in mood, loss of humour and laughter. At the same time, people can be smiling depressives, they can give you one picture when there is something more serious going on. I teach that suicidal thoughts are a medical emergency, must be dealt with without delay, because half the people who commit suicide have seen their GP during the previous fortnight. It's very hard to teach young doctors, who have been in their white coats and walking up and down the ward importantly, to be aware of these personal things.

You can make diagnosis if you listen to the patient in 60 per cent of cases, including clinical illness. Suppose you came to me with indigestion. If I listened as a GP, and I said take this bottle of medicine and go away, that would be a 3 minute thing; but if I spent 20 minutes listening to you as a person, to what you were saying, I would be able to make a full diagnosis.

One of the commonest things we deal with is housewife stress – at least that's what I call it. It's a young woman with two young children, husband goes out at 7 am and doesn't come back until 7 at night and leaves her in a state. The houses on either side are shut up all day because everyone's gone to work. She's got two children and they're pulling at her ... mummy, mummy ... and she can't even go to the toilet without them. She comes into the surgery and says she finds herself standing at the sink like the Pumpkin Eater, tears running down her face, and she finds herself smacking and smacking her children. She's not psychotic or mentally ill, she doesn't need anti-depressants. What she's suffering from is her life. She needs to be able to talk to someone, to be relieved of her worry, and a good doctor can help there because she will probably believe him.

People come in to general practice for support ... it's very important. You know you're not doing anything dramatic and they know you're not doing anything dramatic – it's the continuity and contact that matters. If someone has a breakdown I might say to them 'I think you're having a nervous breakdown', it depends on what I think is the best way to approach things. But I do play it down if I can, especially with employers or insurance companies: I just say it's a reaction to a divorce, for example, especially when the person involved is basically OK, he or she has a good personality. There are some people of course who are always vulnerable, always suppressing the stress of life. In our area we can refer patients directly to a psychologist who works with a psychiatric nurse and can make an assessment about the patient's state. It is so much better than having to go through a psychiatrist: they don't have to wait so long and it can be very informal.

Another big part of general practice is the management of phobic anxiety: helping patients and their families to set up a programme of simple behaviour training. If somebody can't go out I make them walk to the end of the path and then they walk to the nearest lamp-post and then to the end of the road. I get somebody to be at the end of the road to meet them. I get the family in on this, and then I say you're going into town on the bus and your husband will be at Marks and Spencers or at the bus stop.

I think that life is getting more stressful, much more stressful, and these problems for people are increasing; and of course we're much more aware of them. I think the general medical training now does prepare doctors more fully for these kinds of things.

I ask him about breakdown to breakthrough, and he reacts enthusiastically.

One man who had come through a prolonged breakdown said to me recently 'I've only just realised how ill I've been, and how much better I now feel. I can be objective and look back on my life and where I've been. I feel as if a door has opened on my life and I'm coming through.

I'd like to give you a quotation to end with. I often tell people who are having breakdowns that they've been in the trenches too long. And quote to them about chaps in the trenches in World War One. They were OK but when they got back to the rest area then they would break down. You can screw yourself up for so long but in the end something's got to give.

Now, in 1992, Dr Paros is retired but still working with patients. He says, smiling sadly, 'I wish people would open their hearts more.'

If you are lucky enough to have a GP who knows you, has known your family and who has an understanding and flexible approach, you are likely to get all the help you need to begin with. If you have read this book before going to your GP, pick out anything that you feel applies to you and write it down. Make a list of what you want to say in order of priority, or get someone else to help you with it if you don't feel up to it. When you've made the list pick out five main points that you'd like dealt with and go along to your GP armed with this. Most GPs welcome an informed approach from their patients, as long as it doesn't come over bossy and demanding.

Some GPs on the other hand want total control and resent any self-help. If you have a GP like this don't avoid him altogether but see if you can work out just what he or she will be able to give you, given the limitations. It may just be medication and an appointment with a specialist. If you feel that this is appropriate to your needs then it may be possible to use this particular resource, but it is important not to expect anything else. A time of crisis is not the time to try to change a doctor's attitude. And so we have seen from the stories throughout this book, some GPs are not sympathetic to people under life stress: they view their professional work as to do with medicine and curing diseases only. You can of course change your doctor and should endeavour to do so if you are being poorly served, or transfer to another doctor within the practice.

THE PSYCHIATRIST

As with other professionals, psychiatrists are a variable breed. Some are interested only in pills and ECT while, at the other end of the spectrum, some are psychodynamically and psychotherapeutically orientated. A course in psychotherapy is now strongly recommended in psychiatric training and the kinds of courses vary within different areas. Psychiatrists with a more therapeutic approach will be more accessible in terms of understanding and communication, and will tend not to use psychiatric terms rigidly. Terms such as paranoid, psychotic or schizophrenic, which so often tend to stick, can lumber a person with the label and its associated stigma, affecting job prospects, relationships and future visits to outpatients departments. Because psychiatrists are medically trained they look for physical problems which can be treated chemically. This is a special art, and a psychiatrist with a holistic view will be able to place the disorder within the context of the person's whole life. In any individual there may be a part of the person which appears psychotic, disturbed or paranoid; it is a part, not the whole, although at times the disturbed part may eclipse the rest. Breakdown may include disturbed, psychotic or paranoid phases, but it is important that this is seen as a part of the person's experience and not the sum total of the journey.

Dr. Anthony Fry was formerly Consultant Physician in Psychological Medicine at Guy's Hospital, and deputy chairman of the British Holistic Medicine Association. The author of *Safe Space*, he is currently Consultant Psychiatrist at The London Bridge Hospital and Charter Nightingale Clinic.

> For a psychiatrist there are different kinds of breakdown. I'm not so much concerned with the fact that somebody has broken down but as to why they've broken down, why they've stopped functioning. There are as many reasons for breaking down as there are psychiatric diagnoses, from the breakdown of a mother after the birth of a new baby or a reactive breakdown triggered by a life event to an attack of psychotic illness. A very important question for a psychiatrist is 'Is there a history of mental disorder or nervous disorder in your family?' and the common answer is very often 'my uncle had a nervous breakdown in the war' or 'my mother had a nervous breakdown after the birth of her fourth child' .

246

My training in diagnosis is to ask what is the cause: is it that life has been overwhelmingly burdensome or is the person suffering from a chemically related depressive disorder? One of the essential premises of medicine is that if you can explain the process of a disorder you can deal with it. That is not to say we should medicalise all breakdowns – I'm sure we shouldn't – but it is interesting that so many breakdowns tend to take the medical route. One of the major ways of breaking down in our society is to take an overdose: it's as if we find it quite difficult at some social level to accept breakdown, and in order to make a more dramatic statement we need our difficulty to become physical. What's fascinating about the overdose is that it turns mental turmoil into physical damage. It's as if the individual says to society or society says to the individual: 'Look, we can't take you seriously unless you're physically ill.' And having medicalised our pain – by overdose or slashed wrists or whatever – you become firmly embedded in the medicalisation of your distress and then obtain all the privileges of the sick. Whereas making a statement of crisis in other forms – of nerves – could be seen as weakness.

First you look for the cause, some explanation of what's going on. What causes my psychosis? Why do I appear anxious? Why do I not want to go out? These are legitimate questions. The next step is, why has this person broken down? Then we need to provide a whole lot of measures to contain and make safe, to make the person secure, to offer some kind of solidarity, because by definition things have fallen apart and the centre of the person cannot hold. Now a place of safety will involve effort on the part of the individual, the family and friends, and the experts. Many people I contain simply by contact with somebody they trust.

I believe in my own work very much in the concept of safety, in making people safe. In breakdown that is a particular problem, and choosing the appropriate safety according to the needs of the person is vital. For example if it was myself, if I was experiencing breakdown where the cause was that my life was overwhelmingly burdensome and painful and hurting me, then I would like some semi-religious sanctuary somewhere in the country where there was peace and meditation and tranquillity and a degree of comfort and skill. But I would be very worried if my breakdown was a severe depression of which at least a final part was probably a chemically related disorder.

I would be worried if I had that kind of breakdown and somebody sent me off to a retreat because I know (or I believe, though some might not agree) that an untreated depression can last for up to two or three years. We know that from the record of old psychiatric hospitals and in fact some people never come out. Whereas a well-treated depression can be over in eight weeks. Now of course this is blowing the trumpet of medicine, but I think as specialists we need to go beyond telling people they have had a breakdown. When you've got the diagnosis I think that friends and family can be very supportive, but there was a tendency at one stage, I feel, to expect too much of friends, perhaps to burden them in a way that did so much damage in the long term that it didn't do anyone any good. Obviously if someone is in danger, is trying to mutilate or injure themselves, then they should if possible have some sort of material change or move to a hospital or nursing home. Facilities in the Health Service are very variable: some are very good, some leave a lot to be desired and in some places more is needed.

I think different cultural groups in society expect different things, though I know that this is changing rapidly. One person with a breakdown would want to go into a hospital with nurses in uniforms, another would wish to stay at home and see a counsellor and yet another might want something different. One of the great problems that arises in our society, with all its subcultures, particularly in different language areas, is trying to provide appropriate care for everyone. I do have the feeling that the ambiance of the buildings where people go for care is a very important thing. If you are having a breakdown and you go into a ward with 50 other people and several of them are screaming, it can be so unsettling that it makes you feel worse than when you went in there. Whereas if you are in a room with two or three people and you have a sense of peace and private space then I think you have a better chance. My ideal would be a spectrum of care, offering medical care in the very severe cases. I still think that does work and is appropriate for people with psychoses, drug-induced disorders, and so on. And then a sort of half-way house after that which can be a hostel-type environment with small houses and counselling, and after that a way of moving back into the community. I think it's important to have a healthy independent sector where people can pick and choose: there are many groups who have special needs; some people have strong religious beliefs and want support there, some want to see a woman therapist, and so on. It is so very important not to oversimplify.

I think it's terribly important to break the myth that people who break down are weak and pathetic and so on. I don't think breakdown and madness are synonymous ... sometimes breakdown can be the prelude to madness but I don't really like the word. It's dramatic and heavily loaded. I prefer 'losing control' or 'succumbing'. The stigma that the myth about breakdown and madness tends to have in our culture is a way of people distancing themselves from the fear they have of these things. It's a way of saying 'I can handle it, this won't happen to me, I'm not like that'. This whole area is a great problem for people: lots of people are fed up with having it put on their medical records. When I ask people 'When did you last work?' and they say 'Two years ago', I ask 'Why haven't you worked?' and they will say 'Because I've had a mental breakdown, my job prospects are gone.' A lot of patients simply don't admit their history to employers and take that risk because they're fed up with being treated as second class citizens. Only in a few cases is there a serious risk of someone breaking down again.

Breakdown is a communication to other people which may not be permissible in any other way because of culture, family, morals and so on. And breakdown can be a communication to yourself. What we have to do in psychiatry is to get out what it is, to retell the story of the life in a different way, because somehow we have a suspicion that the person is not telling it as it is. Now discovering who you are and where you are is something that can happen through a mystical happening, through a meeting with a special person, through a symbolic experience or through the enlightenment of a doctor. One doesn't want to be oversentimental about breakdowns, some of them are just unpleasant, damaging and so on. Some people very unfortunately are loaded with some tendency to break down more readily than others. But there are a lot of people for whom a breakdown can be a very constructive and rejuvenating experience.

THE 'AGONY AUNT'

Many people who are too shy or unprepared to go to their GPs for help will write to an 'agony aunt'. Many people write or phone in to help lines because they do not feel they are getting the help they need. Agony aunts and help lines do offer a very important resource for people to express themselves and to reach for the help they need. Very often, after talking on the radio or writing to an agony aunt, people begin to feel better: they have begun to put what they are feeling into words.

Claire Rayner is a well known and experienced agony aunt with a great deal of feeling and compassion for people and a deep sense of responsibility which she brings to her work.

My definition of the term 'nervous breakdown' is non-coping, whatever the situation. In some people it's due to a broken leg, in others a severe anxiety attack or panic, or it may be a severe depression when the person withdraws completely. I prefer to call the experience a non-coping crisis. I know the professionals never use it but the patients do. Breakdown is a very good term ... we *do* break down. What worries me is the attaching of 'nervous' in front of it. This makes it sound as if you have technical damage to your nervous system which is a very precise, a specific physiological and anatomical set-up: it makes people think they are really nervous in the pejorative sense of highly strung. Some find that an offensive term, though others hide behind it.

Coping skills are so important. If I could do one thing to improve life in this country I would have built into the syllabus one essential O Level subject along with the English Language and Maths. I would include Social Skills, not because I think it's easy to teach but because if it was in the bloody syllabus they would start to teach it. I'd also like parenting – how to be a parent – to be included.

My mail comes from men and women. I find the Rahe scale of stress very useful because it puts across the idea that stress comes from being successful as well as from terrible disasters. People can understand that bereavement is a bad experience – they can handle it because they know it's meant to hurt. They know and they give themselves permission to be miserable but if they win the Pools or pass an examination, if then they don't feel well, it's monumental.

I speak from total personal experience here. I wrote a book called 'Gower Street'. I'd been coping very nicely with my life – tolerably nicely because I'd had a bad time as a child. Out of the blue I had a call from America one very exciting day which I won't forget, telling me I'd sold the paperback rights of my book for a quarter of a million dollars, which was a lot of money. It was a complete wrench in both our lifestyles. Des's job was no longer crucial to our income: he could do his own thing, which in fact he did. That was a massive change. Very wisely we decided we'd keep the house. The only thing we did was to spend £200 on duvets for every bed in the house. But in the next six months I went into a hypochondriacal state which nearly drove me dotty. I had headaches, not just headaches, I had brain tumours, meningitis, I thought. For six months I managed to sit on the stress, to control it, I knew perfectly well what was going on but I had six months of intense anxiety. I coped in the end. I just kept on working and eventually the newness of it died away and the anxiety too. If you've always had your head geared to a certain income and suddenly it goes way up and you have to make new parameters, new patterns, it seems difficult to do so. I could have broken down but I didn't.

I asked her 'Why didn't you?', 'What stopped you?', 'What helped?'

What helped was years and years of practice at covering up. I had a rough time as a child. I have this theory though I could be wrong! You need to have it rotten at some time in your life and there's a lot to be said for having it when you're young, because it helps you cope with some of the problems when you're older, because you've had the training. I'd been taught painfully, one way and another, to conceal pain, to cover up inadequacies, to develop strategies when I'd have loved to scream and shout.

A good friend of mine said to me years ago 'It's all right for you, Claire, you've made your neuroses work for you' and I think he was right. I think this is what attracted me to the people I write for, talk to or whatever. If you can invest the time, not to mention the money and dig out the sources of your pain, it helps, but learning to live with it is a lot more important. People need different ways to achieve different things. There's a phrase which often crops up in my letters which fascinates me, it explains why so many people turn to food. People say 'I feel so empty' over and over again.

Even semi-literate people refer to this in their letters; people who can barely express themselves. I also get a lot of letters from people using jargon. When I was doing the 'Casebook' series so many people bobbed up who'd learned the 'psycho-babble' language and were hiding behind it, so unreal it was impossible to communicate.

'I'm going to start at the beginning' people say and of course they do, detail after detail, 30 or 40 pages about their father complex and soon I want to say 'Piffle' and 'Now tell me what you *feel*, not what you think you feel – that doesn't help. It's what you feel not what people say you feel that's important.' If their misery gets desperate enough they may be prepared to shift their ground slightly. If they're able to contain their misery just enough by using the old methods they'll go on using them, but if it gets really bad, they will have to change.

Claire feels there are very few places for people to go who feel they might be breaking down or who cannot cope with life.

The first stage is your GP. If you're lucky you may have one of the younger GPs who's had training in this area. There are some group practices which will have a psychotherapist attached to them but there are still far too many GPs who haven't any idea of treating the whole patient.

The next stage is to step outside the NHS and seek counselling. Agony Aunts have done a good job in that we've spread the idea that counselling exists and is a Good Thing, and telling people how to get it. The simplest way is to pick up a phone and dial a Samaritan – they're marvellous. They don't have to do good, they just listen and it's a good beginning. There's Marriage Guidance; I send everyone to Marriage Guidance for everything, they have a network for dealing with relationship problems that includes the relationship with the self which is the first and most important. It's a bit rough on them because they're very short of resources.

Many people are referred to group therapy, not because it's best for them but because it's best for the system. But there are a lot of people who shrivel and die at the thought of group therapy. I couldn't do it – the All Girls Together bit isn't for me. However some thrive on it and it's right for them.

I send a lot of people to some very good medically-trained hypnotherapists. I've a lot of time for hypnotherapy because, in medically qualified hands, it is a short-cut. Very often if you treat the distressing symptom, you haven't altered the cause of the symptom; but if you can get rid of the symptom then the person can get to grips with the problem underneath without concentrating on the symptom.

Hospitalisation poses problems sometimes, especially for young people put into a psychiatric ward full of very disturbed people. I had a girl working for me once to whom this happened and who went into a mental hospital and learned all sorts of florid sickness tricks, who, when life got hard, threw another 'madness' fit. She wasn't mad at all … it was her way of coping. It's also frightening. Mixed subject wards? This may be a terribly involved management difficulty and I'm not sure how you resolve it. Maybe it would be resolved by not putting all one kind of illness together. I don't see why, in the average medical ward, you couldn't put two or three people who are schizophrenic, catatonic or whatever together because keeping them like that would be much less strain on the staff. Patients like that would benefit by being surrounded by 'normality'. I don't like the idea of psychiatric wards as such. I don't see why there couldn't be general wards where some people's illness might be predominantly physical and some people's predominantly psychiatric, and vice versa. In my nursing days you got used to this idea. For example, someone who had a stroke was admitted to a general ward. This was not unusual and the patients were perhaps disturbed but they accepted it and the demented patient coped better than if he had been surrounded by 20 or 30 others in the same state. It also meant that you could look after him individually. I think psychiatric and general patients in general care can cope. We have begun to have male and female patients in one ward so why not psychiatric and physical ones?

I then asked Claire: 'What do you feel about the concept of breaking up to break through?'

Oh yes. I tell people this often. It's the same in a perfectly normal, happy set-up. It's what you do with your children. To help your children grow up you've got to break up the child/Mummy and Daddy bit, the dependent/needing to be relied on kind of relationship – you've got to break that up in order to emerge on the other side in a new relationship which is based on equality and friendship. There's something terribly wrong if as a woman of 30 you still act towards your mother as if you were ten. Breaking up to break through makes total sense.

A lot of helpers are terrified of breaking up. They fear it in their own lives. It was quite a breakthrough for the Marriage Guidance Council when they started teaching their counsellors that their job wasn't just to try to preserve a marriage – it was to help people break up with a minimum of acrimony and pain. Very often a therapist, or for that matter a friend, has to preside at a breakdown: not saying 'There, there' or 'It'll be all right' or trying to advise, but just listening. There's also, with regard to breaking up, this human idea that there is something *wrong* if you want a change, instead of seeing it as a normal, healthy, necessary part of life – and also, there's all sorts of fear of letting go of anything. We should really all make a much wider listening space for everything that happens.

CRISIS

Sometimes we find ourselves in the middle of a crisis and we need help immediately. Some professionals work at the crisis end of breakdown. Sally Berry helped to found the Arbours Crisis Centre in London 15 years ago and helped set up one of the residential homes organised by Arbours. She also works for the Women's Therapy Centre.

Crisis is often a turning point. We try to hold the situation and take in the whole of what is happening, the whole family if possible. Sometimes people are eager to get in touch with the crisis centre when they don't know what to do with people. We try to get people to stay within their setting as much as possible. Obviously if the support system isn't working any more, as when someone is being psychotic, we would take that person into the centre for a while. Medication is no treatment, but there are people whom one cannot contact without medication. I try to get in touch with the part of the person who wants to get well, however disturbed the rest of them might be. I have to see who they were and who they may be. We have the crisis centre and other long term residential places for people who need this.

Mothers are a big group who break down, also people with difficult relationships and adolescents who cannot make the break from home. People experience terrible fear and loneliness. The cultural impact is important: somehow people are not so upset when men stop doing things – they are allowed not to function – but women are not allowed to stop their labours; what gets communicated is that they're irresponsible. When a woman stops, this can trigger off a crisis for a man. Mothers lack acknowledgement for the stress they are under, the impossibility of being a parent. Since the Women's Therapy Centre has opened we get hundreds of letters from women who are so isolated: the possibility that they could come together as a group is wonderful, that they are not so alone.

It is easy to help someone break down and people can easily come apart. It is much more difficult to reconstruct something viable and valuable on the other side of the breakdown – to actually build new aspects, to learn new ways or take the risk of allowing something which has been in eclipse to come through.

There must be places of safety and refuge, where people are allowed to be without intrusion or someone telling them what's happening to them. I think that people do know what's happening to them. I'd like to see and teach a whole group of people to make psychotherapy available. To teach people what it is they can make use of. If people knew more about it and how it works it would perhaps become more available.

Crisis can be like a band aid – you have it, get patched up and go out and experience it all again. The chances for a person are not so good if it keeps on happening and managing might not be such a good thing. It may be a lucky thing to be so disturbed that we breakdown and get a real chance for things to be better. Otherwise we may keep on breaking down and getting patched up for a limited time and the possibility of reconstructing a life gets more and more limited. As we get older we get less malleable; if serious breakdown had happened 15 years earlier we might have had a chance to do something, to change, to let out what's in there. People are not going to get out of their cycles doing the hospital route. New approaches do work and I feel we must try.

In our long term communities people become like an extended family and the job they have is to live there. That's it. Whatever happens day and night has to be constructed by them. The house is deliberately not like a hospital it s hard sometimes to be with yourself and no one telling you what to do. People learn something new then.

I believe in the positive value of crises, people can make fantastic use of them. There is an extraordinarily exciting potential and movement which could never happen in any other way.

COUNSELLING, PSYCHOTHERAPY AND ANALYSIS

Having started your journey on the medical route and obtained a diagnosis, you may decide to stay within these boundaries and be well served by them. However, there may be many kinds of questions you are carrying which you would like time to share with another human being, preferably trained in the art of listening and helping. Your GP or psychiatrist may put you in touch with other people trained as therapists or counsellors and they could include social workers, psychiatric nurses, doctors, occupational therapists or psychologists, who all work within the National Health Service.

At the present time there is very little therapy or counselling available within the National Health Service. Some departments of psychiatry in hospitals do have departments of psychotherapy and this is easily found out. Some areas have health clinics where a psychologist who may be trained in counselling or psychotherapy is employed. Sometimes contact with an individual on a regular basis within the medical framework does work out to be healing and beneficial. Other times contact is broken because of health workers' contracts or because the overstretched state of the Health Service means that appointments are cancelled or units are closed down.

If there are no resources for therapy in your area you may have to look outside the Health Service. There are several ways of finding out what services are available, what they offer and what is involved. Some areas have counselling services run by volunteers for crisis work, with professionals who give their services free. Some are funded by local grant aid and some are charitable trusts. Your GP will be aware of the presence of these centres and so will your local Citizens Advice Bureau and local library. In many areas the church offers counselling services, not necessarily affiliated to particular religious beliefs. Alternatively you could write to MIND (see Useful addresses, p. 275).

Once outside the National Health and in the private sector you might find looking for a therapist or an organisation which runs courses that might suit you is a bit like going on an exploratory shopping trip unless you know someone who has information about what is available and what it is like. There are many different kinds of counselling, psychotherapy and analysis available and they are all extremely varied in approach and method. If you have decided that you would like some therapeutic help it is essential to find out something beforehand of what is being offered. A very useful guide to the different therapies is Lindsay Knight's *Talking to a stranger*. Your local library will have a copy. This sets out in reasonable detail an outline of the different therapies and interviews people who have experienced them.

From my experience, one of the most fundamentally important needs of someone who has suffered a breakdown and is at the dethawing and rebuilding stages is to have continuity with one individual or a group of individuals who remain constant. When someone's inner and outer life has been shattered by a breakdown they need this safe, dependable time to learn to trust themselves, and to trust themselves in life again. The managing skills people can be taught – assertion, social skills, coping, behavioural techniques – are all useful, but only if backed up by the foundation of regular human contact. As we have seen from this book, people tend to break down because the ground in which their original seed has been planted was not conducive to its intended healthy growth. What people need is something near to the appropriate ground they were unable to have so that their roots can settle and their growth be encouraged, fed, watered, nurtured and cherished. Sometimes we don't need all that much, and it is surprising how little people can use of the right kind of encouragement to help themselves recover and grow. But a shifting hotchpotch of different people only exacerbates someone's fragility and keeps them near their breakdown state. For a severe breakdown an individual needs to be able to process what has happened in the safety and confidentiality of a therapeutic alliance with a trained professional.

Before you start looking for help you might like to consider the nature of the different approaches you may come across. The first step in looking for a therapist is to seek out an experienced person who will offer you an assessment and help you look at what you need and what is available, and will explain the procedures and cost involved. It tends to be more useful to find a professional who belongs to an organised body with a code of ethics and colleague supervision. This way you are more likely to get the support and care you need on a serious professional level. Because therapy is not yet subject to certification nationally, anyone can say they are a therapist or counsellor and anyone can advertise in newspapers and shop windows. Some of these people may indeed be helpful, but if you feel you may be approaching a breakdown or know that you have had a breakdown, take it seriously and go through orthodox channels – your GP, psychiatrist or go to one of the nationally recognised bodies with a wealth and history of experience.

Counselling

This covers many different areas: marriage counselling, employment counselling, crisis counselling and so on. It differs from psychotherapy in that the sessions are usually once a week and the work tends to be in the 'here and now' and can involve problem solving techniques; also counselling tends not to last as long (in months or years) as psychotherapy. However there are counsellors who work analytically or psychodynamically, offering a deeper understanding of the psyche and working with the unconscious as well as with conscious forces. As we have seen, in a breakdown we are subject to many unconscious forces which we will need to accept, sometimes befriend and certainly understand. For this reason, counsellors trained with the more in-depth approach will be more help than those working on the more superficial level. This does not discount the enormous value of talking to another person regularly and in confidence, and if this is all that is available, then it may be the one appropriate step forward. Some people are greatly helped by counselling and then become ready to move to a deeper approach with a psychotherapist or analyst.

Psychotherapy

Psychotherapists will have trained with one of the nationally recognised training bodies for psychotherapy. This will include their own psychotherapy, usually three or four times a week for three or more years, and seeing clients for therapy under supervision for two or three years before they are qualified. Psychotherapy can offer sessions from once a week up to five times a week, but tends to concentrate within the once to three times a week period. Sessions tend to last 50 minutes and the therapist and client work together on issues produced by the person's inner life, their outer relationships and on the relationship between therapist and client which tends to constellate some of the client's inner conflicts.

The theoretical approaches behind counselling and psychotherapy

1 The *Freudian* approach tends to be focused on the early years and conflicts with parents. Freud discovered the unconscious and tended to view it as a kind of dustbin into which all matter from early life got dumped. The task of therapeutic work was to deal with the dustbin.
2 A *Jungian* approach, based on the work of Carl Jung, tends to view the unconscious as a compost of potential rather than a dustbin to be sorted out. His view is more positive because he felt that everything that happens to us has a meaning.
3 A *Kleinian* approach will tend to concentrate on our early relationship with mothering, and how as an infant we responded to the good, bad or the good enough aspects of mother.
4 An *Adlerian* approach will focus on our place and significance within the family, our urge towards inferiority or superiority, and social groups.
5 A *humanistic* approach is based on the work of psychologists and therapists in the post-Freudian, post-Jungian eras. They concentrate on the person at the centre of the process of his or her life. Humanistic approaches may include working with the body as in bioenergetic therapy; or working in an active way as with psychodrama, or gestalt.
6 A *transpersonal* approach will include the dimension of man as a spiritual being – a dimension that includes but transcends personality. This approach will work with the individual language and inner world of images and symbols that can be uncovered by active imagination or guided fantasy.

259

7 A *behavioural* approach concentrates on making a plan to change behaviour, in particular phobic behaviour, and will tend to work to a specific plan worked out between therapist and client.

8 A *cognitive* approach will work the way in which a person thinks about and perceives his or her world and offers strategies to change this if it has become negative or problematic.

Some therapies include dance, drama, painting, drawing or acting out; they may include massage, touch, hypnotism, colour or dream work; or they may work on the management of stress, autogenic training, training in self-hypnosis, lifestyle planning and so on. But these methods should be ancillary to the basic relationship between the therapist and client. They are useful skills when used appropriately within the safe context of the main body of work, which is what happens between the two people in the therapeutic alliance and in the process which evolves from the meetings of the two, and the unknown force, that of the journey each are making.

Many counsellors and therapists work with a combination of all these approaches, or they may be traditionally based in one way of working and stick to it rigidly. Therapy is still a young art with its accompanying mixture of science. A good therapist will work with the needs and the individual way of the client, and it will be the client's process which will govern the passage of therapy.

Analysis

Many analysts now work in a psychotherapeutic way but traditionally analysis is divided into three main streams.

Psychoanalysis is based on the work of Freud. Clients tend to be called patients, and usually do their therapeutic work lying on a couch with the analyst interpreting what is being said. *Analytical psychology* is based on the work of C.G. Jung.

Analysis is a much longer process than psychotherapy or counselling, although sometimes the latter two do continue for as long. But by tradition, analysis is a process where the person's journey gradually unfolds within the space and time of the analytic framework. It tends to be a costly process as well as lengthy, but, when completed satisfactorily, is an extremely beneficial experience. When embarking on a journey of this length and commitment it is very important to feel you have found the right analyst. To get the personal trust, liking and individual chemistry right for you is vital, and worth looking for.

Some people feel that analysis is the elite of all the therapies, and many analysts themselves claim that this is so. I do not feel that this is necessarily true. A long analysis with a person not quite right can be much worse than a short psychotherapy with someone who is good enough. Analysis also claims to 'go deeper' than any other therapy, but this may not necessarily be so. Some people, who have had to become very defended in order to protect themselves when they were very small, do need time and safety from which to begin to let go of some of their defences and begin to feel closer to another and to themselves. On the other hand, some of us carry wounds which go very deep, and no amount of time close to another person will make up for past losses. Learning how to carry the wounds we have can be achieved by a period of good psychotherapy.

No therapy should aim dogmatically or rigidly to 'cure' or 'change' because this presumes a model of what should be 'right' and of how people should behave. At its worst, therapy which insinuates an idealised model of 'getting to the bottom of every single disturbance' stimulates a sense of inferiority in the person seeking help, and at the same time can stir up an almost obsessional seeking for what is felt to be enough, which can take over a person's life and dominate them for many years. Therapists are only stepping stones, guides sometimes, midwives at best, who are there to help us understand some of our wounds, to alleviate some of the suffering and to work on strengthening the self inside. Ultimately we go into life on our own. Therapy should never replace life, nor should it make people search endlessly for what might fill them up enough.

Therapy is firstly permission to have an inner life. Secondly to learn to value it through the sharing. Thirdly to become intimate with it. Fourthly to let it show us how to live.

Resources

Medication

DO I NEED IT AND WHAT DRUGS ARE WHAT?

Over the last thirty years the drug industry has changed the face of psychiatry. Doctors and psychiatrists have now a wide-ranging number of drugs to prescribe for their patients. Drugs have different effects on different people. Most people do not like taking medication, they do not trust it or want to become dependent on it. As a psychotherapist I do not prescribe drugs but many of the people I see are taking medication when they begin their therapy. I have mixed feelings about the value of prolonged medication. In the short term, well-chosen drugs picked by a thoughtful psychiatrist who has got to know something of the ways and temperament of the patient can be invaluable. In some cases medication is vital. Severely depressive, manic and obsessional states are intolerable, and make the individual inaccessible to human contact. In these instances medication helps the person to feel sufficiently restored to communicate. But when medication is over-subscribed and goes on for too long, either out of panic at the severity of the symptoms or because it suits the ward routine, the person becomes cut off from their natural reactions and feelings, can become blocked and stupefied like a zombie and cut off from any dream or imaginative life that is not drug-induced.

There is a vast difference in talking with someone when they have weaned themselves off drugs compared to when they are living in a pill-induced world. Some therapists will not work with people on medication. I prefer to work alongside this problem, to see the person

at different times of the day, and see the difference between their pre-
and post-pill times, and to try to encourage that part of the person who
is ready or needs to stop taking the medication. People usually need
help and it is very rewarding to see how different and free a person
can be without medication. Finding the right medication at times of
real need is an art in itself. Used wisely and with the backing of
experience medication can play an important part in recovering from
overpowering symptoms and breakdown.

PILLS AS 'TALISMAN'

Drugs can become a talisman to doctor and patient. The doctor may
view his work as unfinished unless he gives his patient a prescription
to take away and the patient in turn may not feel he is getting proper
treatment unless it is housed in a pill or capsule form. I find that drugs
become very important to people who feel they have nothing much in
their lives.

Drugs become a passport to the hospital community and to the
position as patient – somebody's patient, belonging to someone. Drugs
give people a reason to go to the clinic or the chemist or the hospital
outpatients or pharmacy: they give them a right of passage into
another world. I know a woman whose anti-depressant drugs sat on
her kitchen table so that her husband would see that she needed
looking after, so that he would notice her and take more interest.

In terms of prescribing we have to trust and rely on the knowledge
of the medical profession and each person will vary in their approach.
When I first started working in the Health Service as a therapist in a
psychiatric outpatients I had one or two angry customers who were
hoping to be given something tangible from me: advice about what to
do, or what to say to their angry partners. When I started trying to
get to know them, to understand their lives more and find out what
they felt and thought inside themselves, I got several horrified remarks
like 'Oh you mean I've got to do it all myself?'. People often felt let
down and unsupported. Pills can infantalise us: they can make us
dependent upon them without harnessing other aspects of our person.

It is not surprising that drugs have been produced in the age we are
living. They are on the one hand a magnificent product of a
technological age and they do have wonderful effects on some

illnesses, but unwisely used they also help to maintain a state of inner loneliness and a belief that something outside can make that inner state better. This ignores all the riches and resources that are inside everyone.

A woman who feels her husband does not appreciate her existence can be helped to reach out in her life in an effective way. But if she gets used to the magic potion given by the 'God' doctor she will expect a miracle and not develop within herself. At times, the talisman pill may be the only thing people have in their lives. When they are ready or are encouraged to seek appropriate help they can soon see the part the pill is playing, and let go of it when they have replaced what it represents. I have seen this happen time and time again. We should not be encouraged to give up something until we are ready, and we know what our illness, breakdown or our need to keep pills is about. Many women stay on pills far too long because they don't know how to ask for help appropriately and they fear they will not be heard. They stay in their twilight world with the pills and potions and are kept under in this way.

Medication is a definite interference in our journey in life. Many of the journeys we have seen in this book involved no medication and I have been with people who suffered from almost paralysing symptoms during their breakdown but who were able to stay with them and the support of therapy was enough. However, and this is a personal matter, some stages of a breakdown do need the intervention of medication to help us to be centred enough to cope with what is happening and to be able to talk to others or carry on with our lives. The kind of medication, and the dosage and the period of time during which the medication is taken, is crucial. I believe that everyone should know what pills are what, what possible side effects are and why they are being prescribed. I list here some of the names and purposes of commonly used drugs.

BEFORE YOU TAKE ANYTHING MAKE SURE THAT YOUR DOCTOR TELLS YOU EXACTLY WHY HE RECOMMENDS THIS PARTICULAR DRUG; WHAT IT IS FOR; WHAT SIDE EFFECTS THERE ARE; HOW LONG YOU SHOULD TAKE IT; AND WHAT THE ALTERNATIVE IS.

Medication

SOME DRUGS COMMONLY USED IN BREAKDOWN

Tricyclic anti-depressant drug group

Impramine and Amitriptyline are the oldest and best known.
AMITRIPTYLINE (Tryptizol, Lentizol, Saroten)
Usually taken in 10 mg or 25 mg doses three times a day or 50 mg at night. One at night gives the benefit of a good night's sleep without taking a hypnotic drug and morning agitation and anxiety are relieved.

Side effects

immediate: drowsiness, indigestion, dry mouth, constipation, blurred vision. Driving and alcohol should be avoided until the body has established its reaction.
long term: shaking of limbs, obesity, hypomania.

NORTRIPTYLINE (Aventyl, Allegron)
IMIPRAMINE (Tofranil, Berkomine)
Improvement of depressive symptoms is between 14 to 21 days.
CLOMIPRAMINE (Anafranil)
The only tricyclic anti-depressant which can be given intravenously, sometimes in severe depressive or obsessional states resistant to oral medication.

Side effects

immediate: flushing, hypothermia, hypotension, prolonged dry mouth, sweating, blurring of vision, nausea and vomiting.
DOXEPIN (Sinequan)
DOTHIEPIN (Prothiaden)
Sedative, anti-anxiety
MIANSERIN, NOMIFENSINE (Merital)

Phenothiazines

CHLORPROMAZINE (Largactil, Thorazine)
Usually used for severely disturbed states, for the control and

maintenance of schizophrenia, to promote appetite in anorexia nervosa, for manic states. It has a prolonged quietening effect without the impairment of consciousness.

Side effects

immediate: sedation, dizziness, dry or nasty mouth, indigestion, blurred vision.

medium term: tiredness, stiffness in legs and arms, weight gain, photo-sensitivity (sensitive to sunlight).

long term: when phenothiazines are taken continuously especially in high doses for two years or more rhythmic spontaneous movements occur, especially around the mouth and tongue, but also in the arms, legs and head. Sometimes the jerkiness stops with the stopping of the drug, but it is usually irreversible.

THIORIDAZINE (Melleril)
Given to calm agitation and restlessness. Less likely to produce jerkiness, but can produce some dizziness and muzziness.

PROMAZINE (Sparine)
Used as a tranquilliser often for the elderly.

TRIFLUOPERAZINE (Stelazine)
Used for schizophrenia, alcoholic paranoid states, hallucinosis and anxiety.

PERPHENAZINE (Fentazin)
Similar to Chlorpromazine.

FLUPHENAZINE AND FLUPHENAZINE DECANOATE (Moditen, Proloxin and Modecate)
Can be used orally or given by single injection which gives benefit for 1 to 4 weeks. Used for treatment of schizophrenia.

Side effects

Muscular stiffness and cramps, tremor and restlessness can appear in the two days after the injection and are gone after five days.

Thioxanthenes

Similar to the phenothiazines.

FLUPENTHIXOL (Fluanoxol, Depixol)
Used for anxiety and depression, for schizophrenia and for mania. Can be given orally or by injection. Fewer side effects are produced than with the phenothiazine group.

Anti-parkinsonian drugs

Sometimes drugs are given to combat the side effects produced by the phenothiazine group or by lithium carbonate, and occasionally by the tricyclic anti-depressants. They are called Anti-parkinsonian drugs, and are prescribed when the side effects are pronounced.
BENHEXOL (Artane)
BENZTROPINE (Cogentin)
PROCYCLIDINE (Kemadrm)
ORPHENADRINE (Disipal)
BIPERIDEN (Akineton)
TETRABENAZINE (Nitoman)
Each of this group also has side effects – nausea, drowsiness, dry mouth and constipation.

Monoamine Oxidase Inhibitors (MAOI)

These are often given when tricyclic anti-depressants have failed. They have a slow central nervous modifying action, changing the balance of brain functions. They combine with and activate certain enzymes. Therefore watchfulness about diet is essential. Large quantities of cheese should not be eaten, no Camembert, Stilton or processed cheeses, no Chianti and little alcohol.

Side effects

Ankle oedema, puffy hands due to fluid retention. Should not be combined with other drugs and patients carry a card explaining they are taking MAOI so that other practitioners may be aware of this.
PHENELZINE (Nardil) and ISOCARBOXAZID (Marplan)
Given for depressive states, phobic anxiety.

Side effects

Sweating, dry mouth, weakness, fainting. Avoid meat or yeast extracts, pickled herrings, chicken liver, Chianti, cheeses in large quantities and no Gorgonzola, Brie, Camembert. Stilton or processed cheese.

MAOI stimulant drugs

TRANYLCYPROMINE (Parnate) PARSTELINE
DEXAMPHETAMINE (Dexedrine)
FENFLURAMINE (Ponderax)

Side effects

tiredness, sedation, diahorrea, dizziness, headache.
These drugs are sometimes given to stimulate more neuro-transmitters between the nerve endings as this process begins to relieve depression. Stimulant amphetamine drugs such as Dexedrine are often used illegally to combat fatigue and suppress appetite: tolerance develops rapidly and increased doses risk creating dependence.

Barbiturates

(Sodium Amytal: Nembutal; Seconal Sodium; Soneryl;
Phenobarbitone)
This group used to be frequently used for anxiety and sleeplessness but the medical profession are now aware of the high risk of drug dependence which this group carries.

In psychiatry barbiturates are used for ECT anaesthesia and to control epilepsy and only occasionally for symptom control. When tolerance to the drug develops the same dose no longer relieves the symptoms and dependence on the drug is very quick indeed.

Lithium Carbonate (Camcolit, Priadel, Phasal, Liskonum)

It is unknown how it produces psychiatric benefit but it does, and has many different biochemical actions within the body. Lithium ions

271

rapidly diffuse throughout the whole of the body water. Patients need to have their blood levels monitored regularly to make sure that the dose is correct for them and does not produce unwanted side effects.

Side effects

immediate: nausea, vomiting, sometimes diahorrea.
at any time: clumsy movements, disorientation.

Benzodiazepines (Valium, Librium)

This is the group of tranquillising drugs which are said to be shrouding western countries with their highly addictive and numbing effects.

Valium and Librium have become familiar names since the 1960s when these drugs seemed to be the answer to relieving symptoms of anxiety and depression. It is estimated that some twenty-five million prescriptions a year are issued in Britain for tranquillisers. If the name of the drug ends in 'pam' (Diazepam (Valium) Lorazepam (Ativan) Oxazepam (Serenid) Nitrazepam (Mogadon) Flurazepam (Dalmane) Temazepam (Normison)) they are from the benzodiazepine group which includes Chlordiazepoxide (Librium) and Clorazepate (Tranxene). This group are all closely related: they are hypnotic, minor tranquillising and anti-convulsant drugs; they are easily digested and are prescribed for the alleviation of anxiety, treatment of insomnia, to help cope with stress or induce relaxation. This group is also used for epileptic patients and can be given for *delirium tremens* and abreaction to LSD drugs.

SSRI/Selective Serontonin ReUptake Inhibitor

SSRI's have been hailed as the wonderdrugs of the nineties. Certainly for many people SSRI's have literally changed their life. They work by inhibiting the reuptake of serontonin, a neurotransmitter, thus increasing the amount available at central nerve synapse, in a similar way to tricyclics. The main advantage to this group of drugs is that it isn't fatal in overdose, and because it doesn't affect the reuptake of other central neurotransmitters, there are less side effects. SSRI's are prescribed for numerous conditions from depression, anxiety, bulimia nervosa, compulsive-obsessive disorders, panic disorders with or without agoraphobia. The most famous brand is Prozac.

CIPRAMIL (Citalopram, as hydrobromide)
DUTONIN (Nefazodone hydrochlor.)
EFEXOR (Venlafaxine, as hydrochlor.)
FAVERIN (Fluvoxamine)
LUSTRAL (Sertraline, as hydrochlor.)
PROZAC (Fluoxetine hydrochlor.)
SEROXAT (Paroxetine, as hydrochlor.)

Side effects for these drugs can include: nausea, vomiting, dry mouth, headaches, insomnia, sexual dysfunction, drowsiness, rashes and allergic reactions, mania and hypomania.

ELECTROCONVULSIVE THERAPY (ECT)

ECT treatment is a hotly debated area and most of the general public do not like the idea of it. The image of a patient strapped down and given an electric shock to their brain at a time when depression or disturbance makes them unable to make an informed decision about treatment is a frightening one. ECT has been used too frequently and too carelessly since it was brought into use. Ideally it should only be used as a treatment when a person is dangerously withdrawn (mute) or catatonic (stiff and rigid) or severely depressed and unable to function at all.

ECT is an electric shock given through electrodes directly into the brain to produce an epileptic fit. The aim is to stimulate the non-dominent cerebral hemisphere and to produce more neurotransmitters throughout the nervous system. In depression the neuro-transmission (what goes on between the nerve endings) is slowed down. This process may be speeded up by amphetamine drugs but the drug cannot maintain the high production level for long. It is thought that ECT is much more effective for the production of neuro-transmitters and there are not the side effects produced by long medication. It's a common phenomenon to see dull, mute and depressed faces go into the anaesthetic room for treatment and after gaining consiousness become more livelier and more communicative.

273

Used responsibly and effectively and with a great deal of care and caution ECT has proved to be effective. What we don't know is what would have happened to the person if they had not had it. Some people do feel very bitter about being given ECT because they consider it to be a violation of their freedom and some people do suffer from loss of memory for months afterwards. What we are back to again is how much trust we have in the physician who is taking care of us and in the psychiatrist whom he recommends. Everyone has to sign a consent form for ECT after serious discussion with all the doctors and relatives involved and after the person who is to receive the treatment and his relatives are fully aware of all the procedures.

Useful addresses

CRISIS

ARBOURS ASSOCIATION CRISIS CENTRE
ARBOURS ASSOCIATION, 41a Weston Park, London N8 9SJ
Telephone 0181 340 7646; Crisis Centre 0181 340 8125

The Centre was established in 1973 and provides immediate and intensive personal support and accommodation for individuals, couples and families threatened by sudden mental and social breakdown. The crisis team consists of a resident therapist, a team leader and Arbours trainee or other professional working at the Centre. Initial consultations are often made at the home of the caller or person in crisis.

SAMARITANS
Head Office
10 The Grove, Slough, Berkshire SL1 1QP
Telephone 01753 532713/4
National Helpline 0345 909090 (All calls charged at local rate)

The Samaritans also offer help for people in crisis, or will put you in touch with local organisations who offer specialist crisis help, for example with drugs, with wife or husband battering, with anorexia, with alchohol problems and crisis. The address and telephone number of the Samaritans will be in your local directory. The operator will also put you through free of charge if there is an emergency. There is a 24 hour telephone answering service and most centres are open from 9 a.m. to 8 p.m.

Useful addresses

THERAPY

MIND is the national association for mental health in this country and offers extremely useful help and guidelines for people searching for appropriate resources, in their particular localities.
National Helpline 0345 660163 (All calls charged at local rate)

MIND NATIONAL
Granta House
15-19 Broadway, London E15 4BQ
Telephone 0181 519 2122

REGIONAL OFFICES

Northern MIND
158 Durham Road, Gateshead NE8 4EL
Telephone 0191 490 0109
Fax 0191 477 4481

North West MIND
21 Ribblesdale Place, Preston, Lancashire PR1 3NA
Telephone 01772 821734
Fax 01772 200013

Trent and Yorkshire MIND
44 Howard Street, Sheffield S1 2LA
Telephone 0114 272 1742
Fax 0114 276 2283

West Midlands MIND
20-21 Cleveland Street, Wolverhampton WV1 3HT
Telephone 01902 24404
Fax 01902 713 887

South West MIND
9th Floor, Tower House, Fairfax Street, Bristol BS1 3BN
Telephone 0117 925 0961
Fax 0117 925 5706

South East MIND
Kemp House, 1st Floor, 152-160 City Road, London EC1V 2NP
Telephone 0171 608 0881
Fax 0171 608 3750

If you write to your local address of MIND they will give you the name and address of a therapist working in your area. In some areas MIND organise support groups. They are always helpful and will offer whatever help they are able, including information of services available, useful addresses in your area and leaflets or further reading as appropriate.

RELATE - NATIONAL MARRIAGE GUIDANCE COUNCIL
Herbert Gray College, Little Church Street, Rugby, Warwickshire
CV21 3AP
Telephone 01788 73241

This organisation will offer help to couples whether they are married or not, and single people having difficulty with relationships. Donations are asked for according to means and there is usually a waiting list. You will find their address in your area in the local telephone book listed under RELATE.

LONDON MARRIAGE GUIDANCE COUNCIL
76a New Cavendish Street, London W1M 7LB
Telephone 0171 580 1087
Separate to Relate, this organisation offers a London-based service with national links.

COUNSELLING AND PSYCHOTHERAPY

Here are some of the organisations who offer help with assessment, and with finding a suitable counsellor or therapist in your own area. Most therapists work to fees on a sliding scale according to your means. Some organisations offer clinic places working with trainees under supervision, at greatly reduced fees. Always ask.

BRITISH ASSOCIATION OF PSYCHOTHERAPISTS (referral service)
37 Mapesbury Road, London NW2 4HJ
Telephone 0181 452 9823
The referral service will put you in touch with a local therapist 'assessor' who will give a diagnosis interview for a fee of about £38 and will help to arrange on-going therapy with a suitable therapist. The Association's members cover adult and child psychotherapy using Freudian, Jungian and Kleinian approaches.

Useful addresses

THE BRITISH ASSOCIATION FOR COUNSELLING
1 Regent Place, Rugby, Warwickshire
Telephone 01788 578320

Free information pack sent on receipt of A4, first class, S.A.E. The association also publishes directories of individual counsellors and counselling agencies and organisations.

WESTMINSTER PASTORAL FOUNDATION
23 Kensington Square, London W8 5HN
Telephone 0171 937 6956

Offers counselling individually, in groups, couples or families, for personal, marital or family problems. Will give information on affiliated counselling centres in England and Wales. Eclectic approaches.

WOMEN'S THERAPY CENTRE
6 Manor Gardens, London N7 6LA
Telephone 0171 263 6200 (Not a drop in - calls taken 10.00-12.00 a.m. and 2.00-4.30 p.m. Monday to Friday, or answerphone)

Offers crisis counselling, self-help therapy groups, workshops of various lengths on a wide variety of topics. Psychoanalytic and humanistic approaches. Referral network in London and other parts of the country.

INSTITUTE OF FAMILY THERAPY
43 New Cavendish Street, London W1M 7RG
Telephone 0171 935 1651

Family therapy includes the family as a whole and is offered for a wide range of problems. It can help families share information and find new ways of relating which can reduce problems or symptoms carried by individual members: the 'scapegoats'.

THE LINCOLN CENTRE AND INSTITUTE FOR PSYCHOTHERAPY
19 Abbeville Mews, 88 Clapham Park Road, London SW4 7BX
Telephone 0171 978 1545

A training institute, offering psychotherapy with clinicians and trainees. Analytical psychotherapy and brief psychotherapy. Medical referral needed, sliding scale of fees.

LONDON CENTRE FOR PSYCHOTHERAPY
19 Fitzjohns Avenue, London NW3 5JY
Telephone 0171 435 0873

Mainly London based, psychotherapy, and training, analytically based.

ASSOCIATION FOR GROUP AND INDIVIDUAL PSYCHOTHERAPY
1 Fairbridge Road, London N19 3EW
Telephone 0171 272 7013

Offers analytically orientated therapy after assessment from a senior Association member.

THE CENTRE FOR TRANSPERSONAL PSYCHOLOGY
7 Pembridge Place, London W2 4XB

Network of counsellors using transpersonal perspective, in London and other parts of England. Also a programme of introductory workshops aimed to help personal development. Write, enclosing a stamped addressed envelope.

INSTITUTE OF PSYCHOSYNTHESIS
65a Watford Way, London NW4
Telephone 0181 202 4525

Write for information on courses and style of working. There are short courses, and counselling referral available.

ADLERIAN SOCIETY OF GREAT BRITAIN (ASGB)
77 Clissold Crescent, London N16 9AR
Telephone 0171 923 2472
Referral service for individual psychology, counselling and therapy with fees on a sliding scale. Workshop programme and group work.

ANALYSIS

Freudian Kleinian Schools

LONDON CLINIC OF PSYCHOANALYSIS
63 New Cavendish Street, London W1M 7DR
Telephone 0171 436 1177

Many analysists are medically qualified. Patients are assessed before referral to an analyst. Fees are according to income and there are some National Health Service vacancies.

Jungian Schools

THE SOCIETY OF ANALYTICAL PSYCHOLOGY
1 Daleham Gardens, London NW3 5BY
Telephone 0171 435 7696

Assessment is made before referral.

ASSOCIATION OF JUNGIAN ANALYSTS
Flat 3, 7 Eton Avenue, London NW3 3EL
Telephone 0171 794 8711
- Independent group of analytical psychoanalysts.
Assessment is made by an analyst who is also a psychiatrist.

OTHER USEFUL ORGANISATIONS AND ADDRESSES

THE PHILADELPHIA ASSOCIATION
4 Martys Yd, 17 Hampstead High Street, London NW3
Telephone 0171 794 2652

The Association was founded in 1964 and has fostered 20 community households which offer refuge and asylum to those in distress. At present there are four houses in London, one for teenagers in care, and a small-holding near Oxford. Their approach is based on a phenomenological critique of psychoanalytical practice and theory, and they help people who have been disturbed to gain their own feet in their own time through the accepting therapeutic environment.

THE RICHMOND FELLOWSHIP
8 Addison Road, London W14 8DL
Telephone 0171 603 6373

The Fellowship provides residential homes run as therapeutic communities. There are 40 houses for people of all backgrounds. The Fellowhip, founded in the same year as the Mental Health Act (1959) supports people in their communities who suffer breakdown and helps them to re-orientate to independent life. There are nine houses for older children and adolescents; houses for recovering alchoholics and drug users, and for adults facing all kinds of emotional crises.

THE ARBOURS ASSOCIATION
41a Weston Park, London N8 9SJ
Telephone 0181 340 7646

The Arbours Association offers a consultation service, three therapeutic communities for seven to 10 people, a psychotherapy clinic and a training programme for professionals. The Association was established in 1970 as a registered charity in order to help people in emotional distress and as a alternative to the traditional mental hospital regime. The director of the Association is Dr. Joseph Berke.

ADDICTION TO TRANQUILLISERS

RELEASE
388 Old Street, London EC1V 9LT
Telephone 0171 729 9904
Helpline 0171 603 8654 (24 hours)

RELEASE have self-help groups all over the country. They also supply health information to purchase.

TRANX RELEASE
Council on Addiction, 81 St Giles Street,
Northampton NN1 1JF
Telephone 01604 27027/22121
24 Hour Information Line 01604 26116

ADDICTION TO ALCOHOL

ALCOHOLICS ANONYMOUS
Telephone 01904 644026 (Head office)
Look in your local telephone book for contact number for local group.

ALCOHOL CONCERN
Waterbridge House, 32-36 Loman Street, London SE1 0EE
Telephone 0171 928 7377
Information and advice on all aspects of alcohol use and abuse.

Useful addresses

BEREAVEMENT

CRUSE
Cruse House, 126 Sheen Road, Richmond, Surrey TW9 1UR
Telephone 0181 332 7227 (Helpline)

Counselling and practical help by telephone and through a network of local groups.

COMPASSIONATE FRIENDS
53 North Street, Bristol BS3 1EN
Telephone 01179 539639
A self-help group of parents who have lost a child or children - of whatever age. Network is nationwide.

NATIONAL ASSOCIATION OF BEREAVEMENT SERVICES
20 Norton Folgate, London E1 6DB
Telephone 0171 247 1080

SURVIVORS OF BEREAVEMENT BY SUICIDE (SOBS)
82 Arcon Drive, Anlaby Road, Hull HU4 6AD
Telephone 01482 565387

CANCER

BACUP (British Association of Cancer United Patients)
3 Bath Place, London EC2
Cancer Information Service   Linkline 0800 181199
Cancer Information Service   0171 613 2121
Administration   0171 696 9003
Counselling   0171 696 9000
BACUP has one of the best medically qualified teams of counsellors - most of them are former oncology nurses. They are also headed by medics and have the best approach to bridging the gap between patient and medical staff.

BRISTOL CANCER CENTRE
Grove House, Cornwallis Grove, Clifton, Bristol BS8 4PG
Helpline 0117 980 9505

BREAST CANCER CARE
Anchor House, 15-19 Britten Street, London SW3 3TZ
Telephone 0171 867 1103
Helpline (Nationwide freephone Mon-Fri 9.30 am - 4.30 pm)
0500 245345

CANCER RELIEF MACMILLAN FUND (Macmillan Nurses)
Anchor House, 15-19 Brittten Street, London SW3 3TZ
Telephone 0171 351 7811

THE CANCER SUPPORT CENTRE WANDSWORTH
20 York Road, London SW11
Telephone 0171 924 3924

MARIE CURIE CANCER CARE
28 Belgrave Square, London SW1X 8QG
Telephone 0171 235 3325

EATING DISORDERS

THE WOMEN'S THERAPY CENTRE
6 Manor Gardens, London N7 6LA
Telephone 0171 263 6200

The Women's Therapy Centre run workshops for women with eating problems which have been extremely successful.

EATING DISORDERS ASSOCIATION
National Information Centre, Sackville Place, 44-48 Magdalen Street, Norwich NR3 1JU
Telephone 01603 621414 (8.45 a.m. to 6.30 p.m. weekdays)

Information and support for sufferers from bulimia and anorexia.

PHOBIC ANXIETY

PHOBIC SOCIETY
4 Cheltenham Road, Chorlton-cum-Hardy,
Manchester M21 9QN
Telephone 0161 881 1937

Self-help organisation for people with phobias and other anxiety disorders. Local groups. The Society has some 4,500 members and is always willing to provide advice and information.

POSTNATAL DEPRESSION

THE ASSOCIATION FOR POSTNATAL ILLNESS
25 Jerdan Place, London SW6 1BE
Telephone 0171 386 0868

The Association advises and supports mothers with postnatal illness and runs a national network of supporters.

THE NATIONAL CHILDBIRTH TRUST
Alexandra House, Oldham Terrace, London W6 6NH
Telephone 0181 992 8637

The Trust has volunteers trained to help people with postnatal depression.

MEET-A-MUM ASSOCIATION
Cornerstone House, 14 Willis Road, Croydon, Surrey CR0 2XX
Telephone 0181 665 0357

Nationwide contact organisation designed for both expectant and postnatal mothers who feel isolated and in need of support.

YOUNG PEOPLE

SAMARITANS
(address and telephone number in your local telephone directory)
National helpline 0345 909090

The Samaritans can be visited or talked to in complete confidence (you don't have to give your real name) and will help put you in touch with whatever agency is most appropriate if needed. The Samaritans are all ages and colours and their lines are open 24 hours a day! If you are worried about a friend you may ring the Samaritans and ask for help on their behalf.

CHILDLINE
Telephone 0800 1111

National helpline for this confidential service for children. Call free from any telephone.

YOUNG MINDS
102 Clerkenwell Road, London EC1
Telephone 0171 336 8445
National Helpline 0345 626376
Resource, advice and information, mainly for parents and professionals, about children's problems from birth to 17 years old.

CHILD PSYCHOTHERAPY TRUST
Star House, 104-108 Grafton Road, London NW5 4BD
Telephone 0171 284 1355
Help, information and advice about child psychotherapy.

YOUNG PEOPLE'S COUNSELLING SERVICE
Tavistock Clinic, 120 Belsize Lane, London NW3 5BA
Telephone 0171 435 7111

THE BRANDON CENTRE
26 Prince of Wales Road, London NW5 3LG
Telephone 0171 267 4792/3

INSTITUTE OF FAMILY THERAPY
43 New Cavendish Street, London W1M 7RG
Telephone 0171 935 1651

RE-SOLV
(Society for the Prevention of Solvent and Volatile Substance Abuse)
30a High Street, Stone, Staffs ST15 8AW
Telephone 01785 817885

Re-Solv is a charity solely concerned with solvent misuse. Provides information and advice, publishes leaflets, booklets and videos and know about local agencies who can help.

AUSTRALIA

ASSOCIATION OF RELATIVES AND FRIENDS OF THE MENTALLY ILL
2 Nicholson Rd, Subiaco, WA 6008
Telephone 09 381 4747

Useful addresses

AUSTRALIAN NATIONAL ASSOCIATION FOR MENTAL HEALTH
(ANAMH)
1 Cookson Street, Camberwell, Vic. 3124
Telephone 03 813 1180

CATHOLIC FAMILY WELFARE BUREAU
576 Victoria Parade, East Melbourne, Vic. 3002
Telephone 03 419 5633

CATHOLIC FAMILY WELFARE FAMILY SERVICES
33 Wakefield Street, Adelaide, SA 5000
Telephone 08 210 8200

CITIZENS ADVICE BUREAU: ADELAIDE
44 Pirie Street, SA 5000
Telephone 08 212 4070

CITIZENS ADVICE BUREAU: BRISBANE
69 Ann Street, Brisbane, Qld. 4000
Telephone 07 221 4343

CITIZENS ADVICE BUREAU: NSW
411 Liverpool St, Darlinghurst, NSW 2010

CITIZENS ADVICE BUREAU OF ACT
Griffen Centre, Bunda Street, Canberra, ACT 2601

CITIZENS ADVICE BUREAU: TASMANIA
Eastlands Shopping Square, Rosney Park, Tamania, 7018
Telephone 002 440671

CITIZENS ADVICE BUREAU OF WESTERN AUSTRALIA
33 Barrack Street, Perth, WA 6000
Telephone 09 221 5711

CITIZENS COMMITTEE ON HUMAN RIGHTS
201 Castlereagh Street, Sydney, NSW 2001
Telephone 02 264 5893

COMPASSIONATE FRIENDS (Bereaved parent support)
381 Pitt Street, Sidney, NSW 2000
Telephone 02 267 6962

DIAL-A-MUM OF AUSTRALIA
Palmerston Road, Hornsby NSW 2077
Telephone 02 477 6777

GOOD SAMARITAN HOSTEL
100Malakoff Street, Marrickville, NSW 2204
Telephone 02 569 1883

INSTITUTE OF COUNSELLING
190 High Street, Willoughby, NSW 2068
Telephone 02 417 8352

LIFELINE
148 Lonsdale Street, Melbourne, Vic. 3000
Telephone 03 662 1000

MARRIAGE GUIDANCE COUNCIL
46 Princess Street, Kew, Vic. 3101
Telephone 03 853 5354

MELBOURNE CITY MISSION
Information Centre, 217 Flinders Street, Melbourne, Vic. 3000

SALVATION ARMY COUNCILLING SERVICE
93 Queens Street, North Strathfield, NSW 2137
Telephone 02 743 2831

SMITH FAMILY WELFARE SERVICE
16 Larkin Street, Camperdown NSW 2050
Telephone 02 550 4422

SYDNEY CITY MISSION FAMILY SUPPORT SERVICE
317 Queen Street, Campbelltown, NSW 2560
Telephone 046 280211

SYDNEY CITY MISSION YOUTH SUPPORT SERVICES
The Roslyn, 31 Roslyn Street, King's Cross, NSW 2011
Telephone 02 357 1041

WESLEY CENTRE MISSION
210 Pitt Street, Sydney, NSW
Telephone 02 267 8741

Useful addresses

WESLEY CENTRAL MISSION LIFELINE
Telephone 02 951 5555

WESLEY CENTRAL MISSION YOUTHLINE
Telephone 02 951 5522

NEW ZEALAND

THE MENTAL HEALTH FOUNDATION
PO Box 37-438, Parnell, Auckland

CITIZENS ADVICE BUREAU
305 Queen Street, Auckland
Telephone 773 313

48 Auro Street, Wellington
Telephone 848 287

203 Gloucester Street, Christchurch
Telephone 66 490

ANOREXIC AND BULIMIA SUFFERERS AND FAMILIES SUPPORT
GROUP TRUST
PO Box 21-489, Henderson, Auckland
Telephone 689 743

ANOREXIA NERVOSA SUPPORT GROUP
65 Karaka Street, Wainuiomata, Lower Hut, Wellington
Telephone 646 131

MARRIAGE GUIDANCE COUNCIL
8-10 Roxburgh Street, Mt Victoria, Wellington
Telephone 851 729

SALVATION ARMY SOCIAL SERVICE OFFICE
202-206 Cuba Street, Wellington
Telphone 845 649

SAMARITANS
(Wellington)
Telephone 739 739

LIFELINE
PO Box 5104, Wellsley Street, Auckland
Telephone 795 597

YOUTHLINE
PO Box 1059, Wellington
Telephone 721 888

PO Box 9300 Newmarket, Auckland
Telephone 797 889

Christchurch
Telephone 794 794

Dunedin
Telephone 771 234

Bibliography

General Psychological Reading

Achtenburg, Jeanne, *Imagery in Healing* (The New Science Library, 1985)

Assagioli, Roberto, *The Act of Will* (Wildwood House, 1974)

Balint, E and Norell, J.S., *Six Minutes for the patient* (Tavistock Publications, 1973)

Balint, M., *The Doctor, his Patient and the illness* (Churchill Livingstone, 1957)

Begg, Ean, *Myth and Today's Consciousness* (Coventure, 1984)

Bettelheim, Bruno, *Freud and Man's Soul* (Fontana, 1985)

Bettelheim, Bruno, *The Informed Heart* (Penguin, 1986)

Bowlby, John, *Attachment* (Penguin, 1971)

Campbell, Joseph, *Myths to Live By* (Souvenir Press, 1972)

Clare, Anthony and Thompson, Sally, *Let's Talk about Me* (BBC, 1981)

Cochrane, Raymond, *The Social Creation of Mental Illness* (Longman, 1983)

Cousins, Norman, *The Healing Heart* (W.W. Norton & Co, New York, 1983)

Erikson, Erik, *Childhood and Society* (Triad Granada, 1963)

Field, Joanna, *On not being able to paint* (J.P. Tarcher Inc., Los Angeles, 1957)

Frankl, Viktor E., *Man's Search for Meaning* (Hodder & Stoughton, 1962)

Frankl, Viktor E., *The Unconscious God* (Simon & Schuster, New York, 1975)

Franz, Marie-Louise von, *On Dreams and Death* (Shambhala, 1986)

Fromm, Erich, *To Have or To Be* (Abacus, 1979)

Fry, Anthony, *Safe Space* (Dent, 1987)

Hardy, J.G., *Doctors* (Corgi, 1987)

Harper, Robert A., *The New Psychotherapists* (Prentice Hall, 1975)

Hillman, James, *Re-visioning Psychology* (Harper & Row: Colophon Books, 1975)

Hillman, James. *The Dream of the Underworld* (Harper & Row, 1970)

Jacobi, Jolande, *The Way of Individuation* (Meridian Books USA, 1983)

Jung, C.G., *Analytical Psychology* (Routledge & Kegan Paul, 1968)

Jung, C.G., *Man and His Symbols* (Aldus Books, 1964)

Jung, C.G., *Memories, Dreams, Reflections* (Fontana, 1983)

Jung, C.G., 'Answer to Job' in *Collected Works Vol. XI Psychology and Religion* (Routledge & Kegan Paul, 1958)

Jung, C.G., *Structure and Dynamics of the Psyche* (Routledge & Kegan Paul, 1960)

Knight, Lindsay, *Talking to a Stranger* (Fontana, 1986)

Kohon, Gregorio (Ed.), *The British School of Psychoanalysis* (Free Association Books, 1986)

Laing, R.D., *The Divided Self* (Penguin, 1965)

Littlewood, R. and Lipsedge, M., *The Butterfly and the Serpent: Culture, Psychopathology and Biomedicine* (Reidel Publishing Company, 1986)

McCormick, Elizabeth, report on Oxford Seminar Archetypical Psychology (organised by the Champernowne Trust) September 1985, in *Holistic Medicine* Volume 1 1986

Maslov., A.H. (Ed.), *Toward a Psychology of Being* (D. Van Norstran Co., 1962)

May, Rollo, *The Meaning of Anxiety* (W.W. Norton & Co., New York, 1977)

Miller, Alice, *The Drama of a Gifted Child* (Faber, 1983)

Milner, Marion, *The Hands of the Living God* (Hogarth Press, 1969)

Pietroni, Patrick, *Holistic Living* (Dent, 1986)

Plath, Sylvia, *The Bell Jar* (Faber, 1967)

Rippere, Vicky and Williams, Ruth, *Wounded Healers* (John Wiley & Sons, 1985)

Rowe, Dorothy, *Depression* (Routledge & Kegan Paul, 1983)

Satir, Virginia, *People Making* (Souvenir Press, 1972)

Schaffer, John P.B., *Humanistic Psychology* (Prentice Hall, 1978)

Sheely, Gail, *Passages* (E.P. Dutton, 1976)

Bibliography

Smith, Adam, *Powers of Mind* (Ballantine Books, New York, 1975)

Storr, Anthony, *The Art of Psychotherapy* (Secker & Warburg, 1979)

Suttie, Ian, *The Origins of Love and Hate* (Penguin, 1963)

Szasz, Thomas S., *The Myth of Mental Illness* (Harper & Row, 1974)

Tillich, Paul, *The Courage to Be* (Fontana, 1962)

Totman, Richard, *Social Causes of Illness* (Souvenir Press, 1979)

Ulanov, Ann Belford, *The Feminine in Jungian Psychology and Christian Theology* (Northwestern University Press, 1971)

Wickes, Frances G., *The Inner World of Choice* (Coventure, 1963)

Winnicot, D.W., 'Fear of Breakdown' in *The British School of Psychoanalysis, the Independent Tradition* (Edited by Gregorio Kohon) pages 173-182

Winnicot, D.W., *Playing and Reality* (Penguin, 1974)

Winnicot, D.W., *The Maturational Process and the Faciliatat Environment* (Hogarth Press, 1979)

Ziegler, Alfred J., *Archetypal Medicine* (Spring Publications, Dallas, Texas, 1983)

Addiction to tranquillisers

Gordon, Barbara, I'm Dancing as Fast as I Can (Bantam, 1979)

Hallstrom, Cosmo, 'The Current View on Tranquillisers and New Development' in Postgraduate Doctor Africa Vol. 6 No. 12 (1984)

Loder, M., 'Benzodiazepines - The Opium of the Masses' in Neuroscience 3 (1978)

Trickett, Shirley, Come Off It (Thorsons, 1986)

Bereavement

Bowlby, John, *Loss, Sadness and Depression* (Penguin, 1981)

Lewis, C.S., *A Grief Observed* (Faber, 1961)

Parkes, Colin Murray, *Bereavement ... studies in grief in adult life* (Pelican, 1975)

Ross, Elizabeth Kubler, *On Death and Dying* (Macmillan, 1969)

Tatelbaum, Judy, *The Courage to Grieve* (Heinemann, 1981)

Ward, Barbara, *Healing Grief* (Vermilion, 1993)

Warden, J. William, *Grief counselling and grief therapy* (Tavistock Publications, 1983)

Eating Disorders

Bruch, Hilda, *The Golden Cage ... the enigma of anorexia nervosa* (Vintage Books, 1979)
Buckroyd, Julia, *Eating Your Heart Out* (Vermilion, 1996)
Colcough, Beechy, *It's Not What You Eat it's Why You Eat It* (Vermilion, 1995)
Macleod, Sheila, *The Art of Starvation* (Virago, 1981)
Orbach, Susie, *Fat is a Feminist Issue* (Hamlyn Paperbacks, 1979)
Orbach, Susie, *Fat is a Feminist Issue II* (Hamlyn Paperbacks, 1984)
Orbach, Susie, *Hunger Strike* (Faber, 1986)
Roth, Geneen, *Feeding the Hungry Heart* (Grafton, 1986)
Sours, John, *Starving to Death in a Sea of Objects* (J. Avonson, U.S., 1981)
Woodman, Marrion, *Addiction to Perfection* (Inner City Press Canada, 1983)
Woodman, Marrion, *The Owl was a Baker's Daughter* (Spring Publications, 1982)

Illness

Groddeck, Georg, *The Meaning of Illness* (Hogarth Press, 1977)
Harrison, John, *Love your Disease* (Angus and Robertson, 1984)
Inglis, Brian, *The Diseases of Civilisation* (Hodder & Stoughton, 1981)
Lowen. Alexander, *The Language of the Body* (Macmillan, 1969)

Phobia

Lloyd, Mollie, *You and Your Phobia* (Owl Publications Ltd, PO Box 410, Brighton Sussex. 32p including p and p)
Melville, Joy, *Phobias and Obsessions* (Unwin Paperbacks, 1979)
Vose, Ruth Hurst, *Agoraphobia* (Faber, 1981)
Weekes, Claire, *Agoraphobia* (Angus and Robertson, 1984)
Weekes, Claire, *Help with your nerves* (Angus and Robertson, 1981)

Retirement

Handy, Charles, *Taking Stock: being fifty in the eighties* (BBC, 1983)
Open University Course on retirement
Smith, Maggie, *Branching Out: a workbook for early retirement* (Lifeskills Associates, 1986)

Bibliography

Separation and children

Alvarez, A., *Life after Marriage* (Fontana, 1982)

Dreihurs, Rudolf, *Happy Children* (Fontana, 1964)

Gugenhuhl-Craig, Adolf, *Marriage Dead of Alive*

Hayman, Susie, *The Relate Guide to Second Families* (Vermilion, 1996)

Quilliam, Susan, *The Relate Guide to Staying Together* (Vermilion, 1995)

Vaughan, D., *Uncoupling* (Methuen, 1987)

Winnicot, D.W., *Playing and Reality* (Pelican, 1974)

Stress

Barnes, Trevor, and the Samaritans, *Dealing with Depression* (Vermilion, 1996)

Brasher, R.E., *Hyperventilation Syndrome* (Chest, 1983)

Breton, Sue, *Panic Attacks* (Vermilion, 1996)

Dychtwald, Ken, *Body Mind* (Pantheon, 1977)

Fensterheim, Herbert and Baer, Jean, Don't say *'Yes' when you want to say 'No!'* (Futura, 1976)

Fischer, Harvey J., 'A Psychoanalytic View of Burnout' in *Stress and Burnout in the Human Service Professions* (Pergamon Press, New York, 1983)

Friedman, Mayer and Rosenman, Ray, *Type A behaviour and your heart* (Fawcett Crest, 1974)

Garden, Anna-Maria, *Psychological Precondition of Burnout* (London Business School)

Kirsta, Alex, *The Book of Stress Survival* (Unwin Hyman, 1986)

Le Shan, Lawrence, *How to meditate* (Bantam, 1975)

Lum, L.C., *Syndrome of Chronic Habitual Hyperventilation in Modern trends in Psychosomatic Medicine* (Butterworths, 1976)

McQuade, Walter and Aikman, Ann, *Stress ... How to stop killing your body* Arrow, 1978)

Patel, Chandra, *The Complete Guide to Stress Management* (Vermilion, 1996)

Pelletier, Kenneth R., *Mind as Slayer, Mind as Healer* (Allen & Unwin 1978)

Priest, Robert, *Anxiety and Depression* (Vermilion, 1996)

Selye, Hans, *Stress without Distress - How to survive in a stressful society* (Hodder & Stoughton, 1975)

Smith, Manuel J., *When I say 'No' I feel guilty* (Bantham, 1975)
Wood, Clive, *Living in Overdrive* (Fontana, 1984)

Suicide

Durkheim, Emile, *Suicide* (Macmillan, 1951)
Hillman, James, *Suicide and the Soul* (Spring Publications, 1976)
Kreitman, Norman, *Parasuicide* (John Wiley, 1977)
Schneidman, Edwin, *Definition of Suicide* (Wiley Interscience, 1987)

Women

Brinton Perera, Sylvia, *Descent to the Goddess: A way of initiation for women*
    (Inner City Books, 1981)
Dalton, Katherine, *Once a Month* (Fontana 1983)
Eichenbaum, Luise and Orbach, Susie, *Understanding Women*
    (Pelican, 1983)
Shuttle, Penelope and Redgrove, Peter, *The Wise Wound* (Paladin, 1978)

Glossary

AGORAPHOBIA a fear and dread of the 'market place', i.e. of being in public and of being seen as out of control.

ANABOLIC healthy state of functioning.

ANOREXIA means literally loss of appetite. Anorexia Nervosa refers to a state of refusal to eat to the point of starvation.

BULIMIA a condition in which an individual cannot eat without having to empty themselves afterwards, either through vomiting or laxatives.

CATABOLIC unhealthy state of function.

CATATONIC a state where the voluntary muscle systems become fixed in any one position.

CONSCIOUS means that which we are aware of, we know, we see, we think ... it refers to that which is in 'daylight'.

DEPERSONALISE a state, or feeling, in which an individual loses a sense of reality about themselves.

EGO
the centre of conscious personality through which we mediate conscious life and everyday happenings.

ENDOGENOUS
coming from within, often used by GPs to describe depression which is carried within families.

FALSE SELF
hides the true self or seed because the true self has not yet been mirrored or allowed consciously.

GROUNDED
refers to making an experience 'safe', and I also use the word 'anchored' to the same purpose. When we have a dream we need to write it down so we may remember it and get in touch with what it means or is saying to us: this is 'anchoring'. When we have a powerful realisation or insight we need to 'ground' our experience in what we know as reality – writing, drawing, acting out – so that we bring it into our life and do not leave it in the unconscious. Things appear to us from the unconscious in the form of images, dreams and symbols, so that they are made conscious. Powerful experiences need to be 'grounded' so that we are not swept away by them, and sometimes grounding takes the form of breathing exercises or getting in touch with our bodies in a concrete, very present way. Sometimes intense personal experiences need to be held in a very private way ... not necessarily spoken or shared, but valued and held by the individual in their own way.

HOMEOSTASIS
the balance of the whole.

INNER FIGURES
refer to the forces inside us which direct our behaviour. These usually develop early on when we take in unconsciously some of the dominant

297

facets of parents, teachers, authority figures. Inner figures can be angry, demanding, punishing; or they can be loving, encouraging, supporting.

INNER WORLD   is the place in which we live when we are not connecting with other people: it contains our dreams, fantasies, hopes, fears, beliefs and much of our unconscious life, contains our 'real' self.

LEFT BRAIN   governs the right side of the body, focused, rational, driving, organised.

NUMINOUS   awe-inspiring, indicating spirituality and presence.

PERSONA   is a mask or lens. Most people have several personae with which to present themselves in different situations. Sometimes a persona gets too fixed and confused with what is the real person.

PHOBIA   extensive fear of an object or space leading to aversion and obsessionality.

POLARITY   one end of a magnetic pole that is held in tension by the other end: its opposite. For example, control and chaos; night and day.

PROJECTION   an unconscious idea of our own that we split off and only see in others.

PSYCHE   refers to the whole, to our essential nature, true being, and includes personality, mind, soul, self and individuality. The psyche has self-regulatory properties which are governed by the Self which draw us into experiences which are necessary for us to develop what is our true way or destiny.

PSYCHOPATHOLOGY — making 'disease' out of psychology as in 'mental illness'.

PSYCHOSOMATIC — problems in the body brought on by unconscious mental attitude.

PSYCHOTIC — a term used to describe a mental state containing unconscious material, often flooding normal consciousness, and causing severe disturbance of normal mental function.

RIGHT BRAIN — governs the left side of the body, traditionally diffuse, expressive, creative, able to relax and relate.

SELF — (with a capital S) the inner, ordering and unifying centre of the total psyche (conscious and unconscious) containing the seeds of real self (small s) with which we come into life.

SELF — (small s) the inner seed.

SHADOW — all that is unconscious or has been made unconscious by repression in a person or group.

UNCONSCIOUS — means that which we are unaware of, we don't see ... but which is in the dark or hinted at by moonlight.

Index

Index

food, as symbol, 104–5; see also eating disorders
'free floating' anxiety, 83
Freud, Sigmund, 93, 100, 259, 260
Freudian analysis, 259, 260, 280
friends, coping needs, 225–6, 238–40
Fry, Dr. Anthony, 246–9

Garden, Dr. A.M., 54
general practitioners (GPs), 241–5, 252
grief, pain of, 129
Groddeck, Georg, 100–1
group therapy, 252
guilt, 'magical', 127–9

headaches, and mental distress, 9–10
health breakdown, 92–101
heart surgery, 99
heights, fear of, 87
help, sources of, 241–61, 274–89
help lines, 250
Hillman, James, 6, 222–3
hormones, imbalance, 45
hospitals, psychiatric wards, 253
housewife stress, 243–4
Human Function Curve, 43–5
humanistic approach, counselling and psychotherapy, 259
hyperventilation, 45, 64–5
hypnotherapy, 253
hysterectomy, 97–9

identity crisis, after loss, 130–1
illness behaviour, 97; see also physical ailments
imagination, 9; images from unconscious, 34–5
Imipramine, 268
impasse stage, 209–12
indecisiveness, 57–8
Isocarboxazid, 270–1
isolation, social, 202

journey of your life exercise, 24–8
Jung, C.G., 222–3; analytical psychology, 260, 280; approaches to counselling and psychotherapy, 259; autobiography, 33–4; 'collective unconscious', 101; on life stages, 176

Kfir, Dr. Nira, 220

Kleinian analysis, 259, 280
Knight, Lindsay, 257
Lewis, C.S., experience of bereavement, 124
Librium, 272
life events: as catalyst for breakdown, 12; Rahe scale of stress, 40–1; see also death; divorce; moving house; pregnancy
life journey exercise, 24–8
lithium carbonate, 271–2
Littlewood, Dr. Roland, 194
loss: impact on children, 127–9; meaningful, 122–39; poem, 123; relationships ending, 139–48; see also death

madness, medical emergencies, 223
'magical' guilt, 127–9
manic depression, 68
MAOI stimulant drugs, 271
marriage: coping with partner's breakdown, 228–38; death of partner, 126–7; divorce, 141–8
Marriage Guidance Council, 142, 252, 254
Maudsley Hospital, 119
meaningful loss, 122–39
medical emergencies, 222–3
medical technology, as help in breakdown, 11
medical treatment, 96–9
medication see drugs
menopause, 177
mental distress, expressions of, 9
Mianserin, 268
mid life crisis, 176–82; experiences of, 178–82
Miller, Alice, 74–5
MIND, 257
money, spending, 58
monoamine oxidase inhibitors (MAOI), 270–1
monophobia, 87
mood changes, 59; adolescents, 170–1
mother, separation from, 140; see also parents
mourning, 125; four stages of, 129–39
moving house, as catalyst for breakdown, 148–53
myalgic encephalomyelitis, 101
mythic experiences, 39–40

National Health Service, 256

Index